THE
PREHISTORIC
BRAIN
IN THE
MODERN
WORLD

How to Get Unstuck When
Your Brain is Holding You Hostage

KIRA S. KAYLER

MEDIA.COM

Published by
Illumify Media Global
www.IllumifyMedia.com
"Let's bring your book to life!"

Library of Congress Control Number: 2025903493

Paperback ISBN: 978-1-964251-52-3

Cover design by Debbie Lewis

Printed in the United States of America

Dedications

To my husband, for standing by me through the tears, frustration, and growth and for showing me what love, partnership, and unwavering support truly look like.

To my son, may you grow up surrounded by love, possibility, and the freedom to write your own story. This work is for you, so the messages we once carried can stop with us.

And to my sisters, for the journeys you've walked and the challenges you've faced. My hope is that this book helps us all see new paths forward and reminds us that it's never too late to rewrite our stories.

Contents

Acknowledgments

I am profoundly grateful to my college professors, who challenged my thinking and laid the foundation for my growth. To Mary Steinberg and Margie Jamin, your mentorship and wisdom guided the early steps of my journey and shaped my skills in ways I'll always cherish.

To my clients, thank you for your courage, resilience, and trust. You have been my greatest teachers, sharing your lives and inspiring me every day.

To my friends, colleagues, and supervisees, your guidance, encouragement, and ideas have illuminated my path and enriched this journey immeasurably.

To Stella and Sophie, my ever-faithful companions, your love carried me through countless moments. May you run free and joyful at the Rainbow Bridge.

Finally, to the incredible team at Illumify Media, whose dedication, creativity, and expertise turned this dream into a reality, I am deeply grateful for your support and belief in this project.

Introduction

Understanding the Struggle, Embracing the Change

"The real problem of humanity is the following:
we have Paleolithic emotions, medieval institutions,
and god-like technology."
—E.O. Wilson, evolutionary biologist and naturalist

D o you feel stuck? Are you caught in the same cycles, day after day, where nothing seems to change no matter how hard you try? Maybe it's your job, relationships, or daily routines that feel like a loop you cannot break. You wake up thinking, *Today will be different*, but by the end of the day, you are back to the same old patterns, wondering what went wrong.

Something is holding you back. Voices in your head say things like, *You're not good enough* or *Why bother? It will never work*. Hours slip away as you scroll your phone or zone out in front of the TV, and you are left with that nagging feeling: *What is wrong with me?*

You are not alone. If you are reading this, it means you are still searching for answers. It means you have not given up, which is good. Feeling stuck does not mean you are broken. It means you are trying, even if it does not feel that way right now. You are more resilient than you think. The very fact that you are here, looking for a way forward, is proof of your strength.

I have seen this struggle time and time again. Clients—competent, intelligent, and motivated—came to me desperate for change but stuck in the same frustrating cycles. They were not lazy, and it was not a matter of willpower. They were simply stuck. As I listened to their struggles, I noticed the same patterns in myself.

Why do we sabotage ourselves? Why is change so difficult, even when we know what we want? What keeps us locked into old habits and ways of thinking, even when they no longer serve us?

I started digging. My search went beyond traditional behavior theories and into neuroscience, psychology, and human development. Books and podcasts provided stories of those that rose from the ashes of poverty or trauma and reinvented themselves in midlife or late in life. I asked what, how, and why? What held them back? What propelled them forward? I wanted to understand not just what we do but why we do it. And I discovered that it all comes down to one thing: We have a very primitive brain trying to make sense of a modern world.

Our inner caveperson, the part of our brain wired for survival, reacts to stress as if every challenge were a life-or-death threat. It avoids discomfort, craves immediate gratification, and clings to familiar patterns because they feel safe. While the world has changed dramatically over thousands of years, our brains have not kept up. The wiring that once helped us survive predators and famine now struggles to navigate a world of abundant food, endless information, and complex social lives. This primitive brain sees rejection as a threat to survival, procrastination as a way to avoid risk, and perfectionism as a shield against failure.

But here is the good news. This same brain that resists change is also capable of remarkable transformation. Neuroplasticity allows your brain to adapt, rewire, and form new pathways. The more you understand how your brain works and why it sometimes works against you, the more power you have to make choices that align with the life you want.

Why This Book Is Different

You might be thinking, *There are plenty of self-help books out there. What makes this one different?* That is a fair question. What sets this book apart is that it is not about quick fixes, oversimplified solutions, or sheer willpower. It is about understanding the deeper patterns that keep you stuck and learning how to work with your brain instead of fighting against it.

I wrote this book because I saw a gap. Too often, books explain how your brain works but leave you wondering how to apply that knowledge in real life. Or they give you strategies without addressing the underlying beliefs and habits that prevent follow-through. This book bridges that gap. It weaves understanding and action together, rooted in science and enriched by years of experience working with clients who felt stuck just like you.

This is not about perfection or magically fixing your life overnight. It is about learning to ask the right questions. When you ask your inner caveperson, or your brain, questions like, "Is this true?" "What could go right?" or "What should I really be doing?" you start to notice something shift. That awareness is where change begins. Real transformation happens in those small moments of curiosity when you challenge a long-held belief or when you question whether the first thought in your head is the only truth.

What You'll Discover in This Book

This book is your guide to understanding the intricate connections between your brain, your thoughts, and your behaviors and how to use that understanding to create meaningful, lasting change.

We will begin by exploring the fascinating neuroscience behind why you do what you do. You will learn how your brain's primitive wiring works tirelessly to keep you safe but often sabotages your growth. We will uncover how these forces shape the stories you tell yourself about who you are and what is possible.

From there, we will tackle motivation, habits, and the invisible barriers keeping you stuck. You will discover why willpower alone is not enough and learn how to work with your brain's reward system to break free from cycles of frustration.

Most importantly, this book will move you toward action. You will gain practical tools for rewiring your brain, rewriting your inner narratives, and disrupting habits and thoughts that no longer serve you. Whether it is overcoming self-sabotage, building healthier routines, or feeling more empowered in your choices, this book is here to guide you.

How This Book Will Help You Change

Creating meaningful change can feel challenging, but it starts with understanding yourself. From there, you can step out of old patterns and embrace new ways of thinking and living.

Part I, chapters 1 through 4, sets the stage by explaining the foundational concepts behind why change feels so difficult. It dives into the primitive wiring of the brain, which is shaped by evolution to prioritize safety and familiarity over risk and growth. You will learn how the drives of our subconscious, attachment styles, and cognitive biases form the invisible scaffolding of our daily lives. Using insights from neuroscience and psychology, these chapters reveal the hidden forces keeping you stuck and, more importantly, how to begin shifting them.

Part 2, chapters 5 through 11, takes these concepts from theory to practice. Through engaging, reconstructed examples inspired by real-life scenarios, you will see how individuals like you have grappled with their inner caveperson, rewired harmful habits, and reimagined the stories they tell themselves. These narratives illustrate how the tools introduced in Part I come to life, offering hope and clarity on the path to meaningful change.

This book explores both the why and the how of personal transformation. It equips you with practical strategies rooted in science and enriched by lived experience. From understanding your brain's inner workings to developing new habits and rewriting the narratives that no longer serve you, you will have the tools you need to create lasting change.

Your past does not define your future, and being stuck is not the end of your story. With small, intentional steps, you can move toward the life you want. Let's get started.

You Don't Have to Figure This Out Alone

If the patterns you've just read about sound familiar, you're not alone.

You've probably already done the work. Therapy, self-help, insight, productivity hacks. But you're still circling the same questions: "What's wrong with me?" or "Is this all there is?"

If what I'm teaching is resonating, and you're ready to create a whole new level of success in your life by working to eliminate the prehistoric tendencies from your brain, you're in luck.

I regularly mentor ambitious people who want to unlock the next level of success in their life. Check out this website, watch the training, and set a call with me to explore mentorship opportunities.

Start here: **instincttointention.prehistoricbrain.com**

1

A Prehistoric Brain in a Modern World

"Nothing in biology makes sense except
in the light of evolution."
—Theodosius Dobzhansky,
geneticist and evolutionary biologist

Your brain is an incredible tool shaped over millions of years to ensure your survival in a world far more dangerous and unpredictable than the one we live in today. But the instincts that once kept our ancestors alive can sometimes work against us in modern life, where the threats we face are more emotional, social, or psychological than physical.

Imagine, for a moment, living in a world with no modern conveniences. There are no grocery stores, no phones, no central heating. Your only protection from the elements is what you can find or build. Food and water are scarce, and predators lurk in the shadows, ready to pounce at any moment. This was the reality for our ancient ancestors, a world where survival depended on constant vigilance, quick decision-making, and efficient use of resources.

In this world, every day was a fight for survival. Hunting and gathering required bursts of intense energy followed by rest and recovery. Navigating uncharted territory meant using memory and observation to distinguish what was safe from what was dangerous. Recognizing patterns, like the movement of predators, the seasonal changes in food availability, or the signs of a brewing storm, was crucial for staying alive. Those who could react quickly to danger, conserve energy for critical tasks, and learn from their experiences were the ones who survived and passed their traits down to future generations.

These survival skills became hardwired into our brains, creating what I call your "inner caveperson." This inner caveperson is always on alert, constantly scanning for threats, and influencing your thoughts, emotions, and behaviors, often without you realizing it. It's the voice in your head that whispers (or sometimes screams), *Watch out! This is dangerous!* It can be your ally when it helps you react quickly to danger, but it can also hold you back when it clings to outdated fears or amplifies your self-doubt.

I believe we all carry remnants of this ancient survival wiring inside of us. Our brains, designed for survival in a primitive and dangerous world, now struggle to navigate the complexity of modern life. For example, our brains still respond to perceived threats like a critical email, public speaking, or a missed text message the same way our ancestors responded to a predator lurking nearby. In both cases, the brain releases a flood of chemicals and activates the nervous system, preparing the body to fight, flee, or freeze.

Your inner caveperson plays three roles in your life: a friend, a moderator, and sometimes, a foe.

- **As a friend,** it helps you react instantly to danger or discomfort. It's the part of your brain that causes you to swerve when a car drifts into your lane or to spit out spoiled milk before swallowing.

- **As a moderator,** it encourages you to pause and assess before moving forward. It's the part that says, *Wait a second; this might not be a good idea.*
- **As a foe,** it overreacts to perceived dangers, treating minor challenges like life-threatening crises. It clings to outdated information and distorted memories, keeping you trapped in cycles of fear, self-doubt, and indecision.

I often tell my clients, "Beneath everything is a scared, vulnerable human with a brain that is just trying, every moment of every day, to keep you safe." Your brain isn't the enemy, but it can work against you. Understanding your inner caveperson is the first step to breaking free from the cycles that hold you back.

Four Big-Picture Facts About Your Brain

To understand how your inner caveperson operates, it's essential to explore four key facts about your brain. Each of these traits helped our ancestors survive, but in today's world, they can sometimes create challenges that leave us feeling stuck or overwhelmed.

1. **Your Brain Is Designed to Keep You Safe:** Your brain's primary mission is survival. It is constantly scanning for threats, whether physical, emotional, or social and is constantly triggering protective responses like fight, flight, or freeze.[1] This wiring once kept our ancestors alive by reacting to predators or dangerous situations. Today, the same system reacts to modern stressors like a critical email, an awkward conversation,

3

or a missed deadline as if they were life-or-death threats.

Your brain doesn't distinguish between a lion chasing you and a tense interaction with a coworker. It releases the same flood of stress chemicals, preparing your body to fight, flee, or freeze. As I often remind my clients, "Your brain's goal is to keep you alive, not to help you thrive."

2. **Your Brain Conserves Energy:** Your brain is like an energy-efficient machine, wired to conserve resources by relying on habits, routines, and shortcuts.[2] This efficiency allowed our ancestors to save energy for critical tasks like hunting or escaping danger. For example, walking the same path to a water source became automatic, freeing up mental resources for more urgent challenges.

   However, this energy-saving tendency can make change feel difficult. Whether it's learning a new skill, starting a long-overdue project, or breaking a habit, your brain resists extra effort. It prioritizes rest and routine, even when those routines no longer serve you.

3. **Your Brain Constructs Its Own Reality:** Your brain doesn't just observe the world; it creates your experience of it. By combining sensory input, memories, and expectations, your brain makes its best guess about what is happening. This guessing ability was vital for our ancestors, helping them predict potential dangers. For example, mistaking a stick for a snake was a safer error than missing the snake entirely.[3]

   Today, this same system can lead to unnecessary fear or self-doubt. Your brain might exaggerate risks or jump to conclusions based on incomplete information. Recognizing when your brain is making things up, like assuming your friend is upset, because they haven't replied to your text, can help you challenge these distortions.

4. **Your Memory Is Flexible and Shaped by Emotion:** Your memory isn't a perfect recording of the past. Instead, it is constantly being rewritten, shaped by emotions and current experiences.[4] For our ancestors, this flexibility helped prioritize survival lessons, like remembering where danger lurked, over less critical details.

   Today, it can lead to distorted or exaggerated memories, especially when your inner caveperson amplifies feelings of failure or fear. You might replay an awkward moment from years ago, convinced it defines you, while forgetting the many times you succeeded. Understanding that memory is malleable can help you rewrite the stories you tell yourself and create a more empowering narrative.

When you look at these four facts about your brain, it's clear that so much of what holds you back isn't your fault. It's just the way your brain is wired. Your brain is an amazing tool that's always working to protect you, but sometimes it does so in ways that feel frustrating or limiting.

The important thing to remember is this: You're not stuck with these default settings. Once you start noticing how your brain works, you can begin to work with it instead of feeling like it's working against you. You can learn to challenge the instincts and habits that no longer serve you and take steps toward the changes you want.

Next, we'll dive deeper into the survival instincts that shaped your brain, the ones passed down from our ancient ancestors. These instincts helped humans survive in a dangerous world but now show up in ways that can hold us back. Understanding these traits is the next step to quieting our inner caveperson and creating more freedom in our lives.

Ancient Survival Traits

I often tell my clients that to understand why we are here today, we must know how we got here and where we came from. The thoughts, feelings, and behaviors that shape our daily lives have deep roots in traits developed by our ancestors to survive in a dangerous world. These traits, like the fight, flight, or freeze response, negativity bias, fear of the unknown, disgust, and primitive social skills, were critical to survival. However, in our modern world, they sometimes work against us, keeping us trapped in cycles of self-doubt, anxiety, or indecision. Let's explore these traits and how they show up in our lives today.

Fight, Flight, or Freeze

Have you ever been startled by a loud noise and felt your heart race? Hesitated before making a huge financial decision and noticed how clammy your hands felt? Or ducked instinctively when a soccer ball came flying at you? These are all examples of the fight, flight, or freeze response.[5] When faced with a perceived threat, the brain sends chemical signals like adrenaline to prepare the body for immediate action. Your heart races, your focus sharpens, and your body gets ready to fight, flee, or freeze in place. This response was crucial for surviving life-or-death situations and allowed our ancestors to react quickly to danger, whether that meant dodging a predator or defending a loved one.

In the modern world, however, these same responses are often triggered by situations that are not life-threatening.

Have you ever felt the same sweaty palms and racing heart before speaking in public as you might feel if a car swerved into your lane? Even though the stakes are vastly different, your brain doesn't know the difference. It still reacts as if there is a tiger fifty feet away. This ancient mechanism, while well-intentioned, can keep us stuck in cycles of fear and hesitation, reacting to perceived threats that are not as dangerous as our brain assumes.

The next time you notice your body responding with fight, flight, or freeze, ask yourself, "What am I really reacting to? Is this truly a life-or-death threat?" By identifying the trigger, you can start to reframe your response.

Negativity Bias

Have you ever noticed how one negative comment can ruin your mood, even if you've received dozens of positive ones? Or how your mind tends to dwell on what could go wrong instead of what could go right? If so, you're not alone. This tendency, called negativity bias, is another survival response passed down from our ancestors.[6]

In their world, remembering dangerous situations was far more critical than remembering pleasant ones. A hunter who remembered where a lion was last seen was much more likely to survive than one who only remembered where the prettiest flowers were blooming. Over generations, the brain learned to focus more on potential threats and negative experiences, reinforcing a stronger response to potential dangers.

Think about the last time someone gave you feedback. If it included one small critique among several compliments, what did you focus on? That's negativity bias at work. Understanding this tendency can help you reframe your reactions.

Today, negativity bias might show up in more subtle ways. You might catch yourself replaying an awkward conversation from years ago or assuming the worst when a friend takes a little too long to respond to your text. Your brain's intention is to protect you by preparing for danger, but this bias often leads to overthinking and self-doubt.

This deeply ingrained bias can also make it harder to celebrate your successes or feel confident about trying something new. Even when things are going well, your brain might default to scanning for risks, leaving you feeling uneasy or on edge.

Pattern Recognition

Have you ever spotted a connection between two events and thought, *This must mean something*, only to later realize there was no real link? Pattern recognition, another ancient survival tool, is your brain's way of finding meaning in the world around you.[7] It's what helped early humans figure out which plants were safe to eat, predict the weather, or track animal behavior.

However, this skill sometimes backfires. Your brain is so eager to find patterns, that it can jump to conclusions or create connections that don't exist. For instance, you might see a series of coincidences and think they are signs or warnings, even when they are random events.

I'll share a personal story to illustrate this. When my mother passed away during my graduate school years, it coincided with one of the worst storms back home in California. Overwhelmed with grief and guilt, I couldn't help but feel the storm reflected her anger at how her life ended. My mind wove these unrelated events into a narrative shaped by raw emotion and my brain's need to find meaning. I was convinced she was somehow punishing me and the rest of the world.

At that moment, my brain was doing exactly what it had evolved to do, constructing a story to make sense of the chaos and uncertainty I was experiencing. This same skill that once helped our ancestors connect patterns in nature to avoid predators or find food now led me to connect random events into a narrative that wasn't real.

Have you ever connected unrelated events and let that belief shape your decisions? Understanding this tendency can help you challenge those false conclusions. Perhaps you believed that missing an important call meant you were destined to fail at something larger or that a string of bad luck was a sign to give up. These mental leaps can often feel so real because your brain is wired to find patterns, even when there are none.

While pattern recognition can be helpful, when left unchecked it can fuel fears, anxieties, and false beliefs. When your brain jumps to conclusions that aren't based on reality, it can lead to overthinking, self-sabotage, or unnecessary stress. Recognizing this tendency is the first step to challenging it. The next time you notice your brain creating a narrative, pause and ask yourself, "Is there real evidence for this connection, or is my brain trying to make meaning where there isn't any?"

Fear of the Unknown

Have you ever avoided trying something new because it felt too uncertain or uncomfortable? Maybe you hesitated to apply for a dream job, skipped a big opportunity, or second-guessed reaching out to someone you admire. That little voice in your head might have said, *What if this goes wrong? It's safer not to risk it.*

This fear of the unknown was a survival advantage for our ancestors. Sticking to familiar paths and routines kept them out of trouble. Wandering into uncharted territory could mean walking into a predator's den or running out of resources. The unknown represented potential danger, so avoiding it often meant staying alive.[8]

In today's world, however, this instinct can hold us back. That same ancient fear shows up when you're faced with uncertainty, even when the stakes are much lower. It whispers, *Better to stay where you are. You don't know what could happen if you take that leap.*

Consider how this might play out in modern life. Maybe you want to start a new project or make a big life change, but instead, you find yourself procrastinating or convincing yourself it's not the right time. Or perhaps you send someone a text and start spiraling when they don't reply right away, imagining worst-case scenarios: *Are they mad at me? Did I offend them?*

Fear of the unknown can leave you feeling trapped, cycling through self-doubt and hesitation. Your brain isn't trying to hurt you, it's just doing what it was designed to do: protect you from uncertainty. The challenge is learning to push past those whispers and embrace the possibilities that lie on the other side of discomfort.

Disgust

Another deeply ingrained human survival trait is the visceral reaction we experience when something repels us—disgust.[9]

Picture this: You open the fridge, take a sniff of the milk carton, and immediately recoil with an "Ugh!" That immediate, gut-level reaction is your brain's way of protecting you from consuming something spoiled or harmful. For our ancestors, disgust acted as a built-in safety mechanism. It kept them away from poisonous plants, contaminated water, or individuals with poor hygiene and visible illnesses that could threaten their survival.

What is fascinating is that disgust does not just apply to physical substances. Over time, this safety mechanism expanded to include social and moral values. In today's world, disgust can manifest in visceral reactions to political ideologies, cultural differences, or even how we perceive ourselves.

Have you ever felt a strong, almost physical reaction to something someone said or did, even if it wasn't objectively harmful? Maybe it was a comment that didn't align with your values or an action that clashed with your beliefs. That is the ancient mechanism of disgust at work.

During the political turmoil of 2016 and the later challenges of the COVID-19 pandemic of 2020, I saw firsthand how amplified this response became. People expressed disgust toward others who had different morals, values, or behaviors, sometimes leading to divisions so sharp that families and friendships were torn apart.

But disgust does not only point outward; it can also turn inward, shaping how we see and judge ourselves. I have worked with clients who feel disgusted by their bodies, internalizing societal judgments and turning them into self-loathing. This ancient safety mechanism, meant to protect us, can morph into a toxic inner critic.

The voice of disgust often whispers, *Stay away from that, it is dangerous.* While this might protect us in some cases, in today's world, this voice can lead us to isolate ourselves, harshly judge others, or sabotage our self-esteem. Recognizing this pattern lessens its hold and helps us regain a more balanced perspective.

Primitive Social Skills

Have you ever felt the sting of rejection or the anxiety of being left out? Maybe you hesitated to speak up in a group, fearing judgment, or caught yourself comparing your life to someone else's on social media. These feelings might seem modern, but they are deeply rooted in our ancient need for connection and belonging.

Our ancestors relied not only on physical survival instincts but also on the social structures of their groups to thrive. Strong bonds within these groups ensured cooperation, protection, and mutual support. For them, belonging to a group wasn't just comforting; it was essential for survival in a world full of unpredictable dangers. And while today's world is different, your brain still carries those instincts, whispering that rejection or isolation might be a threat to your safety.

This is why rejection and isolation can feel just as painful as physical harm.[10] While the world looks vastly different from our ancestors' time, our inner caveperson still keeps close tabs on our social standing. It whispers questions like, *Are you fitting in? Do they like you?* and *Are you good enough to stay in this group?*

One way this instinct shows up is through something psychologists call in-group/out-group bias. This is the tendency to align with and favor those in our "tribe" or social group while being more skeptical or even hostile toward those outside of it. For early humans, this instinct helped navigate complex social hierarchies and avoid potential threats from outsiders.

In today's world, this instinct often shows up in ways that create unnecessary stress, anxiety, and feelings of inadequacy. Following are some examples:

- **Comparisons in Everyday Life**: Have you ever found yourself comparing your progress, choices, or circumstances to someone else's? It might happen while scrolling through social media, but it can also occur in your workplace, your friend group, or even at a family gathering. Maybe you see someone land a big promotion and wonder why you're not farther along in your career. Or you hear about a friend's seemingly perfect vacation, marriage, or lifestyle and question whether you're falling behind.

Carefully curated social-media highlight reels often amplify these feelings, but comparisons can also arise in the most ordinary interactions. A casual remark from a coworker or a glimpse into someone else's life can trigger the inner caveperson's voice, whispering, *They're doing so much better than you. You don't measure up.*

Whether it's in person or online, these moments of comparison can leave us feeling like we're not enough. The caveperson's instinct to evaluate our standing within the group was meant to help us fit in and survive, but in today's world, it can create feelings of inadequacy and self-doubt.

- **Fear of Rejection**: Maybe you've stayed in a toxic relationship out of fear of being alone, or pursued a career path you didn't love because it was what others expected of you. The inner caveperson warns, *Don't speak up, or you'll be cast out of the group.*

Does this sound familiar? Maybe you've stayed quiet in a meeting or stayed with something unfulfilling just to avoid rocking the boat. These social instincts might feel safe in the moment, and at one time they were vital for group survival. But now they can lead you to live in ways that suppress your true self, silence your needs, and leave you unfulfilled, stuck in self-doubt, and under pressure to conform.

The good news is that understanding these ancient tendencies can empower us to reclaim our true self. By recognizing that the inner caveperson's fears are often outdated, we can begin to challenge them. With practice, we can replace fear-based messages with ones that foster self-acceptance, authenticity, and a sense of belonging that comes from being true to ourselves.

Energy Conservation

Do you ever wonder why some days you just can't seem to get anything done, even though your to-do list is staring you in the face? Or why your brain seems to take the easiest route whenever possible? It's not laziness, and it's not lack of willpower, it's part of your brain's ancient programming.

The concept of energy conservation is deeply rooted in human evolution. For early humans, conserving energy wasn't just a luxury, it was a survival strategy. Hunting, gathering, and defending the group required bursts of intense effort, followed by rest and recovery. Food was scarce, and wasting energy on unnecessary activities could be life-threatening. Every calorie burned had to count. Tasks like scanning for predators, searching for food, or protecting the group required intense focus and energy, so the brain learned to prioritize what mattered most for survival.

What many people don't realize is that the brain is one of the most energy-demanding organs in the body, using roughly 20% of the body's total energy at rest, despite being only about 2% of your total body weight.[11] Complex thought processes, such as problem-solving, learning new skills, or making difficult decisions, burn significantly more energy than routine or automatic tasks.

This high-energy cost is one of the reasons your brain evolved to automate repetitive and predictable behaviors, such as walking familiar paths or performing habitual tasks. By relying on routines and mental shortcuts, your brain reserves energy for bigger, more unpredictable challenges like spotting predators, navigating new terrain, or solving complex social problems.[12]

Today, your brain still operates this way, focusing on what seems immediately necessary while automating or deprioritizing other tasks. But here's the catch: while this programming served our ancestors well, it can sometimes work against us in the modern world. Unlike our ancestors, we are rarely in life-or-death situations that demand immediate bursts of focus or energy. Instead, much of our modern effort requires prolonged focus, creativity, and problem-solving, all of which burn significant mental energy.

Have you ever noticed how hard it is to start something new, even if you know it's important? Whether it's learning a new skill or tackling a long-overdue project, your brain often resists the extra effort. That's your inner caveperson kicking in, prioritizing rest and routine to conserve energy.

In today's world, food isn't scarce, and physical survival isn't always at stake, but your brain hasn't fully adapted to this reality. Instead of protecting you from predators or food shortages, it works to shield you from perceived mental or emotional "threats" like effort, uncertainty, or discomfort. This is why you might find yourself avoiding a challenging task, even when you know it's essential for your growth or success.

In modern life, this tendency toward energy conservation can show up in ways that frustrate us. It may lead to procrastination, avoidance, or relying on mental shortcuts to get through the day. Your brain is constantly looking for ways to save effort, which is why it creates habits and routines to simplify decision-making. These energy-saving tendencies are helpful, but they can also hold you back when they lead to unproductive or limiting behaviors.

Heuristics: The Brain's Energy-Saving Shortcuts

Heuristics are mental shortcuts that help your brain conserve energy and make quick decisions.[13] While useful, these shortcuts can sometimes oversimplify situations and lead to errors. Below, heuristics are grouped by their purpose, helping us see how they align with specific aspects of decision-making:

Heuristics That Simplify Decisions

These shortcuts reduce mental effort by relying on familiar or straightforward solutions.

- **Familiarity Heuristic:** Your brain gravitates toward what it already knows. For example, you might repeatedly buy the same brand of coffee or choose a familiar route home because it feels predictable and safe. Familiarity allows your brain to conserve energy by defaulting to the known.
- **Anchoring-and-Adjustment Heuristic:** Your decisions are influenced by the first piece of information you encounter. For instance, if a car is originally priced at $30,000 and later discounted to $28,000, you might view it as a great deal, even if it's still overpriced.

Heuristics That Use Emotions or Patterns

These shortcuts rely on emotional responses or pattern recognition to guide decisions.

- **Affect Heuristic:** Your decisions are heavily influenced by your emotional reactions. For example, you might avoid a roller coaster because it looks terrifying, even though it is statistically safe. Your emotional reaction becomes the guiding factor.
- **Representativeness Heuristic:** Your brain categorizes things based on stereotypes or patterns. For instance, seeing someone in a white coat might make you think they are a doctor, even if they aren't.
- **Availability Heuristic:** Events or examples that come to mind easily feel more significant or likely than they really are. For example, hearing about a plane crash on the news might make you overestimate the risk of flying.

Heuristics That Rely on Social Cues

These shortcuts help us navigate group behavior by looking to others for guidance.

- **Social-Proof Heuristic:** You follow the crowd because it feels safer or more acceptable. For example, you might choose a busy restaurant over an empty one, assuming the crowd knows something you don't.
- **Authority Heuristic:** You are more likely to trust, follow, and emulate people who have authority or expertise. For example, you are more likely to believe a doctor wearing a lab coat than a random stranger giving medical advice, even if they both say the same thing.

While heuristics are designed to make decision-making more efficient, they aren't perfect. Recognizing when these shortcuts are at play can help you make more thoughtful and intentional choices.

Cognitive Biases: Built-In Blind Spots

Cognitive biases are systematic errors in thinking that influence how we perceive the world and make decisions. While biases are often helpful for quick decision-making, they can also create blind spots, distort reality, or reinforce limiting beliefs. To make these biases easier to digest, I have grouped them by the roles they play in shaping our behavior.

Biases That Protect Us

These biases evolved to keep us safe by helping us avoid potential threats or negative outcomes.

- **Negativity Bias:** Your brain gives more weight to negative information than positive. For example, one harsh critique might overshadow a dozen compliments, leaving you feeling deflated. This bias ensures you focus on potential dangers but can also hold you back from celebrating successes.
- **Loss Aversion:** The pain of losing something feels stronger than the pleasure of gaining something of equal value. For instance, you might avoid an investment that could earn you $50 because of the possibility of losing $50. This bias can make you overly cautious.

Biases That Reinforce Habits

These biases keep you anchored to familiar patterns, even when they no longer serve you.

- **Status-Quo Bias:** Your brain prefers things to stay the same. For example, you might stick with a subpar insurance plan because it feels easier than researching and switching to a better option.
- **Sunk-Cost Fallacy:** You continue investing in something because of the time, effort, or money you've already spent on it. For instance, you might stay in a job you dislike because you've been there for years.

Biases That Influence Perceptions of Reality

These biases shape how we interpret and remember the world around us.

- **Confirmation Bias:** You seek out information that supports your existing beliefs while ignoring contradictory evidence. For example, you might only read articles that align with your political views and dismiss opposing perspectives.
- **Hindsight Bias:** After an event occurs, you feel as though you "knew it all along." For instance, you might claim you predicted a stock market crash after it happens, even if you didn't see it coming.

Biases That Impact Confidence

These biases affect how we view our abilities and knowledge.

- **Overconfidence Bias:** You overestimate your skills, knowledge, or likelihood of success. For example, you might feel completely prepared for a test after minimal studying because you've done well in the past.

- **The Spotlight Effect:** You believe that others are paying more attention to your mistakes or appearance than they actually are. For example, you stumble over a word while doing a presentation and think that the whole audience thinks the presentation was bad, even though most people didn't notice.

While these are some of the most common biases, there are many others that influence our daily thoughts and decisions. Later in this book, we will also explore cognitive distortions, which are related thought patterns that further shape how we interpret the world. By becoming aware of these mental blind spots, you can start to challenge them and make decisions that align with your goals.

Moving Beyond Autopilot Thinking

These heuristics and biases represent just a small sample of the many mental shortcuts that shape human behavior and create challenges in today's complex environment, keeping us stuck in patterns of thought and actions that no longer serve us.

Recognizing when your brain is operating on autopilot is the first step toward breaking free from its hold. By pausing to reflect on these tendencies, you can make more deliberate, mindful choices that align with the life you want to build.

Instant Gratification

Have you ever found yourself reaching for that extra slice of cake, binge-watching an entire TV series, or endlessly scrolling through social media, even when you know you should be doing something else? You might feel frustrated with yourself afterward, wondering why it's so hard to resist.

But this craving for instant rewards is not a personal failing, it's hardwired into your brain.

For our ancestors, stumbling upon something valuable like ripe fruit, a freshwater source, or safe shelter was a rare and precious opportunity. Their brains rewarded these discoveries with a burst of dopamine, the feel-good chemical that made the experience pleasurable. This reward system encouraged them to seek out similar rewards in the future, ensuring survival in a world of scarcity.[14]

Back then, resources weren't guaranteed. If something good came along, it made sense to take advantage of it immediately. Eat the ripe fruit now before it rots. Drink the water now because it might not be there tomorrow. Rest in the safe shelter while you can. Acting on impulse often meant the difference between life and death.

Fast forward to the modern world, and this same ancient wiring still drives much of our behavior, even though the circumstances have completely changed. Our inner caveperson still urges us to seize pleasure whenever we can. It whispers, *Now, now, now!* So we scroll, snack, shop, or stream, chasing those little bursts of dopamine that momentarily make us feel good.

Today, however, resources are not as scarce, and many of the things we crave—junk food, entertainment, social validation—are constantly available. What once helped our ancestors survive can now trap us in cycles of procrastination, overindulgence, and guilt.

The Downside of Instant Gratification
While there's nothing wrong with enjoying small pleasures, relying too much on instant gratification can make it harder to achieve long-term goals. It erodes patience, self-discipline,

and our ability to delay rewards in favor of something bigger or more meaningful.

For example, think about procrastination. You're faced with a task you don't enjoy, like tackling a work project or cleaning your home. Instead of diving in, your inner cave-person whispers, *That seems like too much work. Let's check Instagram instead!* It promises you immediate relief, even though avoiding the task only creates more stress later.

Or consider overindulgence. Whether it's snacking on junk food, online shopping, or compulsive habits, the brain's reward system keeps urging you to chase that next dopamine hit. Each time you give in, it reinforces the behavior, making it harder to resist the next time.

The more we give in to these temptations, the more we strengthen the habit. Over time, this can create cycles of stress, guilt, or anxiety, leaving us feeling stuck and unable to focus on what truly matters.

Our Dual Natures

Have you ever asked yourself, *Why can't people just be kind all the time?* or *Why did I overreact like that?* As human beings, we are capable of extraordinary kindness, cooperation, and connection, but we are also prone to anger, defensiveness, and even hostility. This dual nature, our ability to nurture deep relationships one moment and engage in conflict the next, is deeply embedded in our evolutionary past.

Humans are among the most powerful and dangerous creatures on the planet.[15] Throughout history, we have done more harm to each other than any predator ever could. As uncomfortable as this truth may be, it stems from the same traits that helped our ancestors survive.

On one hand, survival depended on cooperation. Early humans formed tight-knit social groups to protect one another, hunt effectively, and raise offspring. Collaboration was rewarded by powerful neurochemicals like dopamine, oxytocin, and serotonin,[16] which reinforced feelings of trust, bonding, and emotional closeness. This made connection essential for survival.

At the same time, survival required defending the group's resources. Scarcity of food, fertile land, or shelter often led to conflict, both within and between groups. Fear, anger, and aggression arose to protect one's own. The very same brain mechanisms that fostered love and cooperation could quickly shift to hostility and aggression when survival felt threatened.

The Inner Push and Pull

This dual nature remains with us today. Deep in our brains, bonding and aggression still exist side by side. For example, when you meet someone new and feel a rush of excitement, it is not just bonding chemicals like oxytocin and dopamine at work. Cortisol and adrenaline, stress-related chemicals, are also present. Your brain is preparing for two possible outcomes: connection or conflict.

This delicate balance between unity and defense plays out in countless ways in modern life. Our inner caveperson, driven by survival instincts, can create a push-and-pull dynamic that impacts our relationships and interactions.

Here are some examples of how this tension shows up today:

- **Resource Scarcity**: Think back to the United States's toilet paper shortage of 2020. People hoarded supplies, often to an extreme degree, because their brains perceived a threat to their survival. This reaction was not just about the item itself; it was rooted in the same mechanisms that helped our ancestors secure food, water, and safety.

- **Social and Political Conflicts**: Loyalty to our "in-group" (those who share our beliefs or affiliations) can lead to skepticism or hostility toward "out-groups." Social media often amplifies this divide, creating echo chambers where group loyalty intensifies and aggression toward opposing groups escalates.

- **Reactive Behavior**: The fight-or-flight response can kick in even during minor disagreements. A snide comment or a heated argument might feel like a personal attack, triggering defensive or aggressive behaviors. The brain's ancient wiring is quick to perceive threats, even when no real danger exists.

Modern Complications of Being Human

While these survival instincts served our ancestors well, they can create challenges in today's world. Modern technology, for example, often complicates how we navigate our dual nature. Texting, emails, and social media allow us to connect instantly, but they can also lower our inhibitions. It is easier to lash out, miscommunicate, or say things we would not dare to say in person. Psychologists call this the "online disinhibition effect,"[17] and it is a modern reflection of how our dual nature can lead to conflict.

Understanding our dual nature helps us recognize the inner caveperson's role in these reactions. It reminds us that the push and pull between connection and conflict is not a flaw but a survival mechanism. By becoming more aware of these instincts, we can better navigate our relationships and respond to challenges with greater empathy and control. Instead of reacting defensively, we can pause and ask ourselves, *Is this situation really a threat?* How can I respond in a way that fosters connection rather than conflict? Awareness is the first step to navigating our dual nature with compassion for ourselves and for others.

Epigenetics

So far, we've explored how our brain's wiring reflects the survival needs of our distant ancestors. But what about the survival experiences of our more recent ancestors, our grandparents, great-grandparents, and beyond?

This is where epigenetics comes into play. Epigenetics is the study of how environmental factors, life experiences, and even trauma can influence how our genes are expressed. These changes don't alter the genes themselves but affect how they are "read" or activated by the body, creating marks that can be passed down through generations.[18] These marks shape not just physical traits but also emotional and behavioral tendencies.

Imagine your brain as a blueprint. Your genes provide the design, but the environment, everything from life experiences to stress and trauma, can shape how that blueprint is carried out. The fascinating part is that these environmental changes can influence how certain genes are turned "on" or "off," leaving a legacy that affects future generations. Epigenetics reminds us that the old debate of nature versus nurture misses the bigger picture. It's not one or the other, it's both.

For example, someone who grows up in a chaotic, unstable environment may have stress-related genes "switched on," while someone raised in a peaceful, supportive environment may not. These "switches" are influenced by both inherited and personal experiences, affecting how we respond to challenges and stress in daily life.

The Echoes of Ancestral Experience

Imagine a grandchild who startles easily and experiences heightened anxiety in stressful situations. Now imagine that this grandchild's grandfather survived a brutal war. While the child didn't live through those horrors, the grandfather's experience of stress and trauma might have left a biochemical mark on his genes, one that was passed down through the generations.

Epigenetics shows us that these genetic "marks" can alter how certain genes, including genes related to mood regulation, are expressed. The following are some examples:

- **Alex's Story:** Alex's grandfather endured famine and violence during a war. These extreme conditions likely altered how his body regulated stress and metabolism, creating epigenetic marks that were passed down. Today, Alex notices that he is quick to feel stress and often overeats when anxious. His inner caveperson whispers, *Danger is everywhere, be ready!* This pattern is not just a result of Alex's personal experiences; it is partly an echo of his grandfather's survival strategies.

- **Jamie's Story:** Jamie's mother struggled with chronic depression. As a result, Jamie often feels vulnerable to depressive episodes and hears her inner caveperson say, *You can't handle this, it's too much.* These struggles reflect both inherited tendencies and the environment Jamie grew up in.

Epigenetics helps explain why some individuals feel trapped in cycles of fear, anxiety, or self-sabotage. These patterns aren't simply personal failings; they're often inherited responses, shaped by the challenges faced by past generations.

Breaking the Cycle

Fortunately, epigenetic changes are not set in stone. While trauma and stress can leave their mark, those marks can also be rewritten. Just as the environment can create epigenetic marks, it can also alter or reverse them. New behaviors, choices, and environments can reshape how genes are expressed, creating a ripple effect that can positively impact future generations.

For instance, someone who recognizes inherited patterns of fear or stress can take steps to create a different environment for themselves and their children. By fostering safety, support, and resilience, they can help "turn off" the genetic switches associated with these negative patterns.

Understanding epigenetics allows us to see our struggles in a new light. It helps us recognize that the inner caveperson's voice isn't just shaped by ancient evolutionary history, it is also influenced by the survival strategies of the generations before us. This perspective opens the door to greater compassion, healing, and the possibility of breaking generational cycles of fear and self-doubt.

Key Takeaways

Breaking free from patterns that no longer serve you is not about overhauling your entire life in an instant. It is about noticing the ways your brain's ancient instincts influence your daily decisions and responding to them with awareness and intention. These instincts are not flaws; they are part of what makes you human. But when you begin to recognize their influence, you create space to pause, reflect, and choose a path that aligns with your goals and values. Progress happens one small, intentional step at a time.

- **Know your instincts.** Your brain's ancient instincts influence your thoughts, feelings, and behaviors. These instincts evolved to help our ancestors survive in a dangerous and uncertain world, but they can sometimes hold you back in modern life. Understanding how they operate is the first step toward creating positive change.
- **Name what's happening.** Responses like fear, negativity bias, and instant gratification are not personal flaws. They are survival mechanisms deeply rooted in evolution. By recognizing them, you can begin to challenge these patterns and make more intentional decisions.
- **Awareness is the first step.** Change happens when you approach yourself with awareness and self-compassion. Small, deliberate actions can help you quiet the voice of your inner caveperson and take steps toward a life aligned with your values and goals.

Moving from Understanding to Action

Now that you understand how your brain works, use this knowledge to your advantage. Here are five actionable items that can help you make intentional choices and move you towards the positive changes you want in your life.

Pause and reflect when faced with fear or hesitation. When you notice yourself responding to stress or uncertainty, take a moment to pause. Ask yourself if the situation is truly a threat or if your brain is reacting to outdated instincts.

- **Practice self-compassion.** Remind yourself that your brain's instincts are not a flaw or weakness but a part of being human. Speak to yourself with kindness, especially when you feel stuck or overwhelmed.
- **Start with small, manageable steps.** Choose one area of your life where you feel held back, and commit to making small, consistent changes. Over time, these small actions build momentum and create lasting transformation.
- **Reframe negative thoughts.** When your inner cave-person whispers, *You can't do this* or *This will never work*, challenge those thoughts. Ask yourself, "What is the evidence for this? Is there a more supportive perspective I can take?"
- **Celebrate progress, no matter how small.** Recognize the moments when you step outside your comfort zone or make a more intentional choice. These wins, no matter how small they seem, are proof that change is possible.

While your brain was designed for survival, you were designed for so much more. With awareness, self-compassion, and consistent effort, you can begin to harness your brain's wiring as a tool for growth and transformation. Every small step forward is a chance to rewrite the story your inner caveperson tells. Remember, change is possible, and it starts with the choices you make today.

2

Whispers Across Time: How History and Memory Shape Us

"We're all ghosts. We all carry, inside us, people who came before us."

—Liam Callanan,
novelist

In Chapter 1, we explored how the survival instincts of our ancient ancestors still influence us today. These instincts to fight, flee, or freeze, to scan for danger, and to conserve energy are wired into us, passed down over millennia to keep us alive. But alongside these ancient instincts, we carry another layer of influence.

Have you ever felt a pull to act a certain way but couldn't quite explain why? Or found yourself reacting strongly to something, as though someone else's expectations or beliefs were influencing you? These moments aren't random. They come from the messages, beliefs, and lessons you've absorbed over time, the "ghosts" of the people and ideas that shaped you.[1] They are always with you, shaping how you think, feel, and act, even when you aren't fully aware of it. I often tell my clients, "We are never really alone in a room. We carry with us the voices of parents, ancestors, and the cultural stories that shaped us." It is as if your mind is a crowded room, filled with whispers of advice, caution, encouragement, or criticism. Some of these whispers reflect love and protection, while others grow from seeds of doubt or fear.

Think about it for a moment. These voices might come from a parent's advice, a grandparent's warnings, or even the unspoken rules of a culture you grew up in. They often operate quietly, shaping your choices and self-perception without you even realizing it. Some are kind, cheering you on with affirmations like, *You've got this!* Others are protective, whispering fears like, *What if you fail?* or warnings like, *Don't take risks. It is too dangerous.* Many of these voices are patterns you absorbed long ago, running in the background of your mind like scripts on repeat.

There are several forces that shape the voices you carry with you, including your subconscious mind, the bonds you formed in childhood, the cultural expectations you have absorbed, and the memories that color your view of the world. Each of these layers work together in unique ways to influence your behaviors, beliefs, and sense of self.

As you read, you will see how these influences affect your thoughts, emotions, and behaviors. Subconscious beliefs might amplify lessons from childhood or ancient survival instincts. Cultural scripts may push against personal memories, creating inner conflict. Together, these voices shape the way you see yourself and the world around you. But by understanding where they come from, you can begin to sort through them and decide which ones truly serve you.

This chapter is about uncovering those hidden voices, the ones that add another layer of influence to your inner world. By exploring where these voices come from and why they persist, you can begin to understand how they amplify or contradict your ancient survival instincts. Most importantly, you will learn how to rewrite the voices that no longer serve you. This process isn't about erasing those voices or pretending they don't exist. Instead, it is about recognizing them, understanding their origins, and deciding which ones deserve your attention. By doing so, you create room to hear your own voice more clearly, the one that reflects your values, strengths, and the person you're becoming.

The Hidden Voices: Unveiling the Unconscious

When I began studying psychology over two decades ago, I was taught that roughly 80% of human behavior stemmed from subconscious processes. Today, with advances in neuroscience and brain imaging, researchers now estimate that up to 95% of our cognition and behavior originates in the subconscious mind. In other words, only about 5% of what we do is the result of conscious, deliberate thought.[2]

Conscious behavior operates within our awareness. It is intentional and driven by thoughts and emotions we can readily identify. For example, when you decide to exercise because you want to improve your health or choose to speak up in a meeting to share an idea, you are making deliberate choices, fully aware of your reasoning and intentions.

Subconscious behavior, by contrast, operates below the surface. It is automatic, habitual, and shaped by both evolutionary instincts and a lifetime of experiences, beliefs, and environmental cues, many of which you may not even realize are influencing you. While survival instincts push us toward safety and efficiency, our individual habits and behaviors are shaped by repeated exposure to experiences, relationships, and cultural conditioning. Every belief, habit, and routine you develop contributes to the patterns and instincts that guide your actions, often without your conscious input. Each time you respond to a situation in a certain way, whether it's avoiding conflict, seeking approval, or engaging in a daily routine, your brain strengthens the associated neural pathways, reinforcing that behavior as a subconscious pattern.

For instance, have you ever experienced a wave of comfort or nostalgia when you catch the scent of fresh-baked cookies? That's your subconscious at work, tying the smell to positive memories or feelings from your past, even if you weren't consciously recalling a specific moment. Similarly, when you instinctively feel more relaxed at the sound of waves crashing on a beach, your subconscious is responding to deeply ingrained associations between those sounds and feelings of calm and tranquility.[3]

Even the small habitual actions you perform daily, like brushing your teeth in the same order each morning or instinctively checking your phone when you hear a notification, are largely driven by subconscious patterns. The brain builds these habits through repetition, strengthening neural pathways each time the behavior is performed. Over time, these routines bypass conscious thought entirely, relying on the neural pathways and routines your brain has built over time.

I often refer to the subconscious as "the voices." These are the internal echoes of past people, experiences, and stories that shaped you, often acting in the background as a guide for your beliefs, actions, and behaviors. These voices arise from the unconscious mind, which operates outside of awareness, processing emotions, storing memories, and reinforcing patterns. The voices that surface in your mind—your inner dialogue—are a reflection of these deeper unconscious processes, shaped by years of experiences, influences, and repeated messaging.

These voices might include younger versions of yourself, the guidance of parents or grandparents, the words of teachers, or even the influence of cultural icons. They might whisper subtle instructions like *You're not good enough* or *Don't take risks; it's too dangerous.* Or they might encourage you with uplifting messages like *You've got this* or *Keep going! You're capable.* These messages aren't random; they are expressions of deeper unconscious patterns shaped by past conditioning.

Our subconscious patterns don't just shape how we react in the moment; they also influence how we see ourselves over time. The brain struggles not only to imagine a future self that is significantly different from who you are today but also to store and retrieve memories in a way that accurately reflects personal growth. Instead of offering an objective record of past experiences, memory tends to reinforce our current self-perception. If you believe "I'll always be stuck in this situation," your brain will instinctively recall moments of struggle rather than times when you overcame challenges. This creates the illusion of a static identity, making it harder to envision change, even when you've already experienced it. These subconscious filters can keep you locked in outdated beliefs about yourself, but once you recognize them, you can begin rewriting the story.

Recognizing these subconscious voices is a powerful step in changing their influence. Even though they operate outside of your direct control, bringing them into awareness allows you to challenge, reframe, and replace the messages holding you back. The goal isn't to silence the voices entirely, but to understand their origins and recognize their purpose. Once you know where they come from, you gain the freedom to decide which ones to embrace and which ones to let go of.

Blueprints of the Heart:
How Early Bonds Shape Us

Have you ever wondered why some relationships feel safe and easy, while others leave you second-guessing or pulling away? These relational dynamics often begin earlier than we realize. They often trace back to the relationships you had with your earliest caregivers. From the moment you are born, your brain begins soaking up everything you see, hear, and feel. Over time, it constructs from your genetic blueprints your emotional templates that influence how you build relationships, respond to emotional needs, both your own and others, and handle feelings of vulnerability or trust.[4]

The bonds we form with our caregivers, whether they feel secure and consistent or unstable and distant, become the foundation for how we navigate connection and trust throughout life. These early relationships shape how we see ourselves and other, what we believe we deserve, and how we handle emotional challenges.

As children, we don't have the words or understanding to process these experiences fully. Instead, we internalize patterns of connection based on how we were cared for.

For some, these early experiences provided a strong sense of safety and stability, helping them develop a foundation of trust and resilience. For others, caregiving might have been inconsistent, emotionally distant, or even harmful, creating patterns of insecurity or mistrust that linger into adulthood. If you recognize yourself in this second group, know that these early experiences were not your fault. It is also important to understand that no matter what your early experiences were, these patterns are not set in stone. They can be examined, challenged, and rewritten over time.[5]

Attachment Styles:
Four Patterns That Shape Us

Psychologists often refer to these early relationship patterns as attachment styles. Attachment styles are emotional patterns that shape how you connect with others, trust, and form relationships throughout life.[6] They are formed during childhood, based on how your earliest caregivers responded to your needs. These patterns are open to change, and with effort and self-awareness, they can evolve over time.

Secure Attachment

Secure attachment develops when caregivers are consistently responsive, dependable, and nurturing. When a child's needs are met with care and predictability, they learn that the world is a safe place, that they are worthy of love, and that others can be trusted.

As adults, securely attached individuals tend to feel comfortable with intimacy and are open to giving and receiving support. They can navigate emotional challenges with confidence and resilience. Their internal voices often affirm and encourage them: *I am lovable*, *I can trust others*, and *I am safe*.

People with secure attachment often find it easier to balance independence and connection in relationships. However, secure attachment does not mean someone never struggles. It simply means they have developed a strong foundation of trust and self-worth that helps them recover from difficulties. If you didn't grow up with secure attachment, it's important to know that you can still develop it in adulthood through self-reflection, healthy relationships, and intentional practices.

Anxious Attachment

Anxious attachment develops when caregivers are inconsistent. Sometimes they are present and responsive, but other times they are unavailable, dismissive, or unpredictable. This inconsistency creates a sense of insecurity, teaching a child that love and attention are not guaranteed.

As adults, individuals with anxious attachment often seek constant reassurance and experience a deep fear of abandonment. Their inner dialogue is frequently filled with doubt and worry, including thoughts like, *They might leave me*, *I'm not enough*, or *What if I lose them?*

People with anxious attachment may struggle with trust, self-esteem, and emotional regulation. They can appear clingy, overly sensitive, or even jealous in relationships, not because they are inherently flawed, but because their early experiences shaped their expectations of instability in connections. For example, someone with anxious attachment might check a partner's messages repeatedly for reassurance or feel panicked if a friend cancels plans.

These responses, while challenging, are not fixed. With self-awareness, patience, and a great deal of self-compassion, individuals can work to shift these behaviors and build healthier, more secure relationships.

Avoidant Attachment

Avoidant attachment develops when caregivers are emotionally unavailable, dismissive, or overly critical. In these environments, children learn to rely on themselves and avoid showing vulnerability because they have internalized the belief that others cannot be counted on.

As adults, individuals with avoidant attachment may prefer independence and keep emotional distance in relationships.

Their internal voices tend to say: *I can't rely on anyone*, *It's safer to stay distant*, or *I don't need anyone*.

While their independence can be a strength, avoidantly attached individuals often find it hard to open up, trust others, or form deep emotional connections. For instance, someone with avoidant attachment might avoid discussing feelings in a relationship, fearing it will make them seem weak or too vulnerable. If this resonates with you, it's okay to feel unsure about vulnerability. It is unfamiliar, and that's normal. With the right tools and support, avoidantly attached individuals can gradually learn to take small steps toward emotional connection and intimacy.

Disorganized Attachment

Disorganized attachment develops in chaotic or abusive environments where caregivers are both a source of comfort and fear. This creates a confusing and conflicting internal world, where a child does not know what to expect or how to respond.

As adults, individuals with disorganized attachment may experience a mix of anxious and avoidant tendencies. They might crave closeness but fear it at the same time, leading to unpredictable patterns in relationships. Their internal voices might say: *I'm not safe*, *I don't know what to expect from others*, or *If I get too close, I'll get hurt*.

Disorganized attachment is often rooted in trauma, which can make trust and emotional regulation feel challenging. For example, someone with disorganized attachment might pull away from a partner during conflict, even when they are desperate for reassurance. However, with the right support, attachment styles can be transformed over time. Healing often involves working through past trauma, building emotional safety, and creating a more stable foundation for connection.

Attachment Styles Are Not Destiny

No matter what your early experiences were, your attachment style does not have to define you. These patterns might shape your instincts and responses, but they are not unchangeable. With self-awareness, support, and effort, you can shift toward a more secure way of relating to yourself and others.

A powerful starting point toward making that shift is recognizing your relational dynamics. Once you understand where they come from, you can start to question the stories they tell you about yourself, your relationships, and what is possible. This awareness creates space for change. Then you can step outside the framework you were given and start building something new.

The Voices of Culture: Navigating Inherited Scripts

Beyond our families, the culture we are born into also shapes the voices in our minds. Every culture carries its own set of ideals, expectations, and norms. These cultural influences shape how we see ourselves and interact with the world. They can profoundly impact our identity, behavior, and sense of self-worth, often in ways we do not consciously recognize.[7]

For some people, cultural messages feel like a natural fit. The norms and values you grow up with might be comforting, providing a strong sense of identity and connection. For others, cultural expectations can create tension, especially when the messages from different cultures or communities conflict. Whether you have embraced your cultural narratives or found yourself questioning them, it is worth exploring how these influences have shaped your internal world.

Cultural Dissonance and Overlapping Identities

For many people, cultural scripts are not straightforward. If you've ever felt torn between the values of your parents, grandparents, or culture and the expectations of the world around you, you're not alone. For instance, if you were raised in a culture that emphasizes self-reliance, you might hesitate to ask for help, even when it's deeply needed. First-generation immigrants might feel caught between honoring the traditions of their family and embracing the opportunities of a new society or pursuing their dreams.

Maybe you've felt the tug of competing voices yourself, one urging you to stay close to your roots, while another whispers that you need to follow your own path. Navigating these tensions can feel especially complicated when you belong to more than one identity or community. For instance, you might find yourself adjusting your behavior depending on the people or spaces around you, trying to fit in without losing yourself. If you're a minority professional, you might feel the weight of presenting yourself differently at work than you do in your personal life, trying to balance authenticity with others' expectations. Or, if you're a woman working in a male-dominated field, you might wrestle with doubts about whether you belong there, even though you do.

These inner conflicts can feel exhausting and leave you questioning where you truly fit. Over time, they can shape how you see yourself, how you relate to others, and how you show up in different areas of your life.

Recognizing these intersecting cultural influences is essential for understanding the conflicting voices shaping your choices. By becoming aware of these cultural scripts, you can identify which ones align with your values and which ones you might want to let go of.

The Stories Culture Tells Us

Cultural scripts are often passed down through generations, quietly shaping thoughts, choices, and self-perceptions in ways that may go unnoticed. These scripts might reflect familiar beliefs or unspoken rules, such as:

- *Success means sacrificing everything for your career.*
- *Putting yourself first is selfish.*
- *Your worth is defined by what others think of you.*

These messages can become so ingrained that they feel automatic, as though they've always been part of how life is supposed to work. But when you step back and reflect, you might notice that not all inherited beliefs align with your true self or the life you want to create.

The goal isn't to judge these cultural messages as right or wrong but to bring awareness to how they influence your choices and values. Are they helping you live in a way that feels true to who you are now? Or are they holding you back from becoming the person you want to be?

Moving Toward Balance

When you recognize the cultural stories shaping your inner world, you create space to choose. These inherited narratives don't have to define you forever. But navigating cultural influences isn't about rejecting your heritage or silencing the voices of the past. It's about finding a balance that feels right for you. This means honoring the parts of your cultural identity that still resonate, while also giving yourself the space to question and step away from messages that no longer reflect who you are or who you want to become.

Finding this balance begins with reflection. You might ask yourself the following:

- What values from my culture feel meaningful to me?
- What inherited beliefs or expectations no longer align with the life I want to create?
- How can I make space for both my heritage and my individuality?

It's not about judging these messages as "good" or "bad." It's about understanding which cultural influences support the life you want to live and which ones might be holding you back.

When you take time to reflect, you start to integrate your identity in a way that feels authentic and empowering. This process isn't about getting it right all at once. It's about giving yourself the freedom to grow, shift, and adapt as you continue to align more fully with your true self.

The Architects of Memory: Crafting Our Personal Myths

You might recall from chapter 1, that our brains don't store experiences as perfect snapshots. Instead, they interpret, filter, and often distort reality to create a cohesive story about who we are.[8] This story, our personal myth, is constantly rewritten as we revisit memories and integrate new experiences.[9]

How Memory Shapes Us

Our memories don't store the past objectively. They are reconstructed, filtered, and reshaped to fit our evolving self-narrative. This process influences how we see ourselves and the world, often reinforcing certain beliefs while distorting others. Several cognitive biases shape this process, affecting what we remember, how we interpret it, and how it guides our decisions.[10]

- **Memory Shapes Us Through Negativity Bias and Confirmation Bias**: Your brain prioritizes negative experiences and seeks out information that reinforces existing beliefs.[11] If you believe you are "bad at relationships," you are more likely to recall every failed relationship while ignoring moments of connection and support. This filtering happens automatically, shaping how you see yourself and the world. Confirmation bias strengthens this effect by making you focus on information that aligns with what you already believe, making it harder to see the full picture of your strengths and possibilities.

- **Memory Shapes Us Through Cognitive Dissonance**: When new information contradicts your beliefs, your brain often resists it to maintain a sense of stability. This is known as cognitive dissonance, the mental discomfort that arises when reality challenges your self-perception. To reduce this discomfort, memory can reshape or even dismiss experiences that do not fit. Strong emotions, especially fear or self-doubt, make certain memories more deeply ingrained and harder to change.[12] For example, if you believe you are "not creative," your brain may downplay times when you successfully solved or had an original idea, making it difficult to recognize your own growth.

- **Memory Shapes Us by Highlighting Intense Moments and Endings**: Our memories don't preserve every detail of an experience. Instead, we tend to remember the most emotionally charged moment and how it ended, while much of the in-between fades. A difficult time in life that led to a positive resolution might be remembered more favorably than an overall good experience that ended in disappointment. This can distort how we evaluate past experiences, making them seem better or worse than they really were.[13] For example, a long vacation with one stressful final day might be remembered as unpleasant, even if most of the trip was enjoyable.

- **Memory Shapes Us Through the Way It Reconstructs and Filters the Past**: Memory isn't a perfect record. It's a reconstruction, constantly reshaped by new information, conversations, and even subtle suggestions. Over time, details shift, gaps get filled in, and what we recall may not be what actually happened. Meanwhile, the brain filters out details that seem unimportant or that don't fit our existing self-narrative.[14] While this helps us move on from minor details, it can also cause us to overlook moments that challenge limiting beliefs or offer a more balanced perspective. If you believe you always mess up under pressure, your brain will highlight failures while letting the times you handled things well fade into the background, reinforcing a version of yourself that isn't the full story. This process isn't something we actively control. Our brains automatically filter and reshape memories, often without us realizing it, reinforcing patterns of thought and belief that feel like objective truth.

- **Through the Influence of Current Emotions**: Present emotions can distort how we remember the past.[15] When you're feeling down, your brain tends to recall only failures, reinforcing feelings of inadequacy. Similarly, when you're happy, your brain tends to highlight positive memories, making challenges from the past feel less significant. This means that memory is not just a reflection of the past, but a reflection of how you feel in the present. When emotions shift, so does the way you recall past events, making memory a constantly evolving story rather than a fixed record of what actually happened.

The Science of Memory

The hippocampus processes memory, while the amygdala tags emotional significance to events. This collaboration explains why emotionally charged memories like a breakup or a major achievement are so vivid. Yet even vivid memories are prone to distortion. "Flashbulb memories," such as where you were during a major historical event, feel accurate but are often riddled with errors.[16] Understanding this malleability can help us approach our memories with curiosity rather than judgment.

The Role of Collective Memories and Intergenerational Trauma

Just as personal memories shape individual identity, collective memories shapes communities.[17] This shared history, whether traumatic or triumphant, leaves a lasting imprint on individuals, families, and cultures.

Research has shown that collective memories of trauma experienced by one generation can leave psychological imprints on subsequent generations.[18] For example:

- Children of Holocaust survivors often report heightened anxiety and hypervigilance, even without having suffered their parents' trauma themselves.[19]
- Descendants of enslaved people may inherit fears and mistrust rooted in the memories passed down of centuries of systemic oppression.[20]

These inherited narratives influence how individuals perceive safety, risk, and belonging. At the same time, positive collective memories, like cultural traditions or stories of resilience, can serve as a source of strength and identity.[21]

Moving Forward: Rewriting Your Self-Story

Understanding the layers of voices that shape your inner world is a powerful starting point of transformation. But the real progress lies in consciously choosing which narratives to embrace and which to rewrite. By challenging subconscious patterns, examining cultural scripts, and reframing memories, you can craft a self-story that reflects your true values and aspirations.

Key Takeways

Understanding the influences that shape your thoughts, beliefs, and self-story is not about blaming the past or pretending it doesn't exist. It's about recognizing how the voices of parents, culture, and personal experiences contribute to the patterns you carry today. These influences aren't flaws; they are part of being human. And by bringing them into awareness, you create space to question, reframe, and rewrite them to better align with who you are and the life you want to create.

- **Your thoughts aren't always your own.** You carry a "crowded room" of influences that shape your self-story. Your inner world is not just shaped by your survival instincts but also by the voices of parents, caregivers, cultural norms, and personal experiences. These messages can guide, support, or hold you back, often without you realizing it.
- **Your current identity isn't fixed by your past.** The beliefs you formed to make sense of early experiences can be updated as you grow.
- **Question what you've absorbed.** The lessons and messages you internalized from childhood, culture, and memories may feel permanent, but they are not. Recognizing where these messages come from gives you the power to question, challenge, and rewrite them in ways that align with the person you are becoming.
- **Shine a light on the subconscious.** Bringing subconscious voices into awareness is a key part of the process to bring about change. Up to 95% of your thoughts and behaviors come from subconscious patterns that run automatically. When you identify the voices that

influence you, whether they are supportive or critical, you create space to challenge their hold and intentionally choose the narratives you want to carry forward.

Self-awareness gives us the ability to notice these voices and the stories they tell. But awareness alone doesn't change much. The next step is action: challenging the voices, building new habits, and taking small steps to create the life we want. It's not about changing everything all at once; it's about consistently choosing to take one step at a time toward something better.

Moving from Understanding to Action

Following are five actionable steps to help you take action with your newfound understanding to reframe your narratives, shift old patterns, and create a more authentic and fulfilling life.

- **Identify the voices shaping your decisions.** Pay close attention to the thoughts that arise during moments of self-doubt, hesitation, or overthinking. Ask yourself, "Where is this voice coming from? Is it my own, or does it belong to someone else, like a parent, teacher, or cultural expectation?"
- **Choose one belief to rewrite.** Reflect on a belief or script that holds you back, such as "I'll never be good at this" or "I have to put others' needs ahead of mine." Write it down, then consciously reframe it to reflect your strengths, growth, or new values. For instance, "I'm not good at this" could become "I'm learning and improving as I go."

- **Practice replacing criticizing voices with compassionate ones.** When you notice a harsh or judgmental thought arising, pause and ask: "What would I say to a friend in this situation?" Respond to yourself with kindness instead of criticism. This practice helps quiet old, unhelpful voices and replaces them with a more supportive inner dialogue.
- **Reconnect with your values.** Take some time to reflect on what truly matters to you. What do you want your life to stand for? Which beliefs or expectations feel misaligned with the person you are or the life you're building? Let your values, not the echoes of others, guide your choices.
- **Experiment with small actions that challenge old patterns.** If you tend to avoid risks, try doing something small that feels just outside your comfort zone, like sharing your opinion in a group setting or asking for help on a project. Each small action teaches your brain that it is safe to step outside old beliefs and scripts.

Each of these steps is a small shift in the direction of growth. By practicing these actions regularly, you can begin to rewrite the internal scripts that hold you back and take ownership of your story.

3

The Neuroscience of Motivation: Understanding Why You Feel Stuck

"You don't have to see the whole staircase,
just take the first step."
—Martin Luther King Jr.,
civil rights leader

We've already talked about how ancestral wiring, our culture, heritage, and personal history impact our thoughts and actions. Now we're going to focus on the science of motivation itself. Motivation can feel like a mystery. Some days, it's easy to take on challenges, while other days, even simple tasks feel overwhelming.

Maybe one day you wake up feeling like a 100 lb. weight is pressing on your chest. The goals you set yesterday, or even last week, remain untouched, and the thought of tackling them feels impossible. Your inner voice might whisper, *Why even try? It's useless*, or *I'll never change*. You're not alone. Millions of people experience this cycle of feeling stuck, unsure how to escape. To find the way out, you need to understand what is really happening in your brain when you feel stuck. By exploring how your brain processes goals, rewards, and stress, you'll learn why you sometimes feel paralyzed and what you can do to get moving again.

The Basics of Motivation: Internal vs. External Motivation

Motivation is what helps you take action, whether it's for small, daily tasks or big, life-changing goals. Without it, even simple steps can feel impossible. But when you understand how motivation works in your brain, you can learn how to use it to your advantage.

Motivation isn't about willpower alone. It's shaped by how your brain responds to different kinds of rewards and challenges. Sometimes, motivation comes from outside you, like an award, a deadline, or wanting to meet someone else's expectations. Other times, it comes from within, a desire to grow, learn, or feel a sense of accomplishment. When you can understand what drives you in different situations, you can take steps to tap into that drive and keep moving forward.

Let's start with what comes from the outside, or external motivation. Think about a time when you worked hard toward a goal because there was a clear reason to do it. Maybe you wanted to get in shape for a wedding or class reunion? What about working harder because a promotion was on the line? This type of motivation is fueled by external factors, things outside of yourself that push you to act. It can be powerful because it often provides a clear and immediate reason to get started.[1]

Now think about a time you did something just because it felt good or meaningful to you. Maybe you started gardening because it brought you peace, or you stuck to a new habit like journaling because it helped you feel more grounded. Maybe you picked up a new hobby because it sparked your curiosity, or you kept exercising because it gave you a sense of accomplishment. This is internal motivation. It comes from within, a desire to do something because it aligns with your values, interests, or goals.[2]

Both types of motivation have their place. External motivators are helpful for pushing us to action, especially when you're struggling to begin. Internal motivators, however, are often what keep you going over the long term. When something truly matters to you, it's easier to stay committed even when it gets hard. Both are important, and understanding how to use them together can make a big difference in how you approach your goals.

Here's the tricky part. Your brain is naturally drawn to external motivators because they promise quick results. Throughout history, our ancestors relied on short-term rewards like finding food or gaining approval from their group to survive. Today, the same system in your brain responds to external rewards by releasing dopamine, the chemical that makes you feel good and reinforces the behavior.

Internal motivators, on the other hand, don't always come with instant gratification. Goals like improving your health, building meaningful relationships, or developing a skill require time and patience. Because they don't provide that immediate feel-good response, they can be harder to sustain.

Here's the good part: you don't have to rely on just one type of motivation. You can use both together to stay on track. Here is an example: If you're struggling to start a long-term goal that's meaningful to you, add an external reward to make the first step easier, like taking a break or treating yourself after completing a task. You can also choose external rewards that connect your actions to a deeper reason or purpose, reminding you of why the long-term goal matters, like rewarding yourself after a set number of visits to the gym with a framed picture of an activity you want to be able to do.

Now that we've explored the basics of motivation, let's look at how your brain's chemistry shapes what you feel motivated to do. In the next section, we'll dive into the science of dopamine, your brain's reward chemical, and explore how it can both help and hinder your progress.

Your Brain on Motivation: Dopamine and the Reward System

Dopamine gets a lot of attention these days. People call it the "feel-good" chemical, but that is only part of the story. Dopamine is not just about pleasure; it is about wanting, craving, and motivation. It's what makes you feel excited about a reward and gets you to take action.[3] Think of dopamine as your brain's way of saying, *This could feel good! Go for it!* Without it, it would be hard to start anything at all. In studies, mice that could not produce dopamine would not move to get food, even when they were starving. But when food was placed in their mouths, they ate it, showing they still experienced pleasure. Without dopamine, they lacked the motivation to seek it out on their own. This experiment shows that dopamine is not just about feeling good, it is what pushes us to take action.[4]

When you accomplish a task, enjoy a great meal, or achieve a personal goal, your brain releases dopamine. This gives you a sense of satisfaction and reinforces the behavior, encouraging you to repeat it. For our prehistoric ancestors, this system was essential for survival. Dopamine motivated them to hunt, forage, and form social bonds, all of which required sustained effort.[5] However, because rewards were unpredictable and often required struggle, dopamine was naturally regulated. The brain would release it in bursts when an opportunity was near, driving action, but these surges were balanced by long periods of effort, preventing overstimulation. Unlike today, where rewards are available at the tap of a screen, our ancestors had to work for them. Hunting, gathering, and forming social bonds took time and effort, which meant dopamine was released in smaller bursts rather than all at once. Because rewards were unpredictable and required persistence, their brains naturally cycled between effort and reward, preventing the constant overstimulation we experience today.

Today, that same system still motivates us, but our environment is very different. Instead of foraging or hunting, we now live in a world full of quick and easy rewards. Checking your messages, snacking on chips, or watching just one more episode of your favorite show can all give your brain a small boost of dopamine without much effort.[6]

These quick hits feel good in the moment, but they do not bring the same lasting fulfillment as working toward something meaningful. Over time, your brain can become conditioned to prefer these easy rewards over bigger, more challenging goals, even when those goals would make you happier in the long run. This happens because the brain adapts to frequent dopamine spikes by reducing receptor sensitivity.[7] Unlike our ancestors, who had natural breaks between dopamine-releasing activities, modern life bombards us with constant stimulation. As a result, everyday experiences that once felt rewarding, like reading a book or having a conversation, may start to feel less engaging in comparison to high-dopamine activities. The more you flood your brain with easy dopamine, the less satisfying everyday life can feel.

In chapter 1, we talked about how your brain automates the things you do repeatedly. If you have gotten into the habit of checking your phone every time you feel bored, your brain will make that behavior automatic. Before you even realize it, you are scrolling through videos or checking your news feed.

This doesn't mean you are lazy or unmotivated. It just means your brain is wired to seek out predictable rewards with the least effort possible, a mechanism that helped our ancestors survive but can work against us in a world of instant gratification. But there is a catch: The more we chase pleasure, the more the brain tries to restore balance by increasing pain or discomfort. This is why too much of a good thing, whether it's screen time, junk food, or video games, can actually leave you feeling worse afterward.[8]

You may have also heard of something called a "dopamine detox." The idea is that by stepping away from activities like social media or video games, you can reset your brain's dopamine levels. While the concept sounds nice, it oversimplifies how dopamine works. Dopamine does not need to be reset. It is always at work, helping you focus, make decisions, and stay motivated. However, when the brain is overstimulated by constant rewards, reducing exposure to high-dopamine triggers allows your reward system to recalibrate, helping you find pleasure in everyday experiences again. In other words, stepping away from high-dopamine activities does not "reset" your brain, but it can help restore balance, making simple joys feel rewarding again.

What people actually experience during these so-called detoxes is not a reset, but rather a chance to reduce overstimulation, giving their brain the space to recover its ability to enjoy simpler, more sustainable sources of pleasure.

This doesn't mean you have to avoid everything that feels good. That would not be practical or enjoyable. Instead, it's again about finding balance. Ask yourself how often you reach for easy rewards, like your phone or junk food, and whether those habits are getting in the way of the things you care about. If they are, try replacing those quick fixes with something more meaningful. For example, instead of scrolling through social media when you feel bored, go for a walk or call a friend. These activities might not feel as instantly satisfying, but they help you build healthier habits and focus on what really matters to you.

Another way to work with your brain's reward system is to make difficult tasks more enjoyable. If you don't like cleaning, listen to your favorite music while you tidy up. If you are trying to stick to an exercise routine, pair your workout with a podcast or audiobook you love. This way, you introduce a reward into the process, making it more engaging.

Dopamine is not the enemy. It is your brain's tool for helping you take action and build habits. The key is making sure those habits align with what you truly want. By paying attention to how dopamine influences your choices, you can shift your focus from quick distractions to activities that bring lasting fulfillment. Over time, this helps you stay motivated because you won't have to rely on willpower alone. Your brain will be working with you to create a life that feels meaningful.

While understanding dopamine can help you take charge of your reward system, there is another big factor that often blocks motivation: stress. Stress changes how your brain functions, making it harder to focus, take action, or even care about your goals. In the next section, we will dive into why stress makes motivation harder and what you can do to overcome it.

Why Stress Makes Motivation Harder

Stress plays a huge role in how motivated you feel. When you're stressed, your brain releases cortisol, a hormone designed to help you handle immediate threats. In small doses, stress can sharpen your focus and get you ready to act.

But when stress lingers for too long or your brain mistakenly interprets it as danger, it stops helping and starts to hurt.[9]

This is because your body operates on a system called allostatic balance. Allostatic balance is your brain's ability to maintain stability while adapting to stress. When stress is occasional, your body can recover and return to equilibrium. But when stress becomes too frequent or prolonged, it leads to allostatic load, a buildup of stress-related wear and tear that disrupts normal function. Over time, this depletes your mental and physical resources, making it harder to focus, make decisions, and stay motivated.

Chronic stress can mess with your brain and motivation in ways that leave you feeling stuck, overwhelmed, or just plain worn out. Maybe you've had days where you feel like you're running on empty, struggling to get anything done even though you know there's so much waiting for your attention. It's not just in your head. It's your brain responding to stress in a way that makes it harder to focus, think clearly, or take action.

Stress doesn't just sit quietly in the background. Its voice can be loud and relentless. It might whisper, *You're not doing enough*, or shout, *You're going to fail!* Sometimes, it screams, *This is too much! You can't handle it.* These aren't just random thoughts. They are part of your brain's survival system trying to keep you safe. The problem is that survival mode wasn't designed for modern life. It is supposed to help you run from predators, not juggle overflowing to-do lists, manage financial stress, or navigate complicated relationships.

Here's what's happening behind the scenes. When you're stressed to the point that your inner caveperson feels like you are running from a predator, your brain prioritizes safety over everything else. The fight, flight, or freeze response kicks in, and cortisol floods your system. This puts your brain on high alert, ready to respond to danger. But instead of protecting you, this constant state of vigilance ends up hurting your ability to think clearly or act at all. Chronic stress impacts your brain in several ways:[10]

- **Cognitive function suffers**: Chronic cortisol can damage the prefrontal cortex, the part of your brain responsible for decision-making, planning, and self-control. This makes it harder to focus, weigh your options, or figure out what to do next. You may forget tasks, feel indecisive, or avoid things altogether.
- **Your memory takes a hit**: Stress can shrink the hippocampus, the memory center of your brain, leading to forgetfulness and trouble recalling tasks or conversations.
- **Motivation tanks**: Prolonged stress lowers dopamine, the chemical that makes you feel motivated and makes you enjoy things. As allostatic load builds, the cumulative strain of chronic stress disrupts your brain's ability to regulate dopamine properly. This makes activities you normally enjoy feel pointless or exhausting, leaving you unmotivated and emotionally drained.
- **Burnout sets in**: Over time, constant stress drains your energy and emotional reserves, leaving you physically and mentally exhausted.
- **You become hypervigilant**: The amygdala, your brain's fear and emotion center, stays on high alert, scanning for threats even where there are none. Everyday problems start to feel like life-or-death emergencies, increasing anxiety and keeping you stuck in survival mode.

It's easy to see how chronic stress can trap you in a cycle of inaction, but thankfully, it doesn't have to control you. Once you understand how stress works, you can start working with your brain instead of against it.

Small steps can make a big difference. Taking a walk, practicing mindfulness, or spending time with someone who makes you laugh can help calm your nervous system and lower cortisol levels. Regular exercise, deep breathing, and even jotting down your thoughts in a journal can give your brain the reset it needs to think more clearly and act more intentionally.

Stress is your brain's way of saying, "Hey, I'm trying to protect you," but sometimes it gets it wrong. By learning to manage stress, you can quiet that voice of panic and start making decisions from a calmer, clearer place. It's not about eliminating stress entirely. It's about learning how to handle it, so it doesn't handle you.

Understanding how motivation works and how stress impacts your ability to act is important to getting unstuck. But how do you actually create lasting change when your brain seems determined to stick to its old habits? In the next chapter, we'll explore the science of neuroplasticity, your brain's ability to rewire itself, and how you can use it to rewire unhelpful patterns, form new habits, and reimagine what's possible for your life.

Key Takeaways

Motivation can feel like a mystery, but when you understand how your brain works, you can take charge of it and start moving forward. Here are three key insights:

- **Motivation is shaped by both internal and external drivers.** External rewards give you the push to start, while internal values sustain you over time. Understanding what motivates you helps you balance short-term rewards with long-term fulfillment.
- **Dopamine is a guide, not a shortcut.** Dopamine helps you take action, but modern distractions can hijack this system. Redirecting your focus toward meaningful goals makes it easier to stay on track.
- **Stress interferes with motivation by putting your brain in survival mode.** Chronic stress makes it harder to focus, plan, or enjoy the things that matter to you. Learning how to calm your nervous system can help you reset and take intentional steps toward your goals.

By understanding the forces that shape your motivation, you can work with your brain, not against it, to create the momentum needed for meaningful progress.

Moving from Understanding to Action

Knowing how motivation works is only part of the puzzle. To move beyond feeling stuck, you need intentional actions that align with how your brain functions. Here are five strategies to put these insights into practice:

- **Explore what energizes you.** Take time to notice which activities leave you feeling motivated and fulfilled versus drained or distracted. Write down what gives you energy and how you can incorporate those things into your daily life.

- **Reframe your relationship with stress.** Instead of avoiding stress altogether, try reframing it as a signal that something matters to you. Acknowledge the stress, then focus on calming practices, like deep breathing or mindfulness, to shift out of survival mode and back into clarity.

- **Experiment with different motivators.** Ask yourself, "What would make this task easier to start?" Pair your goals with small, enjoyable incentives or connect them to a purpose that matters to you. Experiment to find what works best for you.

- **Audit your distractions.** Take inventory of activities that provide instant gratification but might interfere with your long-term goals. For example, track how much time you spend on your phone or watching TV. Identify one area where you can set limits and redirect your focus.

- **Reconnect with what you've already accomplished.** When you feel stuck, reflect on the goals you've achieved or challenges you've overcome in the past. Remind yourself that you've succeeded before and can do it again. This builds confidence and reinforces your capacity for progress.

Motivation isn't about forcing yourself to act. It's about creating an environment that supports your brain's natural tendencies while directing them toward what truly matters. By experimenting with new approaches, reflecting on what works, and learning to manage stress, you can shift out of inertia and move toward a life of purpose and fulfillment.

4

Your Brain's Power to Change

*"We cannot always control what happens to us, but we can
choose how we respond, and our responses can either open us up
or close us off to possibilities for growth."*

—Daniel J. Siegel,
psychiatrist and author

Even though your brain's prehistoric wiring prioritizes
safety and familiarity, making change feel like a threat, it
is actually capable of remarkable transformation. Dan Siegel's
words remind us that while we can't always control life's
circumstances, we do have a choice in how we respond, and
those choices can reshape our reality. This isn't just a feel-good
statement; it's grounded in science. Your brain is incredibly
adaptable. Thanks to something called "neuroplasticity," you
have the power to break old cycles and create new patterns.[1]

Neuroplasticity refers to your brain's ability to reorganize
itself by forming new neural connections throughout life.[2]
This means your brain isn't fixed—it can adapt, rewire, and
create new pathways no matter your age or circumstances.

Think of those deeply ingrained habits, whether it's procrastinating, overthinking, or automatically doubting yourself, as being stuck in "neural cement." These are thought
patterns and routines your brain has repeated so many times,
they've become automatic. Like a well-worn trail in a forest,

it feels easier to keep walking the same path than to forge a new one.[3]

The good news? Cement can crack. It may feel hard as stone, but with the right tools, like curiosity and consistent effort, it can break apart and soften over time.

Curiosity is the key to unlocking neuroplasticity.[4] It helps you question your automatic responses and explore different ways of thinking and acting. Without curiosity, change can feel like a chore or a punishment. But with curiosity, you approach it as an adventure, an opportunity to learn something new about yourself.

Neuroplasticity is at its peak during infancy and adolescence, allowing us to develop new skills and adapt to the world at lightning speed. But while this capacity slows as we age, it doesn't disappear. Modern neuroscience shows that even as adults, we can change the structure and function of our brains through consistent, intentional effort.

Every time you make a conscious choice to think or act differently, you strengthen new neural pathways. Over time, these pathways grow stronger, while the old, unhelpful patterns weaken. It's not magic; it's biology. This gradual rewiring process is at the heart of personal growth and transformation.

But here's the catch: To truly harness neuroplasticity, you need to address the stories you tell yourself. If you're stuck in narratives like "I can't change" or "This is just who I am," your brain will continue to reinforce those beliefs. But by challenging those stories and replacing them with more empowering ones, you can reshape your self-perception and your reality.

Neuroplasticity empowers us to unlearn old habits, overcome emotional barriers, and build the life we want. Change isn't immediate, but with patience and consistency, you can transform both your brain and your life.

Neuroplasticity shows us that change is possible, even when the odds seem stacked against us. But how do we know it works in real life, not just in theory? In the next section, we'll explore some incredible stories of how people have harnessed the brain's ability to adapt under extreme circumstances. These modern-day examples will show you just how powerful your brain can be and inspire you to apply neuroplasticity to your own life.

Incredible Stories of Brain Adaptation

Sometimes it feels impossible to believe that real change can happen. But when you hear the incredible ways the brain can adapt, even under the most extreme circumstances, it's hard not to feel hopeful. The following stories aren't just inspiring, they prove that the brain is capable of more than we can imagine.

Take Mora Leeb, for example. At just nine months old, she had a surgery called a hemispherectomy, where doctors removed the left side of her brain to stop severe seizures. The left side of the brain controls speech, so doctors didn't think Mora would ever talk. But her right brain had other plans. It rewired itself to take over, and by age fifteen, Mora gave a speech at her Bat Mitzvah, proof of just how adaptable the brain can be.[5]

You might not be recovering from surgery, but the same principle holds true: Your brain is always capable of adapting and learning, no matter where you're starting from.

Or think about Mark McEwen, a former news anchor who suffered a debilitating stroke at age fifty-one. He lost his speech and mobility, but through years of rehabilitation and persistence, Mark regained much of his independence.

Today, he's a motivational speaker, sharing his journey of recovery and resilience.[6]

And then there's Sharon Stone. At age forty-three, the celebrated actress had a stroke that left her struggling with speech, vision, and balance. Recovery wasn't easy; it took years of therapy and determination. But she came back stronger, using her platform to advocate for stroke awareness and the power of perseverance.[7]

What these stories show is that even in the face of incredible challenges, the brain has an astounding ability to adapt. If someone with half a brain can relearn how to speak, or a stroke survivor can rebuild their life, imagine what's possible for you.

These incredible stories show us that change is not only possible, it's built into the very biology of our brains. While neuroplasticity provides the foundation for transformation, the habits we form play a critical role in reinforcing the paths we take. In the next section, we'll explore how habits shape our daily lives, why they're so hard to change, and how you can use the science of habits to create new, positive patterns that align with your goals.

Habits: The Patterns That Shape Your Life

You might remember from chapter 1 how your brain loves habits because they save energy. Instead of using mental resources to figure out how to tie your shoes or drive to work each day, your brain automates these behaviors through the basal ganglia.[8] This part of your brain acts like an efficiency expert, offloading repetitive tasks so you can focus on more immediate or complex challenges. This automation is what makes habits so powerful, whether they help or hurt you.

As we discussed earlier, your brain is inherently neutral. It will create a habit out of whatever you do most often, whether it's going for a walk every morning or scrolling on your phone. These habits form the foundation of your daily routines, keeping your life running smoothly and freeing up mental space for bigger decisions.[9] But the same system that helps you build positive routines, like exercising or brushing your teeth, can also trap you in cycles you'd rather break, like procrastinating or doomscrolling. While habits let your brain operate on autopilot, which is great for efficiency, it also means ingrained patterns can feel nearly impossible to escape.

Why Habits Stick and Why They're Hard to Break

Habits stick because they're built right into the way your brain works. Every time you do something over and over, your brain strengthens the connection between the trigger (what prompts the habit), the action (what you do), and the reward (why it feels good). This cycle is called the habit loop, and it runs on your brain's reward system, especially dopamine, the chemical that says, *Let's do that again!*[10] The more you repeat a habit, the more automatic it becomes. Over time, it's like carving a trail in your brain, it gets easier to follow, but harder to change direction.

For example, imagine you're feeling stressed (that's the trigger), so you reach for your phone and start scrolling social media (that's the action). Maybe you laugh at a funny video or feel distracted from whatever was bothering you (that's the reward). Your brain logs this as a win and says, *Next time you're stressed, do that again!* Over time, this response becomes so automatic, you don't even think about it, you just grab your phone without realizing it.

You might think of these neural pathways as "cemented" habits. They can feel solid and unchangeable, but as we've already established, cement can crack. With curiosity, patience, and consistent effort, you can loosen the grip of old patterns and create new ones.

This is where neuroplasticity comes in. As we've discussed earlier, your brain is constantly rewiring itself in response to your experiences and behaviors. Breaking a habit involves weakening the old neural pathway and building a new one. This process takes time and effort, but it's absolutely possible. Each time you consciously choose a new behavior, you're strengthening a new "trail" in your brain, and over time, that new pathway can become the default.

The Link Between Habits and Self-Concept

Habits don't just influence what you do, they shape how you see yourself. If you've developed a habit of procrastinating or skipping workouts, it's easy to start telling yourself a story: "I'm lazy" or "I'm not disciplined." Over time, these habits reinforce what you believe about yourself and your abilities, and your brain locks you into a self-concept that feels unchangeable.

This is what we explored earlier when we talked about the personal myths and voices in your head. These are the stories your brain tells you based on your past experiences and routines. Your habits and self-concept are part of a feedback loop: Your habits influence how you see yourself, and how you see yourself influences your habits. For example, if you think of yourself as someone who "can't stick to goals," you're more likely to avoid making new changes because you've already decided you'll fail.

But just as habits can reinforce limiting beliefs, they can also help you rewrite your self-concept. When you make small, consistent changes, like going for a walk after dinner or sticking to a five-minute mindfulness practice, you're not just building a new habit. You're proving to yourself, "I'm someone who takes care of my health," or "I'm capable of making positive changes." Over time, these small wins can chip away at old labels and help you see yourself in a new light.

This is where it helps to remember your past victories. Even if your brain tends to fixate on failures (thanks to negativity bias), you've faced challenges and overcome them before. The fact that you're reading this now is proof that you're willing to learn and grow. When you reflect on those wins, even the small ones, you can remind yourself that change is not only possible, it's something you've already done before.

Why Change Feels Hard and How to Make It Easier

So why does changing a simple habit, like eating healthier or worrying less, feel so difficult? Part of the answer lies in your brain's wiring. As we touched on earlier, your brain is still guided by its "inner caveperson" a survival mechanism that prioritizes safety and familiarity over risk and uncertainty. Even when a habit isn't serving you, your brain may interpret change as a potential threat, making you feel anxious or resistant to trying something new. This is why even small shifts, like skipping dessert or waking up earlier, can feel uncomfortable at first.

The key to working with your brain, instead of against it, is to start small. When you aim for big, sweeping changes, your brain goes into overload, and the effort feels unsustainable.

But when you focus on small, manageable steps, like drinking a glass of water before your morning coffee or spending two minutes tidying your workspace, you're showing your brain that change is safe and achievable. These tiny wins may not seem significant at first, but they add up, creating momentum and building your confidence.

Another way to work with your brain is to replace old habits instead of erasing them. Your brain is wired to seek rewards, so rather than trying to stop a habit cold turkey, focus on finding an alternative behavior that satisfies the same need. For example, if you're trying to stop scrolling through social media before bed, you might replace that habit with reading a book or journaling instead. By swapping the routine while keeping the reward, you're making it easier for your brain to adapt to the change.

Finally, remember that curiosity is your best ally. When you approach your habits with curiosity instead of judgment, you can start to understand the cues and triggers behind them. Why do you reach for your phone when you're bored? What are you really craving when you snack late at night? When you treat your habits as puzzles to solve, rather than personal failures, you create space for experimentation and growth.

Habits aren't just about routines; they're also closely tied to the emotional and cognitive patterns your brain uses to navigate the world. When you're stuck in an unhelpful habit, it's not just the behavior that holds you back, it's the emotional cues and automatic responses wired into your brain.

For example, think about the habit of procrastinating. It's not just about putting things off; often, it's triggered by anxiety, fear of failure, or feeling overwhelmed. Your brain's reaction to those emotions can push you into autopilot mode, cycling through the same familiar (but unhelpful) behaviors.

This brings us to an important question: How does your brain decide whether to act out of instinct or pause to make a thoughtful choice? Understanding how your brain processes emotions, fear, and decision-making is essential to breaking free from unhelpful patterns. In the next section, we'll explore two distinct pathways your brain uses to process these experiences: the fast, reactive "low road" and the slower, deliberate "high road." By understanding these systems, you'll gain new tools to regulate your emotions, respond more thoughtfully, and pave the way for lasting change.

Paths Your Brain Takes: Instinct vs. Intention

You just learned about strategies you can use to make it easier to start changing habits. But while habits are a huge part of your daily life, not everything you do is a result of a habit. Sometimes your brain has to make decisions on the fly, deciding between reacting instinctively or taking a more thoughtful approach. But which one wins, your gut reaction or your intention?

It turns out, your brain has two pathways for responding to the world around you: one that's quick and automatic, and another that's slower and deliberate. Neuroscientists often refer to these as the low road and the high road. Think of them as your brain's two options for navigating challenges, one gets you out of immediate danger, and the other helps you carefully plan your next steps.

The Low Road:[11] Fast but Reactive

The low road is the brain's fast lane. It's powered by the amygdala, the part of your brain responsible for fear and emotional reactions. The low road works in milliseconds. Its job is simple: keep you alive. It's automatic and unconscious, meaning it doesn't take much thought to leap into action when something feels threatening.

This response was critical for our ancestors. When faced with a predator, the low road allowed them to react immediately, fight, flee, or freeze. In today's world, the same pathway still serves a purpose, but as we've established, modern stressors aren't usually life-or-death. Unfortunately, the low road doesn't know the difference. Whether it's a scary email from your boss or someone cutting you off in traffic, the amygdala treats it as a saber-toothed tiger, triggering a flood of stress hormones and making you react without much thought.

Think of a moment when you've reacted emotionally, maybe you snapped at someone, fired off a hasty reply to a message, or spiraled into anxiety after a small setback. That's the low road at work. It prioritizes speed over accuracy, meaning you might act before you've had time to think it through.

The High Road:[12] Slower but Intentional

The high road, on the other hand, is your brain's scenic route. It's powered by the prefrontal cortex, the part of your brain responsible for reasoning, decision-making, and self-control. The high road takes its time to process what's happening, giving you space to pause, assess the situation, and respond thoughtfully.

Let's say you're walking through a dimly lit parking lot and notice a shadowy figure. Your low road might immediately kick in, flooding your body with adrenaline and preparing you to run. But then your high road steps in. You notice the figure is wearing a security uniform and carrying a flashlight. With this new information, you calm down and realize there's no danger. The high road lets you think things through and choose your response, rather than reacting out of instinct.

Why the Low Road Often Wins

If the high road is so much wiser, why do we so often default to the low road? The answer lies in biology. The low road is fast and easy; it's always on standby to handle emergencies. The high road, on the other hand, takes time and effort, which can feel like a luxury when you're stressed or overwhelmed.

When your brain perceives something as a threat, even if it's just a looming deadline or an awkward social interaction, it prioritizes safety. The amygdala hijacks your thinking, pushing you to act quickly. This makes sense in situations where speed is critical, but in daily life, it can leave you feeling reactive, anxious, or stuck in unhelpful patterns.

Shifting from Instinct to Intention

Here's the good news: While you can't eliminate the low road (and you wouldn't want to; it has its purpose), you can learn to strengthen your high road. The more you practice pausing, reflecting, and choosing your responses intentionally, the more natural it becomes to rely on the high road in moments of stress or uncertainty.

For example, mindfulness practices like deep breathing or meditation can help you slow down and notice when your low road is taking over. By creating space between a trigger and your response, you engage your prefrontal cortex and give yourself the chance to respond thoughtfully rather than react impulsively.

And just like with habits, repetition is key. The more you practice engaging the high road, the stronger those neural pathways become. Over time, this makes it easier to stay calm, think clearly, and act with intention, even in challenging situations.

Understanding how your brain processes decisions is a powerful step toward living more intentionally. But how do these pathways influence the way we interact with others? Relationships are one of the most complex areas of our lives, and the brain plays a huge role in how we connect, empathize, and sometimes clash with the people around us. In the next section, we'll dive into the fascinating neuroscience of relationships and why understanding your brain can help you navigate even the trickiest dynamics.

Why Relationships Are So Complicated (and So Worth It)

I personally believe that being human is at its most complicated in the context of relationships. Something happens when we interact with others; it flips a switch in our brains. At a sensory level, we become acutely aware of potential threats or rewards, and our instincts kick in. Remember the dual nature we talked about back in chapter 1? That constant push and pull between fear and connection? That is part of it. Remember when I said humans are the most dangerous creatures on the planet? That is part of it too. And remember when I said we are wired to connect? That is at the core of it all.[13]

If you want to turn on your inner caveperson, go out and talk to a stranger or stand in a crowded room. Relationships, whether with friends, family, coworkers, or strangers, complicate things more than anything else in life. They can make us happy, drive us crazy, or push us to the brink of frustration. And I am not just talking about romantic relationships here. Relationships of any kind are the battleground where so much of our brain's wiring plays out.[14]

It's amazing and infuriating what people can do to one another. We're messy, ugly, immature, superbly intelligent, and graceful, and we just don't always do or say the right thing. Sometimes we make things up. Sometimes we feel driven by other people to do things that can be wonderful or horrible. My clients and I frequently get into theoretical conversations about the world around us, about why "Karens" behave so absurdly, why people snap in traffic, or why we all do the things we do.

I tell my clients that it's all in our wiring.

How Your Brain Responds to Relationships

At its core, the way we engage in relationships is influenced by the structure and chemistry of our brains, much of which was shaped by our ancestors' survival needs. Relationships, whether with a partner, a coworker, or even a stranger, activate key regions in your brain that are designed to detect danger, interpret emotions, and seek connection.[15] Take the amygdala, for example. This part of your brain acts as an alarm system, constantly scanning for potential threats. If someone raises their voice or sends you a curt text, your amygdala might react instantly, treating the situation as dangerous and triggering your fight, flight, or freeze response. In our ancestors' world, this response helped them avoid harm, but today it can misfire, making us feel defensive or anxious over everyday misunderstandings.[16]

Then there is the prefrontal cortex, the logical and deliberate part of your brain. While the amygdala is quick to react, the prefrontal cortex helps you pause, reflect, and decide how to respond thoughtfully. If the amygdala is your inner caveperson, the prefrontal cortex is like your wise elder, reminding you to take a breath and think: *Was that comment really an attack, or am I taking it too personally?*[17]

And let us not forget mirror neurons, the parts of your brain that help you empathize with others. These specialized cells allow you to feel what someone else is feeling. When someone smiles at you, your mirror neurons light up and encourage you to smile back.[18] They are why emotions, both good and bad, are contagious. If you have ever felt your mood lift after spending time with a happy friend or felt drained after being around someone who is stressed, those are your mirror neurons at work.

How Brain Chemicals Influence Connection

Relationships are not just shaped by the structure of your brain. Neurochemicals also play a huge role in how you connect with others. For example, oxytocin, often called the bonding hormone, is released during moments of closeness, like hugging, sharing a meaningful conversation, or even making eye contact with someone you trust. Oxytocin fosters connection and reduces stress, telling your brain, "This person makes you feel safe."[19]

Dopamine, the brain's reward chemical, motivates you to seek out positive interactions. It reinforces social behaviors by giving you little hits of pleasure when your efforts pay off, like laughing with loved ones or getting a thoughtful reply to a text.[20]

Serotonin, often called the mood stabilizer, helps you stay calm and measured in social situations. When serotonin is balanced, you feel steady and in control. But when serotonin is low, it can lead to irritability, social anxiety, or heightened sensitivity to rejection.[21]

Why Relationships Can Hurt

These brain systems are what make relationships so powerful, but they also explain why relationships can be so overwhelming. The same wiring that helps you bond with others can also amplify feelings of rejection or conflict. For instance, social rejection does not just hurt emotionally; it activates the same neural pathways as physical pain.[22]

This is why a harsh comment, being excluded from a group, or feeling misunderstood can feel like a gut punch. Your brain interprets these experiences as threats, and your amygdala kicks into overdrive. The voice of rejection might whisper, *You are not good enough*, or *This always happens to you*. These feelings are not just in your head; they are wired into your biology.

Rewiring Your Brain for Better Relationships

So how do you start rewiring your brain for better relationships? It begins with self-awareness. When you recognize your patterns, like always avoiding conflict or struggling with trust, you gain the power to change them. Practice pausing before reacting, challenge the stories you tell yourself about others, and intentionally nurture connection, even in small ways. Relationships might be complicated, but they are also one of the richest opportunities for growth.

Your Brain, Your Story

The habits we form, the narratives we tell ourselves, and the relationships we cultivate all shape our lives. None of these are unchangeable. Thanks to neuroplasticity, you can rewrite your story. By making small, consistent changes, you can strengthen new pathways in your brain, create healthier habits, and build a life aligned with who you truly want to be.

Neuroplasticity shows us that our brains are not static. They are adaptable and capable of rewiring and creating new possibilities at any stage of life. When you recognize that your brain's prehistoric wiring, your habits, and your inner narratives are not your destiny, you begin to reclaim your agency.

By challenging old patterns, engaging the high road, and fostering self-compassion, you can write a new story that aligns with the life you want to live. Change takes time, and setbacks are part of the process. Each small choice you make to act differently, think differently, or see yourself differently strengthens the neural pathways that support growth and resilience. Over time, these small choices lead to lasting transformation.

Your brain is not holding you hostage. It is waiting for your direction. With patience, consistency, and intention, you can harness its incredible adaptability to release old cycles and step into a future that reflects your truest self.

Key Takeaways

Understanding your brain's ability to alter your habits, beliefs, and relationships can empower you to make lasting changes. Here are the key insights from this chapter:

- **Your brain is built for change.** Neuroplasticity proves that it can rewire itself at any age. Old patterns aren't indelible; with effort and consistency, you can break habits and develop new, healthier pathways.
- **Habits are powerful, but can be reshaped.** They are created through repeated behavior, forming automatic pathways in your brain. However, small, consistent actions can weaken old pathways and replace them with new ones that align with your goals.
- **Relationships shape your brain.** And the way you connect with others is deeply influenced by your brain's wiring. Positive interactions release chemicals like oxytocin, which foster trust and connection, while conflicts can activate the brain's fear responses. By practicing self-awareness and intentional communication, you can rewire how you respond to and engage in relationships.
- **The stories you tell yourself shape your behavior.** Your inner narratives, like *I'm not disciplined*, or *I can't change*, reinforce limiting beliefs. By questioning these stories and rewriting them with curiosity and self-compassion, you can create space for growth.
- **Small steps are the key to lasting change.** Transformation doesn't require huge, momentous efforts. Every small, intentional choice you make strengthens new neural connections and gradually rewires your brain for the better.

Change is not about perfection or instant results; it's about progress. By leveraging your brain's ability to adapt, improving your relationships, and taking small steps forward, you can unlock new possibilities and create the life you truly want.

Moving from Understanding to Action

Your brain's ability to change is one of its most powerful traits, but turning that knowledge into action requires intentional effort. The following action items are designed to help you harness neuroplasticity, rethink habits, and reshape your self-concept in practical, meaningful ways.

- **Use curiosity to explore a habit you want to change.** Instead of immediately trying to break a habit, spend a week observing it with curiosity. Keep a journal to track the triggers, routines, and rewards of the habit. Ask yourself questions like, "What purpose is this habit serving?" "What feelings or needs drive it?" "What alternatives could I try?" This reflective practice can build awareness and loosen the grip of old patterns.
- **Experiment with a replacement habit for one trigger.** Identify one specific habit loop you want to interrupt, such as reaching for a snack when bored or scrolling through your phone when stressed. Replace the habitual action with a healthier or more intentional behavior that fulfills the same need, like drinking a glass of water or journaling. Note how this new behavior makes you feel over time.
- **Reframe a story you tell about yourself.** Choose a limiting belief tied to your self-concept, like "I'm not

good at sticking to goals" or "I'm always too reactive." Write down counterexamples from your life where you succeeded despite challenges. Reflect on how those moments prove your capacity for growth, and use them as daily reminders to challenge unhelpful narratives.

- **Reflect on relationship patterns with a trusted person.** Ask a trusted friend, partner, or family member how they perceive your relationship habits. Do you tend to avoid conflict, overthink conversations, or have difficulty trusting others? Use their perspective as a starting point to identify patterns you may not notice on your own. This feedback can help you better understand your responses and create space for change.

- **Strengthen your "high road" responses with one weekly challenge.** Practice pausing before reacting in emotionally charged situations. When you feel an urge to respond impulsively, take three deep breaths and ask yourself how your "wise elder" (prefrontal cortex) would handle the situation. This could be during a disagreement, a minor inconvenience, or a moment of stress. Reflect afterward on how choosing the high road felt and how it changed the outcome.

By applying these actions, you'll strengthen your ability to adapt and grow. Remember, your brain thrives on consistent, intentional effort. Each small step you take builds momentum, rewiring your habits, reshaping your self-concept, and creating deeper connections with yourself and others.

This Might Be the Moment You Stop Spinning

You've seen the pattern and now you recognize what might be holding you back. You're not making this up. Your brain is just doing what it was built to do.

If what you're reading is making sense, I've made a video training for people who want to set big goals this year and actually achieve or exceed them.

Check out the training at my website and if what I teach makes sense, book a call to speak with me about mentorship opportunities.

Start here: **instincttointention.prehistoricbrain.com**

5

Why We Doubt Ourselves: Unpacking the Roots of Self-Doubt

"Doubt kills more dreams than failure ever will."
—Suzy Kassem,
writer and philosopher

Self-doubt often begins as a whisper. A quiet voice in the back of your mind, so subtle that you almost miss it. It says, *Are you sure?* or *You're not good enough.* It threads itself through your thoughts, planting seeds of insecurity that take root before you even realize they're there.

Your brain, wired to detect potential threats and avoid failure, often magnifies these doubts, interpreting them as signals to stay safe. This is your nervous system's response, an ancient survival mechanism trying to protect you from the risk of making mistakes or being judged.

Over time, this whisper becomes more than just a fleeting thought. It transforms into a tightness in your chest, a flutter of anxiety in your stomach, or a hesitation in your step. These physical sensations are your body's way of responding to perceived threats, a process driven by your autonomic nervous system.[1] Without realizing it, that questioning voice becomes a reflexive pattern, automated by neural pathways that have been strengthened through repetition. Your thinking becomes foggy, your decisions feel riskier, and what once seemed clear and achievable now seems overwhelming.

Inner uncertainty comes from many places. It often starts in childhood when the messages we get from caregivers, teachers, and peers shape how we see ourselves. If those messages are critical, dismissive, or inconsistent, we may start to question our worth. Our developing brain, always searching for connection and approval, absorbs these signals. When validation is missing or mixed, self-questioning steps in to fill the gaps. It whispers questions that echo in your mind. *What am I doing wrong? How can I do better? Why didn't they see me?* These questions can become relentless, like a tape looping over and over. Each time they play, they reinforce the idea that you are not enough, that you are somehow falling short. The need for connection and approval remains unmet, and doubt becomes the filler for those empty spaces.

But it doesn't stop there. The world around us reinforces these feelings in powerful ways. Society, culture, and media set standards for who we should be. They show us images of success, confidence, and perfection. When we look at these, it is easy to feel like we do not measure up. Scrolling through social media can feel like everyone else has life figured out while we are just struggling to keep up. This comparison trap convinces us that we are falling short, even when reality tells a different story.

Remember our primitive brain, the inner caveperson, from chapter 1? Here it is again, showing up just when we are trying to step forward. Our brains, wired for survival, add another layer to self-doubt. The amygdala, the brain's fear center, works tirelessly to keep us safe by spotting danger. But it cannot always tell the difference between a real threat and an imagined one. When we doubt ourselves, it is like our inner caveperson setting off an internal alarm, warning us to stay small and avoid risks.

This alarm might have been useful when real dangers lurked around every corner, but today, it tends to fire off in situations where the only risk is emotional discomfort. Over time, these false alarms create well-worn pathways of self-questioning and hesitation. Even as adults, these old patterns can trap us, making us react to the world as if we are still that younger, vulnerable version of ourselves.

The brain likes what is familiar, even when what is familiar is a story of inadequacy. This is how we end up sabotaging our own growth. We protect ourselves from threats that no longer exist, while holding ourselves back from possibilities that do. It is not that the threat is real. It is that we are not perceiving the world as it really is. We are not the failure we think we are. We are caught in old patterns, reacting to shadows from the past rather than the reality in front of us.

And so, we find ourselves returning to these deep-seated beliefs: the inner voice, the inner caveperson, or the stories that shape how we think, feel, and act. But these stories can be revised. Self-doubt may feel like a fixed part of who we are, but it is not a reflection of our abilities, our worth, or our potential. It is simply a response, a learned way of protecting ourselves from discomfort, insecurity, or shame.

Doubt itself is not inherently bad. In fact, it can help us pause, reflect, and improve. But when it becomes the loudest voice, drowning out our confidence and keeping us stuck, it no longer serves us. Reassuringly, nothing about this process is set in stone. The brain that built these loops is also capable of changing them. Once we understand where our doubt comes from and why it shows up, we can begin to loosen its grip.

You are not the failure you think you are. You are not trapped in this story forever. With awareness, curiosity, and self-compassion, you can challenge the narrative that holds you back. You can rewrite your story, not by erasing the self-crticism, but by giving space to other voices, voices of courage, possibility, and self-trust.

This journey is not about eliminating uncertainty completely. It is about learning to recognize it, question it, and decide when it deserves your attention. Because beyond the noise, there is a part of you that knows you are capable, worthy, and enough. And that part of you is always there, waiting to be heard.

In this chapter, we will explore the roots of self-doubt and learn how they hold us back, and how we can release ourselves from their hold.

Your Inner Caveperson: How Ancient Instincts Fuel Modern Self-Doubt

Self-doubt doesn't exist in a vacuum. It's deeply connected to how our brains evolved to handle risk and uncertainty. The same mechanisms that kept our ancestors safe by prioritizing immediate survival often misfire in modern life, convincing us we're incapable of or doomed to fail. This cycle can feel insurmountable, but understanding its roots can provide clarity and a path forward.

Take Dahlia, for example. She struggled with dieting and exercise for years, feeling as though she was caught in a loop of trying and failing. Each misstep reinforced her belief that she was destined to fail. It wasn't just her choices or willpower holding her back; it was her brain working overtime, driven by instincts designed for survival, not modern-day challenges.[2]

"This is the week!" she would tell herself every Sunday, determined to watch what she ate and start exercising. She'd succeed for a few days, only to slip back into old patterns by midweek. Soon, she'd be reaching for cookies or skipping her walks entirely, feeling defeated and even more depressed than before.

"I don't know what's wrong with me," she admitted in one of our first sessions. "I feel incapable of sticking to anything. I self-sabotage every time. I'll do okay for a few days, and then something changes, something switches in me, and I feel ravenously hungry. I'll think, *Just one cookie*, and before I know it, I've eaten the whole box and feel horrible and guilty."

This cycle had been repeating for years, and Dahlia felt stuck. "Why can't I stay consistent? Why do I keep doing this to myself?"

When I work with clients like Dahlia, I always make sure we talk about neuroscience, our wiring, and our ancestral traits. I explain how the brain's primary job is to keep us safe. This safety mechanism creates warning signals that can show up as self-doubt, cravings, or even self-sabotaging behavior. I often tell my clients about their inner caveperson. I make sure they understand that the brain doesn't always get it right. Sometimes it makes things up. Feelings aren't facts, and not everything we think is true.

For Dahlia, we explored how her inner caveperson was influencing her behavior. To begin, we talked about how her struggles with food and dieting were tied to ancient survival mechanisms.

Our ancestors lived in a world of scarcity, where food came in waves. Sometimes there was plenty, and other times, there was almost nothing. During times of abundance, they would eat as much as possible, storing energy as fat to survive the leaner times. That wiring still exists in us today. When we diet or restrict food, our brain interprets it as a potential famine.[3] This triggers the inner caveperson to sound the alarm: *Must eat! Must survive!*

I explained to Dahlia that this is why, when she deprives herself of certain foods, her hunger signals become louder and harder to ignore. Her brain is reacting to what it perceives as a threat to survival, even though food is always available in her modern world.

Stress also plays a significant role in this dynamic. For our ancestors, stress was often tied to physical danger, like hunting or escaping predators. After such a stressful event, the brain would signal the body to refuel with high calorie foods to recover. Today, our stressors are different. They are deadlines, arguments, or financial worries, but the response is the same. The brain still craves comfort foods after stressful situations because it is trying to restore energy and maintain balance.

Like many of us, Dahlia's inner caveperson was responding to stress by reaching for quick, high-calorie comfort foods. This was her brain's way of saying, *Eat now; you've just escaped danger.* In reality, the "threat" was no longer a life-or-death situation. It was simply a bad day at work or a moment of self-criticism.

Another challenge Dahlia faced, one that many of us struggle with, is the brain's natural inclination to conserve energy. After a long day, Dahlia would often come home with the intention of exercising. Instead of lacing up her sneakers, she would find herself sitting on the couch, watching Netflix with her dog.

"Well," I told her. "This is complicated, but it's also completely normal. Your inner caveperson has a lot to do with it."

Our ancestors couldn't afford to expend energy without a clear purpose because survival demanded efficiency. They saved their energy for hunting, gathering, or escaping predators. This energy-conserving instinct still exists in us today, making it difficult to stay motivated to exercise, especially when the benefit isn't immediate.

I explained to Dahlia that her fatigue at the end of the day was also tied to her body's natural rhythms. Our ancestors relied on the sun to guide their activities, conserving energy in the evenings when it was safest to rest. This evolutionary tendency still affects us today, making it harder to engage in physical activity after work when our energy naturally dips.

On top of that, our brains favor habits and routines because they conserve mental effort. For Dahlia, the routine of coming home and unwinding with Netflix or cuddling with her dog felt comforting and familiar. Starting a new routine, like exercising after work, requires more cognitive effort, which her inner caveperson was naturally resisting.

Once Dahlia understood the evolutionary forces influencing her behaviors, she began to see her struggles in a new light. They weren't signs of weakness or failure. They were simply the result of her brain doing its job. Ancient survival mechanisms were influencing her thoughts and behaviors in ways she didn't fully understand. This realization became the first step toward changing her story.

Narratives of Self-Doubt: How Our Stories Keep Us Stuck

Self-limiting beliefs and behaviors often grow from the stories we absorb throughout our lives. We've already discussed how these stories come from what we experience in our families, communities, and culture, shaping how we see ourselves and what we believe we can achieve.[4]

Dahlia, for example, had absorbed powerful stories about her worth long before she realized it. During one of our sessions, I asked her to reflect on her childhood and the messages she picked up from her family.

"I can't remember my mom ever not being on a diet," she said. "She was always talking about needing to lose weight, and looking back, I see now that she struggled just like I do. But the memory that really sticks with me is when my parents had an argument. My mom told my dad she wouldn't be seen with him unless he lost weight. I will never forget the look on his face."

Her mother's focus on dieting and her criticisms about appearance sent a clear message that love and respect were tied to physical looks. Over time, these subtle yet powerful messages became ingrained in Dahlia's mind: I am not attractive enough, and I have to be thin to be loved. These ideas were the seeds of Dahlia's self-doubt, growing into self-limiting thoughts about her worth and abilities. These early narratives took root and shaped the way she saw herself, laying the foundation for the self-doubt she experienced in adulthood.

These stories have deeper origins, and they aren't unique to Dahlia. Many of us carry similar narratives rooted in early experiences. Maybe you heard a parent dismiss their achievements with phrases like, "I just got lucky," leading you to believe you shouldn't feel proud of your accomplishments. Or perhaps you watched your parents avoid conflict and suppress their feelings, shaping your belief that your emotions aren't important.

Even if these messages weren't spoken directly, they influence how we live our lives. They seep into our thoughts and decisions, subtly dictating our choices. These internalized stories are the foundation of self-doubt, whispering that we aren't good enough, smart enough, or worthy enough. We hold back from applying for promotions, expressing our needs, or trying new things because of these deeply held beliefs.

What narratives are you carrying just beneath the surface of your awareness that might be holding you back?

For Dahlia, her story was amplified by her inner critic, a voice that often mimicked her mother's. As children, we develop inner speech by first talking aloud to ourselves and eventually internalizing this process. This inner voice helps with reflection, planning, and decision-making. But when it's shaped by negative experiences, it can turn into a relentless source of self-judgment.[5]

Her inner critic fueled her self-doubt, constantly reminding her of her perceived flaws. Dahlia's inner voice would whisper things like, *You shouldn't have eaten that; you're weak*, or *If you're not perfect, you're not worthy*. These thoughts felt like her own, but they were echoes of the messages she absorbed growing up. What started as a mechanism to help her navigate the world became a constant source of self-criticism and insecurity.

Of course, family isn't the only source of these stories. Society and culture add their own layers of judgment and expectation. Dahlia reflected on how, during her teenage years, magazines and TV shows promoted the idea that success and beauty meant being thin.

"When I was in high school," she told me, "Everywhere I looked, models looked fragile and flawless. It felt like if you didn't look like that, you weren't attractive or successful." These cultural messages reinforced her self-doubt, making her feel she would never be enough.

For Dahlia, believing her worth was tied to her appearance affected her eating habits, her relationships, and how she saw herself. Her inner critic kept her trapped, always striving for an unattainable version of perfection and fearing that she wasn't worthy of love or success. For someone else, the story might sound like, *I'm not smart enough to succeed* or *I don't deserve happiness*. These beliefs fuel self-doubt, keeping us stuck in patterns that are difficult to break.

As you reflect on Dahlia's experience, consider your own. What stories have you absorbed about your abilities, worth, or potential? Were they spoken directly, or did they form through observation? These beliefs often feel so ingrained that we accept them as truth. But the reality is, they are just stories. And like any story, they can be rewritten.

For Dahlia, recognizing the origins of her beliefs was a turning point. She realized that her self-criticism wasn't truly hers. It was the echo of her mother's voice and societal expectations.

The stories we tell ourselves are powerful, but they aren't final. Once we identify where our beliefs come from, we can start to challenge them. By questioning these narratives and reframing the messages we've absorbed, we create space for a life guided by our own truth, not someone else's. This is how we begin to loosen the grip of self-doubt. Instead of thinking, *I am not good enough*, we can remind ourselves, *I am enough*.

Trapped by Our Expectations: How Self-Doubt Becomes Self-Fulfilling

As we grow older, the voices in our heads that whisper doubt or criticism often seem to grow louder and more authoritative. Over time, these voices shape how we see ourselves and our abilities. The beliefs we hold about who we are influence the choices we make, the risks we take, and the way we approach life's challenges. This is the power of a self-fulfilling prophecy. When we expect failure or inadequacy, we unconsciously act in ways that make those expectations come true.

Jacob's story illustrates this process. Growing up, Jacob internalized the belief that intelligence was not something his family valued or possessed. During one of our sessions, he explained, "In my family, it was all about hard work. Being smart wasn't something anyone talked about. We weren't 'that kind of family.' "

These deeply held family values weren't arbitrary. They were survival strategies that were passed down through generations. In times when survival depended on physical labor and perseverance, intelligence might not have seemed as critical. Jacob's brain adopted this survival-based mindset, making it difficult for him to see other paths.

This belief became cemented early in Jacob's life. In fourth grade, he performed poorly on a standardized test. When his teacher remarked, "Not everyone is good at these things," Jacob took it as confirmation that he was not smart. That moment became a defining one for his self-perception. Because the experience directly impacted his sense of identity and self-worth, his brain prioritized it through something called "self-referential encoding."[6] This process makes memories tied to our sense of self more vivid and easier to recall.

His inner voice began echoing this belief, whispering, *You're not smart enough*, whenever he faced a challenge. From then on, he avoided situations that might challenge his intellect and began seeing himself as "just a hard worker" rather than someone capable of learning and growing. Jacob's self-doubt was not shaped by one event alone. It was reinforced by deeper, inherited influences, such as his grandparents' struggles during difficult times. These experiences, passed down through generations, contributed to a deeply ingrained fear of failure and a belief that hard work, not intelligence, was the only path to survival. Jacob's avoidance of intellectual challenges wasn't just about self-doubt; it was his brain's way of protecting him.

Just like our ancestors avoided dangerous situations to stay safe, his brain perceived failure as a threat and steered him toward the safer path of not trying. His brain naturally organized this experience into a coherent story about his abilities through narrative formation. This defining moment became a pivotal chapter in his internal narrative, one he frequently revisited, reinforcing his belief that he lacked intelligence.

This belief pattern was also fueled by overgeneralization. When Jacob struggled with one test or assignment, he drew a broad conclusion: "I failed this, so I'm going to fail everything." Instead of seeing each challenge as a separate event, his brain applied the outcome of one experience to everything else. This distorted way of thinking solidified his self-doubt and made it harder for him to take risks.

Jacob also fell into emotional reasoning. Because he felt incapable, he believed he truly was incapable. His feelings of inadequacy seemed like undeniable proof, even when the evidence suggested otherwise. When he did succeed, he brushed it off, saying, "I just got lucky," reinforcing his belief that he wasn't really smart.

Another force at play was cognitive dissonance. This occurs when new experiences conflict with existing beliefs, creating discomfort. Each time Jacob succeeded, it clashed with his belief that he wasn't intelligent. To ease this discomfort, he dismissed his success as a fluke. It felt easier to cling to his old belief than to accept a new possibility that challenged his self-doubt.

Each time his inner voice repeated, *You just got lucky*, it reinforced his original belief, creating a cycle that felt inescapable. This self-fulfilling prophecy wasn't "just happening" to Jacob. He was actively participating in it. By avoiding challenges, dismissing his successes, and interpreting his experiences through the lens of self-doubt, he unknowingly created the very reality he feared.

His brain's confirmation bias ensured that he only noticed evidence that supported his belief while ignoring anything that contradicted it. The more he focused on his failures, the more his belief in his inadequacy grew.

Can you relate to this? Maybe there was a moment in your life when you felt like you didn't measure up. A time when you tried something, stumbled, and thought, *I guess I'm just not good at this*. That voice of doubt often grows louder with each experience, making you hesitate or avoid challenges altogether.

Over time, Jacob's repeated struggles and avoidance created a pattern of learned helplessness. After facing so many setbacks, he started to believe that no matter how hard he tried, things would never change. Each challenge he avoided or success he dismissed reinforced this belief. Instead of seeing failure as a chance to learn, Jacob saw it as proof that he wasn't smart enough. The more he felt stuck, the more he avoided trying, and the more his belief that he couldn't succeed was confirmed.

By the time Jacob reached high school, his self-fulfilling prophecy was in full effect. He avoided advanced classes because he did not want to risk failing. When he performed well on an assignment, he dismissed it as luck or credited help from others rather than seeing it as the result of his own effort.

"I didn't think I was smart, so I never really tried," he admitted. "Whenever I did succeed, I figured it was just a fluke."

Breaking this cycle begins with awareness. During one session, I asked Jacob a simple but powerful question: "Have you ever been wrong about what you're capable of?" He paused and then mentioned the debate competition. For the first time, he allowed himself to consider that his success might not have been a fluke.

How about you? Can you think of a time when you were wrong about what you thought you could or couldn't do? What might happen if you gave yourself permission to try, even if you're not sure of the outcome?

Jacob's story shows how internal doubt, shaped by biases and survival instincts, can create a cycle that feels impossible to break. The beliefs we hold influence the opportunities we pursue and the reality we experience. But these beliefs can be revised.

When we start to question our beliefs and the narratives we've internalized, we can disrupt the cycle. Instead of accepting self-doubt, we can ask, "Is this really true?" or "Is there another way to see this?" These small acts of curiosity help us recognize when our inner voices and fears are shaping our realities.

Your beliefs influence your actions, and your actions create your world. By challenging the thoughts that hold you back, you give yourself the freedom to try, learn, and grow. Change doesn't happen instantly, but each small step chips away at the old story, making space for new possibilities. The power to rise above self-doubt lies in knowing you can choose to see yourself differently and can take action accordingly.

Why We Stay Stuck in Self-Doubt: The Brain's Hidden Mechanisms

Being caught in patterns of self-doubt is frustrating, isn't it? By now you see these cycles are not about willpower alone. Your inner caveperson, internalized stories, and self-fulfilling prophecies contribute to these cycles because they are deeply rooted in the way your brain is wired, how your neural pathways form, and how your brain chemistry responds to stress and repetition.

Jacob and Dahlia's experiences illustrate how these brain processes work. In fourth grade, Jacob performed poorly on a standardized test. When his teacher remarked, "Not everyone is good at these things," it created a flashbulb memory, a vivid, emotionally charged moment that left a lasting imprint. His brain registered this experience as a threat, locking in the belief that he was not smart enough.

Maybe you can relate. Perhaps a harsh comment from a teacher, coach, or parent stuck with you longer than it should have. These moments, even if they seem small, can become anchors for self-doubt.

From then on, whenever Jacob struggled with a task, his brain's amygdala, the emotional processing center, became highly active, triggering a stress response. This released cortisol and adrenaline, chemicals that heighten awareness of potential threats. His brain interpreted failure as danger, reinforcing his belief in his inadequacy.

This happens because of Hebbian learning,[7] often summarized as "cells that fire together, wire together." Each time Jacob thought, *I'm not smart enough*, while struggling with a task, his brain strengthened the connection between difficulty and self-doubt. It was like carving a trail through a forest. The more he walked that path, the clearer it became. Over time, avoiding challenges felt automatic because his brain was wired to protect him from the "threat" of failure.

Similarly, Jacob's brain also struggled under stress and overwhelm. His amygdala's activation triggered his brain's fight-or-flight response, making it harder for his prefrontal cortex, the part of his brain responsible for rational thinking and decision-making, to stay in control. This is an example of bottom-up processing, where automatic emotional reactions override rational thought. Instead of facing the challenge, his brain defaulted to avoidance as the safer option.

Have you ever avoided something difficult just because it felt easier not to try? That's your brain's protective mechanism kicking in, even if it isn't serving you well.

Dahlia's experience followed a similar process to Jacob's, but her brain's way of handling stress led to a different pattern. When her amygdala signaled her brain's reward system, it prompted the release of dopamine, giving her a quick sense of pleasure or relief. This reinforced the habit of reaching for comfort food to ease her stress.

As we discussed in chapter 3, chronic stress doesn't just disappear. It builds over time, creating what is known as allostatic load. This happens when the body endures prolonged stress without enough recovery, wearing down both the brain and body. The more this stress accumulates, the harder it becomes to regulate emotions, focus, or take action.

As allostatic load increases, the brain shifts into energy-conserving mode, looking for the easiest way to relieve discomfort. For Dahlia, that meant falling into automatic habits that provided quick comfort, like reaching for food when she felt stressed. Even minor stressors felt overwhelming, making it more likely that she would react impulsively instead of responding thoughtfully.

When stress reaches this level, the brain stops prioritizing long-term solutions and instead looks for the quickest way to feel better. Each time Dahlia reached for comfort food, her brain reinforced the habit, making it feel like the safest and most reliable way to ease her anxiety. The more she relied on this pattern, the harder it became to do anything different. Her brain, trying to protect her, had locked her into a cycle that felt impossible to escape.

Our brains are built for efficiency, and as we've discussed before, this efficiency can sometimes work against us. Neural pathways automate thoughts, actions, and reactions to conserve energy. It helps us respond quickly to familiar situations, like tying our shoes or driving a car, but when these responses are shaped by unhelpful patterns, like avoiding challenges or seeking comfort in food, they can keep us stuck.

Implicit memory also plays a role in these responses. Unlike explicit memories, which you can consciously recall, implicit memories work in the background, shaping how you feel and react. For Jacob, memories of struggling in school left a lasting emotional imprint. Even if he could not remember the exact details, his brain accessed that feeling of inadequacy whenever he faced a challenge. For Dahlia, years of hearing subtle critiques about her appearance created implicit memories that fueled her automatic responses to stress.

To make things more challenging, these memories can be reinforced over time through memory reconsolidation. Each time Jacob or Dahlia revisited these memories, their brains reactivated and strengthened the pathways connected to them. This made their beliefs and reactions feel even more automatic and difficult to change.

What about you? Are there automatic responses that seem to take over when you are stressed or facing a challenge? Maybe you freeze before speaking up in a meeting, or you reach for your phone whenever you feel overwhelmed. What belief might be driving these reactions? What small steps can you take today to create a new path for your brain to follow?

Once we see how these tendencies form, we can start creating new ones. It's not about making huge leaps all at once. It's about taking small, deliberate steps and repeating them until they stick. Jacob began to focus on his successes instead of dwelling on his struggles, reminding himself that intelligence isn't fixed. Dahlia worked on being kinder to herself when she felt stressed and found new ways to soothe her emotions without turning to food.

Change is rarely easy, and it doesn't happen all at once. But by understanding how our brains keep us stuck, we can begin to shift. Our habits and beliefs can be updated. What's empowering is that we can challenge implicit memories, engage in intentional top-down processing, and use deliberate memory reconsolidation to rewire our neural pathways.

By practicing new thoughts and behaviors, we harness neuroplasticity, the brain's ability to change and adapt. In other words, we can use our brain's own processes to shift from automatic, limiting patterns to conscious, empowering choices.

With curiosity, patience, self-awareness, and consistent effort, we can build new patterns that support us instead of hold us back. Our brains are designed to change, and every small step you take today brings you closer to a better outcome tomorrow.

Changing the Story: How to Rewrite Limiting Beliefs

The stories we tell ourselves about who we are and what we can achieve often feel as if they are carved into stone. But as you've seen, these stories are not fixed. They can be rewritten. When we understand how they were formed and why they feel so convincing, we realize we are not powerless. We have the ability to take control and create new, more empowering narratives.

For Dahlia, rewriting her story meant recognizing how her beliefs about herself had been shaped by her past. Her inner critic, which echoed her mother's voice, had taken hold in her brain's language-processing centers. When she caught herself thinking, *You shouldn't have eaten that; you're weak,* she paused and asked herself, "Is this really true?" or "Would

I say this to someone I love?" These small moments of curiosity helped her shift from self-punishment to self-kindness. Over time, she began to see that these critical thoughts were not her own but messages she had absorbed. This moved her toward change.

Dahlia also learned to recognize when her primitive brain, or inner caveperson, was driving her reactions. When she felt stressed and the urge to reach for comfort food kicked in, she asked herself, *Is this a response to what is happening right now, or is this an old pattern from the past?* Instead of automatically reacting, she experimented with healthier responses, like going for a short walk, journaling, or practicing deep breathing. These small actions reinforced her new story: I am capable of caring for myself in healthy ways.

For Jacob, the belief that he was not intelligent had held him back for years. His first step in rewriting his story was to get curious about his thoughts. When he thought, *I can't do this*, he paused and asked, "Can I look at this another way?" or "Is this really true?" This simple questioning helped him challenge his automatic assumptions. He also began to notice when his inner caveperson was steering him toward avoidance. When a task felt difficult, his brain treated it like a threat, and he would retreat. Recognizing this primitive reaction helped him choose a different path. He reminded himself that the discomfort was not a real danger, just an opportunity to grow.

Jacob also worked on identifying when implicit memories were influencing his reactions. Memories of past failures often resurfaced when he faced a challenge. Instead of accepting these memories as proof of his inadequacy, he asked, "Is this memory guiding me, or is this the truth of the present moment?" By staying curious and open, he started taking small risks, like speaking up in meetings or learning a new skill. Each success chipped away at his old story and reinforced a new one: I can learn and grow.

Rewriting these scripts is not about flipping a switch or becoming someone new through one big shift. It is about taking small, deliberate steps and repeating them consistently. These actions may seem insignificant at first, but they add up over time. Every time Dahlia chose self-kindness over criticism, or Jacob chose to try instead of avoid, they created new experiences that reinforced their new stories.

This process requires patience and self-compassion. Old stories do not let go easily, and it is natural to fall back into familiar patterns. When this happens, approach yourself with curiosity rather than criticism. Ask, "What is driving this reaction? Is it my inner caveperson or an old memory?" Setbacks are not failures; they are opportunities to learn and practice again.

Think about the stories you tell yourself. What beliefs are holding you back? Are there small steps you can take today to challenge those beliefs? Maybe it is speaking up in a meeting, setting a boundary, or choosing kindness when your inner critic gets loud. Each small step is a chance to create new evidence for your brain and build a story that reflects your true potential.

Rewriting your story is not about erasing the past. It is about discovering who you really are, free from the limiting beliefs that have held you back. You have the power to write a narrative that supports your growth, your worth, and your abilities.

Key Takeaways

Self-doubt often feels like a defining part of who we are, but it is not. By understanding its origins and the ways it takes hold, you can begin to unravel its power. The truth is that self-doubt is malleable, and with awareness and effort, it can be reshaped. Here are the three most important ideas to take away from this chapter:

- **Self-doubt is a survival instinct, not a reflection of your worth.** Your brain is wired to protect you from danger, but it often misinterprets emotional risks, like failure or rejection, as threats. This can make you feel incapable, but it is just your brain's way of keeping you safe. Recognizing this helps you see self-doubt as a reaction, not a measure of your abilities.
- **Childhood messages and societal pressures reinforce self-doubt.** The way you were treated or spoken to as a child shaped your beliefs about yourself. Negative messages, even subtle ones, can linger in your mind, influencing how you see your abilities. On top of this, societal ideals about success and perfection amplify these feelings, leaving you stuck in a cycle of comparison and doubt.
- **Self-doubt can be unlearned by challenging your inner stories.** The narratives that fuel self-doubt are not facts; they are learned responses. Through curiosity, patience, and intentional action, you can rewrite these stories. Small steps, like questioning the origin of your doubt or practicing self-compassion, teach your brain to trust in your ability to grow and adapt.

Self-doubt is not who you are; it is simply a habit of the mind shaped by your past. By recognizing its roots and understanding how your brain works, you can begin to change the way you respond to it. The voice of self-doubt does not have to be the loudest one. With time and effort, you can create a new, empowering narrative that reflects your true potential.

Moving from Understanding to Action

Understanding where self-doubt comes from is empowering, but true transformation requires action. Here are five practical strategies to help you challenge self-doubt and build new patterns of self-trust:

- **Name your inner critic and start a dialogue.** Give your self-doubt a name or identity, like "The Doubter" or "The Critic." When negative thoughts arise, address them directly: "Thank you for trying to protect me, but I'm choosing to see this differently." This separates you from your doubts and helps you take control of the narrative.
- **Create a "proof list" of past successes.** Write down a list of moments when you succeeded, overcame challenges, or accomplished something you doubted you could. Review this list regularly, especially when self-doubt creeps in, to remind your brain of what you're capable of.
- **Practice asking, "What's the worst that could happen?"** When self-doubt stops you from taking a step forward, ask yourself this question. Often, the worst-case scenario is far less catastrophic than it feels.

By imagining it clearly, you reduce the power of fear and open yourself to taking small risks.

- **Lean into discomfort intentionally.** Identify one thing that feels intimidating but manageable, like speaking up in a group or trying something new. Take small, intentional steps toward it. Each time you face discomfort and survive, you teach your brain that fear and self-doubt don't have to stop you.

- **Start a daily "self-kindness" practice.** At the end of each day, write down one thing you did well, one kind thing you said to yourself, or one moment you showed self-compassion. This practice rewires your brain to notice progress and kindness instead of focusing on criticism or failure.

With consistent practice, these small, intentional steps help you loosen the grip of self-doubt and build a foundation of self-trust. Change takes time, but every effort you make moves you closer to living with confidence and courage.

6

When Relationships Hurt: Breaking the Patterns and Finding Connection

"Family dysfunction rolls down from generation to generation, like a fire in the woods, taking down everything in its path until one generation has the courage to turn and face the flames. That person brings peace to their ancestors and spares the children that follow."

—Terrance Real,
relationship expert and author

Terry Real's words remind us that challenges we face in relationships are often passed down, not born in the moment. Maybe you have felt this in your own life, a sense that you are caught in patterns that came from somewhere else and that you can't seem to break. Even so, with courage, as Terry Real would say, you can turn and face those flames, bringing peace to yourself and those who come after you.

Have you ever wondered why the people you love the most can also trigger your strongest, most defensive reactions? One moment, you feel close, connected, and secure. The next, you are snapping, withdrawing, or shutting down. You think to yourself, *This isn't helpful,* or *They should love me enough to come rescue me.* When this happens, it's automatic, and you just react. You might ask yourself, "Why do I keep doing this? Why do my relationships feel so hard, even when I care so deeply?"

To say that relationships are complex is a profound understatement.

Relationships are our life force. They bring joy, intimacy, and connection. But they also activate our deepest survival instincts. As previously discussed, we all have a dual nature. Part of us longs to love, nurture, and connect. Another part is constantly scanning for threats, ready to defend and protect. This mix of tenderness and self-protection is what makes relationships both beautiful and hard.

Our brains, wired for survival, add another layer of complexity. For our ancestors, staying connected to others was essential for safety. At the same time, they had to stay alert for danger, even within their own groups. In today's world, that wiring is still active. A missed text, a cold response, or a canceled plan can trigger those ancient alarms, making us feel like we are under threat. This is your inner caveperson trying to protect you, even when the danger isn't real.

Modern relationships are also more complicated than those of our ancestors. We are not just managing basic survival anymore. We are balancing emotional closeness, texting and social media, expectations from friends and family, and our own personal growth. Our brains, wired for a simpler way of life, can struggle to keep up. The very instincts that once kept us safe now clash with all the ways we try to connect. What used to be a straightforward need to stay close and protected has become tangled with fears, worries, and the need to be understood.

This is why something as small as a missed text, a cold response, or a canceled plan can feel so unsettling. Our brains interpret these moments as potential threats to connection and safety. That internal alarm, your inner caveperson, kicks in, trying to protect you, even when the danger isn't real.

And, if you remember from the first part of this book, our ancestors also relied on familiarity to stay safe. They stuck to what they knew because the unknown could be dangerous. This instinct still influences how we choose partners today. I often tell my clients that we need to adjust their "picker" in order to have healthier relationships. We are often drawn to people who feel familiar, even if that familiarity comes from unhealthy dynamics. If you grew up with emotionally distant caregivers, you might find yourself attracted to emotionally distant partners. The pattern feels predictable, even if it is not good for you.

And yet, there is more! These survival instincts are just one part of the story. The other part comes from our early experiences. The ways we bonded, or struggled to bond, with our caregivers set the stage for how we connect as adults. When people come to me individually or as couples to figure out why their relationships feel lonely, broken, or superficial, I often respond with something like, "Well, let's start at the beginning."

As we discussed in chapter 2, these early bonds shape our attachment styles. If your caregivers were consistent and nurturing, you likely developed a secure attachment style, feeling that closeness and connection are safe. If love and care were inconsistent, you may have developed an anxious attachment style, always worrying about being abandoned and seeking reassurance. If your caregivers were emotionally unavailable or rejecting, you may have developed an avoidant attachment style, learning to rely only on yourself and avoid emotional intimacy. Some people experience a mix of these styles, known as a disorganized attachment style, where the need for connection collides with a fear of being hurt.

In previous chapters, we also learned that these early experiences don't just shape how we connect; they affect the stories we tell ourselves about who we are and what we are worth. And those stories can produce limiting beliefs that negatively impact our relationships. These beliefs might sound like any of the following:

- *I'm not lovable.*
- *I can't trust others.*
- *I can't rely on anyone else.*
- *People aren't safe.*
- *I will be abandoned.*

These narratives can run beneath the surface of our awareness, shaping how we respond to others and how we interpret their behavior. They are attempts by our brain to protect us from future pain, but instead, they often keep us trapped in patterns of fear and disconnection. Once you recognize these beliefs, you can begin to understand how they are influencing your relationships today.

Hyperawareness, which may have helped protect us as children, can later manifest in adult relationships as a need to manage or control others' emotions. This often leads to patterns of codependency. You may feel responsible for your partner's happiness or find that their moods dictate your own. Without realizing it, you absorb each other's emotions, a process called emotional contagion.[1] If your partner is anxious or stressed, you might feel anxious or stressed too.

But emotional contagion can also work positively, spreading joy, calm, and connection when the relationship is healthy. This instinct, rooted in our primitive survival wiring, helped early humans stay connected and aware of group threats. In modern relationships, it can spread both stress and joy, making small problems feel much bigger or amplifying moments of connection.

To make things even more complicated, we often use our relationships to fix old wounds without realizing it. Instead of healing, we end up recreating the very dynamics that caused us pain in the first place. Changing these cycles begins with recognizing and taking accountability for them. This awareness empowers us to show up differently, both for ourselves and for the people we care about.

You might wonder, why do I keep ending up in these patterns? Why does it feel like I am repeating the same story over and over? You are not alone in this struggle. The tension between connection and self-protection is deeply human. These reactions are not a reflection of your worth or your ability to have healthy relationships. They are your brain's way of trying to protect you, shaped by millions of years of evolution and your earliest experiences.

The remarkable thing about the brain is that it's capable of change. With awareness, curiosity, intention, and a little courage, you can form new pathways and habits. You can learn to pause, reflect, and respond differently. You can build relationships that reflect who you truly are and what you truly need and that are grounded in trust, safety, and authenticity.

In this chapter, we will explore how our relationships reflect the survival traits, attachment patterns, and limiting beliefs we've just talked about. Through real-life stories, we'll see how these dynamics can keep us stuck in unhealthy patterns, making connection feel hard and conflict feel inevitable. More importantly, we will look at practical interventions to help break these cycles, so we can build relationships that are healthier, stronger, and more fulfilling. By understanding what keeps us stuck, we open the door to change, growth, and the possibility of connection that feels secure, authentic, and grounded in trust.

Your Inner Caveperson: How Ancestral Traits Influence Modern Love

Our greatest strengths and weaknesses in relationships really do come from the same place: our need to connect and our fear of being hurt. We want closeness, but that desire also opens us up to pain. When we sense even the slightest risk, our inner caveperson, wired to keep us safe, steps in. This instinct, while trying to protect us, often creates patterns that keep us stuck. These patterns can be hard to spot because they feel so automatic, but once we begin to notice them, we can start to understand why we react the way we do.

To see how these survival instincts play out in real life, let's look at Emma's story, a young woman who came to me after a painful breakup.

When asked why she came to therapy, Emma said, "I'm having a hard time after my boyfriend broke up with me. He said I was too much to handle, too needy. I just want to be happy in a relationship. Why don't my relationships ever work? Am I really too much for people?" As we explored her recent relationship and those that came before it, a clear pattern began to emerge.

Emma's inner caveperson was always on alert, ready to protect her from any perceived threats. Growing up with a mother who was emotionally unpredictable and who would disappear for hours after arguments taught Emma that the world was unsafe and people were unreliable. Her brain adapted by creating a heightened sense of hypervigilance. For our ancestors, this kind of hyperawareness was a survival mechanism that kept them safe from danger. For Emma, it meant constantly feeling on edge in her relationships, always looking out for signs of abandonment or betrayal.

Have you ever felt like you were walking on eggshells, trying to predict someone's mood to avoid conflict or pain? That is exactly what Emma's brain was doing. It was trying to protect her from the same emotional wounds she experienced as a child. Her need to analyze every word, tone, or silence was not because she was "too much." It was because her inner caveperson was still working hard to keep her safe.

One story she shared particularly stood out. She remembered being eight years old when her parents had a huge argument. Her mother stormed out of the house and disappeared for hours. Emma sat by the window, terrified her mother would not come home. In that moment, she felt completely alone. Her brain learned to stay on high alert to avoid feeling that kind of abandonment again. These early experiences left deep marks on her mind, reinforcing the belief that being left alone was a threat to her safety.

Feelings of rejection can be overwhelming, and for good reason. For our ancestors, being excluded from the group was not just painful; it could be life-threatening. Survival depended on connection, protection, and shared resources. If you have ever felt a surge of anxiety when someone pulls away, your brain is likely responding to that ancient instinct to stay connected at all costs.

As a teenager, Emma felt like she was constantly on guard around her mother. One day her mother would be warm and casual, and the next she would be cold and critical. Emma's brain adapted by becoming hyperaware of her mother's moods. Managing other people's emotions became her way of feeling safe. Maybe you have found yourself doing the same thing, trying to keep the peace or anticipate someone's reactions because it feels like the only way to avoid conflict. This is a form of codependency, and while it may have kept you secure in childhood, it can be exhausting in adult relationships.

This instinct to cling to what feels familiar, even when it is painful, can make change seem impossible. Our brains try to protect us by rationalizing why we stay. Thoughts like *I can't afford to leave, I won't find anyone else*, or *Things might get better* are ways your inner caveperson tries to keep you safe from the unknown. These justifications are your brain's way of avoiding the discomfort of uncertainty.

As an adult, Emma's inner caveperson kept sending warnings. *Be careful; they might leave you*, or *Watch out; this could go wrong*. These messages, meant to protect her, trapped her in cycles of anxiety and insecurity. Her constant need for reassurance from partners was her brain's way of sounding the alarm.

These survival mechanisms do not just show up in romantic relationships. You might notice them in your professional life too. Maybe you feel hyperaware of your boss's reactions during a meeting, interpreting a frown or distracted look as a sign that you are in trouble. Or perhaps you constantly seek validation from coworkers, worrying that you are not doing enough. These behaviors come from the same place of insecurity and fear of rejection. Your inner caveperson is working overtime to keep you safe.

Even in social settings, your inner caveperson can take charge. If a friend cancels plans or seems distant, you might feel a surge of anxiety, wondering if they are mad at you or if they no longer like you. This can lead to overcompensating, like frequently reaching out or trying too hard to please others. These reactions, sometimes called fawning, are attempts to maintain connection and avoid rejection.

Understanding that these behaviors are rooted in ancestral wiring was a breakthrough for Emma. It helped her see that her relationship challenges were not personal failures but natural responses to her brain's attempts to protect her. Imagine her relief in knowing that these patterns could be changed. With awareness, Emma could begin to shift them. This new perspective allowed Emma to release shame and start making choices that aligned with who she wanted to be.

Reflecting on how your inner caveperson influences your relationships can be a powerful exercise. While these dynamics are deeply rooted, they can be understood and transformed. With awareness and intention, you can begin to build the secure, connected relationships you deserve.

Rewriting the Stories Your Inner Caveperson Tells You

As we've established, the stories we tell ourselves shape how we experience the world, especially in our relationships. These stories are built from childhood experiences, the way you were treated by those you loved, those who loved you, and those who were supposed to love you. They are also influenced by societal expectations, cultural norms, peer interactions, and the messages we absorb from the media. These stories operate quietly in the background, shaping your emotions, behaviors, actions, and choices even when you are not aware of them. When left unexamined, they can lead to habitual responses that keep you stuck in patterns of fear, shame, and insecurity.

Let's look at Kris's story. She came to therapy following a panic attack at work. The panic attack had been triggered by a fight with her boyfriend, during which he threatened to leave her. At work the next day, she kept ruminating on their argument, vacillating between anger and fear, until she ultimately froze. She described the experience as "a complete meltdown. I couldn't breathe, my chest was pounding, and

I fainted. To make things worse, this was in front of my boss!" Understandably, Kris was embarrassed and confused by what had happened. She had never experienced anything like it before.

You might know this feeling: when emotions seem to hijack your body and leave you spiraling. It can be disorienting and frightening, especially when you pride yourself on staying composed. But this doesn't mean something is wrong with you. It means your brain is trying to protect you, even if it's using outdated methods.

The first step was helping Kris understand the neurobiology of a panic attack so she could recognize and prevent it if she felt one coming on again. I explained that a panic attack is like your inner caveperson sounding the alarm, signaling danger. In Kris's case, her body had moved from stress to "I am going to die." The problem was, there was no tangible threat to escape from. Her inner caveperson, overwhelmed and confused, had decided she was in immediate danger.

I also explained that under normal circumstances, emotions last about ninety seconds from the initial trigger to resolution. Neuroscientist Dr. Jill Bolte Taylor discovered that if left alone, emotions will naturally pass. You might try this yourself. The next time you feel a disruptive emotion, pause and see what happens if you don't feed it with more thoughts. Can you let it move through you and resolve itself?

As we explored Kris's story, we found that her belief that she couldn't rely on others was rooted in her early life. Perhaps you can relate to this, those moments in childhood when you reached out for comfort and were met with silence, dismissal, or frustration. One parent, who was emotionally volatile, would sometimes respond to her feelings with anger or unpredictability. The other parent, though well-meaning, was often distant or unavailable. When Kris sought comfort, her needs were met with responses like "You're overreacting" or "You'll be fine." These moments taught her that expressing emotions would only lead to more pain.

This belief followed her into school. Her internal narrative became *I can't rely on others, and I don't matter.* Maybe you've felt this too, a sense that keeping quiet was safer than risking rejection. Kris's quiet, withdrawn nature made it difficult for her peers to connect with her. Her aloofness was misread as disinterest, leading to more exclusion. Each experience reinforced the idea that she was on her own and that relying on others would only lead to disappointment. When a teacher she trusted moved away without saying goodbye, it felt like another painful reminder that depending on others was futile.

But here's where the story began to change. Kris had to recognize that her belief, "I can't rely on others," was being reinforced by some early experiences, but it wasn't the entire story. Start noticing the contradictions in your own life. Kris had other relationships and people who had been consistent and supportive in her life. At work, she had colleagues who trusted her and continued to engage with her. There were childhood friends who still kept in touch. You might notice similar patterns in your own life, identifying people who have been reliable even when it feels like you've never had anyone, times when you were accepted just as you are even though it feels you've always been rejected.

When Kris and I looked at these other examples, she realized that she had been telling herself a story based on a few painful moments, but it didn't account for the many times she had been supported by others.

I explained to Kris that it was important for her to notice discrepancies between the story she told herself and her actual experiences. While her brain's narrative was "I can't rely on anyone," the reality was that many people in her life had remained consistent and supportive and had been there for her.

To protect herself from the ongoing disappointment of those few painful moments, Kris had unconsciously adopted an avoidant attachment style. She learned to suppress her emotions and avoid expressing vulnerability, believing that staying quiet, self-reliant, and composed would protect her from hurt. When she felt scared or insecure, she retreated inward, hiding her true feelings.

This is where awareness made a difference. While it may have been hard for Kris to recognize at first, her pattern of withdrawal was actually fueling her belief no one was available or reliable for her. She was unintentionally creating the very distance she feared. In her relationship, when her boyfriend had threatened to leave, Kris withdrew emotionally. She didn't express her fear or talk about her need for reassurance. This withdrawal was misinterpreted by her partner as a lack of care or interest, which led him to feel frustrated and distant.

The cycle of withdrawal and frustration deepened the disconnect between them. Is this something you recognize in your own relationships? Withdrawing, shutting down, and remaining silent are common ways that people "do conflict." Sometimes we think to ourselves, *I just want them to come and apologize, or see me*, but our behaviors and demeanor send the opposite message: "Leave me alone." And that is exactly what our partners do. Have you ever withdrawn, thinking it would help, only to find that it only made things worse?

Here's where things can change. Kris's panic attack was a wake-up call, a sign that her old patterns were no longer serving her. Recognizing the difference between her partner's words and his actions helped her understand her fear wasn't rooted in reality. His words, "I'm going to leave," didn't match his behavior, which showed he was still there.

This realization is powerful. It allowed Kris to question her beliefs and shift her behavior. While I do not often use reality testing to determine if a partner is going to stay or leave, in this case, I used it to illustrate a point to Kris. Instead of withdrawing, she began to pause and express her feelings more openly. This small change created a shift in their dynamic.

You can make these shifts too. Start by challenging the stories you've been telling yourself. Are they truly based on the facts, or are they shaped by past hurts? By questioning these stories, you can rewrite them and show up differently in your relationships.

In relationships, it's easy to get stuck in a cycle of fear and self-protection, but by recognizing these defenses, you can choose differently. What is the story you're living by? Is it time to write a new one, one where you no longer fear rejection and instead embrace connection with confidence and vulnerability?

When Beliefs Become Reality: Self-Fulfilling Prophecies in Relationships

As we talked about earlier, a self-fulfilling prophecy happens when a belief you hold, even if it is false or based on misleading information, leads you to act in ways that make that belief come true. The way you perceive a person or situation shapes how you respond, and your actions influence the outcome. In relationships, this can create a cycle that reinforces the very fears you are trying to avoid.

Think about a time when you believed someone wasn't fully invested in your relationship. Did you notice how that belief affected your behavior? Maybe you started acting distant or defensive without even realizing it. Those actions likely caused the other person to pull back, confirming what you feared all along. This is how a self-fulfilling prophecy works.[2]

Your belief shapes your behavior, and your behavior shapes the result, creating a loop that can feel impossible to break.

This cycle can be tricky to spot because it feels like the outcome is proof that the belief was true all along. But here's the truth: It's often the belief that creates the situation, not the other way around. When you recognize this pattern, you can pause, question your assumptions, and choose actions that reflect what you want to create rather than what you are afraid of.

Kris's story illustrates this well. She believes that she cannot rely on others and that sharing her emotions will only lead to being let down. This belief stems from her childhood experiences of reaching out for comfort and being met with silence, dismissal, or frustration. As we have seen, early experiences shape the way we interpret and respond to relationships, often outside of our awareness.

Stan Tatkin, a well-known couples' therapist, explains that we encode our partners so deeply into our memories that they become part of our nervous system.[3] Their voice, expressions, and even small shifts in body language can activate old emotional patterns in an instant. When conflict arises, we are not just responding to the present moment. We are reacting to the past.

When Kris and her partner argue, her body tenses, and she feels the urge to pull away. Her nervous system is not just reacting to him. It is responding to past moments of feeling ignored, dismissed, or unheard. Without realizing it, she withdraws, shutting down instead of expressing what she needs. Her partner, feeling the distance, reacts with frustration or hurt. To Kris, his reaction confirms what she feared all along, that she cannot rely on anyone. In reality, her withdrawal is helping create the very disconnection she is trying to avoid.

Several cognitive biases and mental shortcuts, or heuristics, keep Kris stuck in this cycle. Confirmation bias makes her focus on moments when her partner seems distant or frustrated, while overlooking times when he shows care and support. Negativity bias causes her to dwell on difficult moments more than positive ones, reinforcing her fear of disappointment.

Her brain also relies on the availability heuristic, a mental shortcut where she uses easily remembered past experiences to interpret what is happening now. Because Kris remembers times when people let her down, she expects the same from her partner. The representativeness heuristic leads her to generalize her current partner's behavior based on those past experiences, even when the situation is different.

These mental habits do not just affect romantic relationships. Maybe at work you avoid asking for help because you believe you will be let down. Or perhaps in friendships, you interpret someone's silence as a sign they are upset with you. These unconscious beliefs and shortcuts shape how we interpret situations and how we respond, often without us realizing it.

Emma's story shows a different but equally destructive pattern. Emma believes she is "too much" and that people will eventually leave her. This belief comes from her childhood experiences with an emotionally unpredictable caregiver. When her partner seems distracted or takes longer to respond, Emma's sensory nervous system reacts to those old memories, not the current situation. Her brain jumps to the worst-case scenario, a process known as catastrophizing. She thinks, *He is pulling away. He is going to leave me.* This fuels her anxiety and leads her to cling tightly for reassurance.

Emma's thinking is also shaped by emotional reasoning, a cognitive distortion where she believes something is true because she feels it. In her mind, feeling rejected means she is being rejected, even when there is no real evidence to support that conclusion. Her emotions feel like facts, and that makes her fear of abandonment seem real. She also engages in mind reading, assuming she knows what her partner is thinking. When he comes home and is quieter than usual, she tells herself, *He must be annoyed with me* or *He does not love me anymore.*

When she feels or thinks this way, she begins to question her partner relentlessly. Her behavior becomes more clingy and even intrusive, as she asks for repeated reassurance and looks for hidden meanings in his words and actions. No matter what her partner says, she does not feel reassured. Her need for constant validation becomes overwhelming. Her partner, feeling pressured and smothered, eventually withdraws to create space for himself. To Emma, his withdrawal confirms her belief that she is too much and destined to be abandoned, even though her behavior contributes to the very distance she fears.

In both Kris's and Emma's cases, their brains are reacting to old stories and unconscious beliefs, not the reality of their current relationships. These automatic responses are attempts to protect themselves, but instead, they keep them trapped in cycles of fear and disconnection. They are living out their self-fulfilling prophecies.

Luckily, these reactions can change. The key to transforming them is to become aware of them. When you feel the urge to withdraw like Kris or seek constant reassurance like Emma, pause and ask yourself, *Is this fear based on what is happening now, or is it rooted in past experiences?* Are you falling into confirmation bias, the availability heuristic, catastrophizing, or mind reading?

Imagine responding differently. Instead of shutting down, try expressing how you feel. Instead of clinging for reassurance, remind yourself of times when your partner has been there for you. These small shifts can interrupt the cycle and create new patterns of trust and connection.

If you have ever felt stuck in these stories, know that you are not alone. These reactions are common, and now that you recognize them, you are not trapped by these old stories and mental shortcuts. By understanding cognitive biases like confirmation bias, negativity bias, and the availability heuristic, you can change how you respond and build healthier, more authentic relationships.

Our brains are wired to hold on to these ingrained patterns, but they also have the capacity for change. In the next section, we will explore the neuroscience behind these behaviors and how our brain wiring and neuroplasticity can help us override these habits. With awareness, intention, and practice, you can rewire your brain and create relationships grounded in trust, connection, and safety.

Why We Stay Stuck in Unhealthy Relationships

As we have acknowledged, relationships can be complicated. Whether we're trying to leave or trying to stay and make things work, the idea of change, any change, can feel overwhelming. Sometimes, like Kris, we find ourselves stuck. Not because we don't care, but because we're caught in patterns that make it hard to move forward. Even when we know what we need to do, something keeps pulling us back, leaving us wondering why it feels so impossible to make things better.

When Kris talked about her seven-year relationship, she admitted she wasn't happy. On some days, she thought about leaving and starting fresh. On others, she wanted to stay but couldn't seem to stop the behaviors that were causing so much conflict. "I know what I should be doing," she said, "but in the moment, I just can't seem to follow through."

What Kris didn't realize was that her brain was playing a much bigger role in this than she thought. Over time, her brain had developed strong patterns around her relationship, making both staying and leaving feel like monumental challenges. Every time Kris chose to stay, her brain reinforced the habit. This is something our brains are wired to do. It's called synaptic plasticity,[4] and it's the process where the more you repeat something, whether it's a thought, behavior, or emotional response, the stronger the connection becomes in your brain. For Kris, staying had become her brain's default setting. Even though the relationship wasn't fulfilling, it felt familiar, and the familiar feels safe.

But it wasn't just habit that kept her stuck. The idea of leaving triggered something much deeper. Did you know that our brains process social loss the same way they process physical pain? It's true. When we lose someone close to us, or even imagine it, the same areas of the brain light up as when we experience physical pain. For Kris, just thinking about leaving made her brain interpret it as a threat, something to avoid at all costs. The fear of that kind of pain was enough to keep her where she was, even when she felt unhappy.

It didn't help that Kris's stress response kicked into overdrive whenever she considered leaving. The amygdala, the brain's alarm system, flooded her with fear and anxiety, making it hard to think clearly or rationally. The amygdala's job is to protect us, but it doesn't always get it right. For Kris, the thought of losing her partner triggered the same response as being in actual danger. Her body went into fight-or-flight mode, pushing her to stay where things felt stable.

And then there was the way her brain had adapted to the stress of the relationship. Through a process called allostasis, her brain adjusted to the constant tension, treating it as the new normal. Allostasis isn't just about enduring stress, it's about how the brain actively adapts, recalibrating emotions and physiology to maintain balance.[5] But that adjustment comes with a cost.

The idea of change, whether leaving or making things better, felt disruptive, like more stress than her brain could handle. Because her nervous system had recalibrated to expect tension, anything different felt unfamiliar, even unsafe. This is one of the reasons we cling to situations, even when they aren't good for us. The brain convinces us that staying in familiar discomfort is safer than stepping into the unknown.

Even when Kris wanted to stay and improve the relationship, her brain got in the way. Over the years, she had developed habits—snapping during arguments, shutting down emotionally, or avoiding hard conversations—that were deeply ingrained. These weren't conscious choices. They were automatic responses shaped by her brain's wiring. When conflict arose, her amygdala activated, flooding her with stress hormones and making it nearly impossible to think calmly or rationally. Instead, she reacted defensively or withdrew altogether, repeating the same behaviors that kept her relationship stuck.

Her brain's reward system didn't make things any easier. Every time she avoided a hard conversation or deflected blame, her brain gave her a hit of dopamine, the feel-good chemical. That momentary relief reinforced her avoidance, even though it created more problems in the long run. The brain loves short-term comfort, and for Kris, these little dopamine bursts made it harder to choose the more difficult path of addressing issues directly.

Kris's past experiences added another layer to this. She had grown up in an environment where expressing emotions often led to conflict, so her brain learned early on that avoiding confrontation was the safest option. These implicit beliefs, the subconscious lessons we absorb in childhood, were stored in her brain's fast, automatic systems. Without her realizing it, they were shaping how she reacted to her partner.

Even her partner's emotions influenced her in ways she couldn't control. Have you ever noticed how you tend to mirror the emotions of someone you're close to? As we mentioned in an earlier chapter, that's thanks to mirror neurons in the brain, which help us connect and empathize. But for Kris, these neurons often amplified tension. When her partner was frustrated, her brain mirrored that frustration, escalating the conflict instead of calming it.

Kris felt stuck on both sides. Leaving felt impossible, and staying felt equally challenging. But when she started to understand how her brain worked, she realized something important: her brain wasn't trying to sabotage her. It was just doing what it was wired to do, protect her, keep her safe, and cling to the familiar. That shift in perspective made all the difference.

Kris began taking small steps to retrain her brain. When she wanted to leave, she reminded herself that the pain her brain anticipated was real but temporary, not everlasting. When she wanted to stay, she started practicing pausing during arguments to calm her stress response before reacting. She began questioning her automatic reactions, asking herself, "Is this really true, or is this just my brain trying to protect me?" Each small step helped her create new pathways in her brain, making change feel less overwhelming.

Whether you're struggling to leave or trying to stay and make things better, it's not about willpower or knowing what to do. It's about understanding how your brain keeps you locked in patterns and how you can work with it to create new ones. Your brain might resist at first, but it's capable of remarkable transformation. With patience and intention, you can recode the habits that hold you back and build a path toward the life and relationships you truly want.

Transforming the Way You Love: Creating Modern Love

Kris and Emma both came to therapy wanting better relationships, but they had no idea how much their past experiences and internal narratives were influencing their present patterns. With time and work, both began the process of rewriting the stories they told themselves, creating new relational patterns that reflected who they wanted to be, rather than who they feared they were.

For Emma, this meant addressing the hypervigilance that had shaped her relationships since childhood. Her inner caveperson, constantly on high alert for threats, caused her to misinterpret neutral or even positive behaviors from her partner as signs of rejection. Through therapy, Emma learned to recognize when her brain was overreacting.

One of the first tools Emma used was grounding. When she felt her anxiety rise, she practiced grounding techniques such as deep breathing and focusing on the present moment to calm her nervous system. Over time, these practices helped her create space between her emotions and her actions, allowing her to respond thoughtfully rather than react impulsively.

Emma also worked on challenging the voice of her inner caveperson. "Just because I think it, doesn't make it true," she began to tell herself whenever old fears of abandonment surfaced. By questioning her automatic thoughts, she began to replace them with more balanced and compassionate beliefs.

For Kris, the process of change began with recognizing the feedback loops in her relationship. Her belief that she was unlovable and would always be abandoned led her to cling to her partner and overreact to perceived threats, which in turn pushed him further away. Therapy helped Kris identify this pattern and take responsibility for her part in the relationship dynamics.

"I didn't realize how much my actions were contributing to the cycle," Kris admitted.

One of the most potent tools Kris used was memory reconsolidation. By revisiting painful memories of abandonment and reframing them considering her current life, she began to see herself and her relationships through a different lens. For example, Kris realized that not everyone had abandoned her. She had several long-term friendships and family members who had consistently supported her. Focusing on these positive relationships, Kris started challenging the belief that she was destined to be left.

Both Kris and Emma worked on amplifying positive voices in their heads while turning down the volume on their inner critics. For Emma, this meant practicing affirmations like "I am worthy of love" and visualizing healthy relationships. For Kris, it meant acknowledging her strengths and celebrating small wins, such as communicating her needs without fear.

In addition to changing their internal narratives, Kris and Emma also developed new patterns of behavior in their relationships. Emma practiced setting boundaries with her partners, something she had struggled with in the past. By learning to say no and prioritize her own needs, she created a sense of safety and stability for herself. Kris focused on reducing her reactivity by pausing and asking herself, "What's really happening here?" before responding to her partner's behavior.

Both women also worked on building resilience, a key factor in creating healthier relationships. They practiced self-compassion, reminding themselves that change takes time and that setbacks were part of the process.

In therapy, Kris and Emma came to understand the power of neuroplasticity and the brain's ability to change and adapt. By consistently practicing new thoughts and behaviors, they were literally rewiring their brains for healthier relationships. This process wasn't easy, but it was transformative.

"Now when I feel anxious in a relationship, I stop and ask myself, 'Is this my inner caveperson talking?' " Emma shared during one of our sessions. "It's amazing how much better I feel when I realize it's not reality; it's just an old fear."

Kris echoed with a similar sentiment. "I'm learning to focus on the positive relationships I have, instead of obsessing over what could go wrong. It's like I'm finally seeing things clearly."

For both women, the process of rewriting their internal narratives and developing healthier patterns wasn't about achieving perfection. It was about creating relationships that felt safe, supportive, and fulfilling.

Transforming the way you love begins with understanding the stories you tell yourself and the patterns you unconsciously repeat. Like Kris and Emma, you might find that the beliefs you have carried for years about love, worthiness, or trust are shaping your relationships in ways you hadn't realized. But just as they discovered, change is possible. By examining those beliefs, challenging the ones that no longer serve you, and taking small, deliberate steps, you can begin to create the relationships you want.

This process is about creating meaningful change, not achieving an ideal or being a "perfect" person. It is about learning to pause, reflect, and respond differently when old fears or patterns resurface. Like Kris, you can reframe the painful memories that once felt so defining. Like Emma, you can start recognizing when your inner caveperson is overreacting and create space to respond thoughtfully. Every time you challenge an automatic thought, set a healthy boundary, or celebrate a small win, you are rewiring your brain for healthier, more fulfilling relationships.

So what about you? What story are you telling yourself about your relationships? What patterns are you ready to change? Transformation starts with small steps, moments of awareness and action that slowly build a new path forward. The question is: What step will you take today?

Key Takeaways

Relationships are deeply shaped by our past experiences and the ways our brains are wired for connection and survival. Here are three insights to help you better understand why relationships can feel so challenging and how to move toward healthier patterns:

- **Your instincts can get in the way of connection.** The same survival instincts that helped our ancestors stay safe—hypervigilance, fear of rejection, and a preference for the familiar—can make relationships today feel complicated. These automatic reactions often misinterpret minor disagreements or emotional distance as threats, leading to conflict or disconnection.
- **Attachment styles reflect how we learned to love and trust.** Early experiences with caregivers shape how you connect with others. If you felt secure as a child, you likely trust and seek closeness in relationships. But inconsistent, rejecting, or chaotic caregiving can lead to patterns like avoiding intimacy or craving constant reassurance. Understanding your attachment style is the first step toward making conscious choices about how you connect now.
- **Old stories about love can keep you stuck.** Beliefs like "I have to be perfect to be loved" or "People will always let me down" often come from childhood experiences or past relationships. These stories shape how you behave in the present, creating self-fulfilling prophecies. But beliefs are not facts. With awareness, you can rewrite these narratives and create healthier patterns in your relationships.

Understanding these ideas can help you recognize the underlying forces at play in your relationships. By gaining clarity on where your patterns come from, you can take meaningful steps toward change.

Moving from Understanding to Action

Insight alone is not enough to transform your relationships. You need to take consistent, intentional steps to break old cycles and build new ways of connecting. Here are five actionable strategies to get started:

- **Pay attention to what triggers you in relationships.** Keep a journal or take mental notes about moments when you feel upset, anxious, or withdrawn. Ask yourself, "What am I feeling, and what story is my brain telling me right now?" Recognizing your triggers is essential for shifting to responding instead of reacting.
- **Reflect on the dynamics you recreate.** Think about how your early caregiving experiences show up in your relationships today. Do you find yourself chasing people who feel emotionally unavailable or shutting down when someone gets too close? Identifying these patterns helps you understand what feels "familiar" but may no longer serve you.
- **Practice naming your feelings out loud.** Instead of withdrawing or letting emotions fester, try saying something like "I'm feeling hurt because I felt ignored earlier" or "I'm feeling overwhelmed and need a little space." Naming your feelings helps others understand what is happening without them having to guess.

- **Replace assumptions with curiosity.** When conflict arises, pause before jumping to conclusions about someone's intentions. Instead of thinking, *They don't care about me*, ask, "What else could explain this behavior?" Curiosity opens the door to connection and reduces unnecessary misunderstandings.

- **Develop healthier ways to self-soothe.** When you feel overwhelmed by relationship stress, take a moment to ground yourself. Try simple techniques like breathing deeply, going for a walk, or writing down what you are feeling. By calming your nervous system, you create space to respond with clarity instead of reacting impulsively.

These steps are not about perfection or instantly repairing relationships. They are about breaking old cycles and building new habits one small action at a time. With consistency and self-compassion, you can transform the way you show up in your relationships and create deeper, more fulfilling connections.

7

Why We Avoid: Overcoming Procrastination and Reclaiming Focus

*"Failure is simply the opportunity to begin again,
this time more intelligently."*

—Henry Ford,
founder of the Ford Motor Company

Have you ever found yourself putting off something important, even when you knew it would only make things harder later? Maybe you promised yourself you would tackle that big project today, only to end up scrolling through your phone, cleaning the kitchen, or watching another episode of your favorite show. If so, you are not alone. Procrastination is something we all experience, and for most of us, it feels frustrating and almost impossible to control.

It also often sneaks up on you. One moment, you're ready to dive into a task, and the next, you're avoiding it completely. Sometimes I sit down at my computer to do a project and find myself two hours later researching the best way to clean my grout. Has something like that ever happened to you?

You might think you're just being lazy or that you don't have enough time. But procrastination isn't about laziness; it's about how our brains work. Imagine this: You've got a mountain of laundry staring you down. You know it needs to be done, but your brain immediately thinks, *Ugh, this is going to take forever, and it won't even be fun.*

Meanwhile, your brain notices something more exciting, like your favorite show or cuddling with your dog. In that moment, it prioritizes immediate comfort over effort, convincing you that something easier is suddenly more urgent. This is procrastination in action. Your brain evaluates the effort required and opts for a shortcut to something easier and more immediately rewarding. And here's the kicker, your brain actually rewards you for avoiding the task.

Remember our friend dopamine from chapter 3? The neurotransmitter responsible for motivation and reward? Well, it turns out dopamine has a lot to do with procrastination too. When we anticipate a difficult, uncertain, or effortful task, dopamine levels stay low, making the task feel overwhelming and unappealing before we even begin.[1] Since dopamine is the key driver of motivation, that low dopamine response makes the task seem like trudging uphill through knee-deep mud with no clear reward in sight.

But the moment we choose to avoid the task and do something easier like checking social media or reorganizing a drawer, dopamine spikes. The brain rewards this decision with a rush of feel-good neurotransmitters, reinforcing the choice to put off the harder task.[2] Each time we do this, we strengthen a neural pathway, making avoidance feel instinctive and automatic.

Think of it like digging a trench in your brain. Every time you avoid something difficult, you reinforce the neural pathway of avoidance, making it deeper and more ingrained. Over time, your brain carves out a shortcut: *discomfort* → *avoidance* → *instant relief.* The more we procrastinate, the stronger this response becomes, and the harder it is to start.[3]

And yet, that relief is only temporary. The moment the distraction is over, dopamine levels crash again, leaving us feeling guilty, unmotivated, and even more resistant to starting. This is why we don't magically feel readier hours or days later; the very act of avoiding the task deepens our resistance. Our brains are wired to crave immediate rewards, and the more we indulge in procrastination, the harder it becomes to change course.

Procrastination can take different forms. For some, it's avoidant procrastination, where we fear failure or the task feels so daunting that we push it aside.[4] For others, it's emotional procrastination, where we put off tasks because they trigger anxiety, stress, or feeling overwhelmed. Some individuals fall into decisional procrastination, struggling to commit to a task due to uncertainty about how to start or what the best approach is.[5] Finally, there's active procrastination, where people deliberately postpone tasks, believing they work best under pressure, though this can sometimes lead to last-minute stress and mistakes.[6]

Now, I know you remember this from previous chapters: Procrastination is not just a modern problem. It's deeply tied to our evolutionary wiring. Our ancestors evolved to prioritize immediate rewards like finding food or avoiding danger, because survival depended on it. Tasks that didn't offer a tangible, short-term benefit were often pushed aside.

That same instinct still shapes our behavior today. When we face a task without an immediate payoff, the brain may classify it as less urgent, nudging us toward something easier and more instantly satisfying. This is why distractions feel so appealing. Our brains are wired to seek quick rewards over delayed gratification.

The problem is what once helped our ancestors survive doesn't always serve us well today. Avoiding discomfort made sense in the wild, but in modern life, it can keep us stuck. Many of the tasks we procrastinate on, like writing a report, exercising, or working toward a long-term goal, aren't life-threatening. Yet our brains still treat them as if they are, triggering the same avoidance patterns that were once necessary for survival.

Other factors can keep us stuck too. Fear of failure, fear of perfectionism, and feeling mentally overloaded often fuel procrastination. You know that feeling when you stare at a blank page and think, I don't even know where to start? The weight of that first step feels heavier than the task itself. And when faced with that discomfort, our brains instinctively look for an easier escape route—which is why instead of starting, you find yourself rearranging your bookshelf or organizing your desk. The big project doesn't feel rewarding enough in the moment, so your brain nudges you toward a "quick win" instead.

This is where self-regulation comes in. Self-regulation is our ability to manage impulses, emotions, and behaviors so that we can follow through on tasks, even when they feel overwhelming or uncomfortable. When self-regulation is weak, the brain struggles to override the instinct to avoid effort. Instead of pushing forward, we default to what feels easier in the moment.[7]

That's why you might think, *I'll start tomorrow when I'm in the right headspace*, only to find yourself repeating the same cycle the next day. The brain prioritizes short-term relief over long-term success, making it harder to stay on track when a task feels daunting or emotionally draining.

Sometimes, procrastination is also tied to how we view ourselves. If we believe we're just "bad" at managing time or we've had past experiences where we struggled to complete tasks, procrastination can become a way of protecting our self-esteem. We might delay doing something because we're afraid we won't do it well or that we won't be able to meet our own standards.

In the moment, procrastination can feel like a solution. Delaying a task offers instant relief, even though it creates bigger problems down the line. That momentary escape feels good initially, but it leaves you with growing stress, unfinished projects, and a lingering sense that you have no control over your time or energy.

Here's the good news: procrastination isn't a personal failure, and it's not something you're stuck with forever. Once you understand why it happens and how it works, you can start to take control.

In this chapter, we'll dive deeper into what procrastination really is and why it keeps showing up. We'll also discuss how you can change the patterns that keep you stuck. By understanding what drives procrastination, especially how your brain is wired to seek quick rewards, you'll be able to make better choices and move forward with confidence (without waiting until tomorrow).

Your Inner Caveperson: How Our Primitive Brain Fuels Fear and Procrastination

Do you have that one project that you have wanted to start for months, or even years, that you are still waiting to start? Did you get a new assignment but just can't seem to get started? Maybe you want to share an idea or apply for a new job, but instead, you find yourself frozen, overwhelmed by some invisible force. The more you want to move forward, the stronger the urge to delay or avoid becomes. It can feel confusing, even frustrating, like you're at war with yourself.

As we just talked about, procrastination, self-doubt, and avoidance are not personal failures. They are natural responses shaped by the same survival instincts that once helped our ancestors stay safe. But while those instincts were useful in life-or-death situations, today they can hold us back from the very things we want to achieve. We have already explored how these primitive survival patterns influence the way we interact with others. Now, we will look at how they shape procrastination, even when we genuinely want to move forward.

Noelle's story is a perfect example of how these instincts can interfere with our ability to take action. She came to see me, feeling frustrated and angry with herself. She had a dream of starting a blog, a website, and a consulting business focused on conservation, but every time she tried to begin, she felt paralyzed. She had successfully pushed through difficult projects at work before, so she couldn't understand why this felt so different. The anxiety she experienced felt overwhelming and out of place. It was as if something unseen was holding her back.

Noelle grew up in a loving home where her parents encouraged her to work hard and praised her successes. Despite their support, they often nudged her to do even better. Comments like "This is great, but next time try for 100%" planted a seed of perfectionism in her mind. Over time, this belief ignited her primitive survival instincts. Her brain unconsciously linked her abilities to her being accepted. If she didn't perform perfectly, she feared disappointing the people she relied on for belonging and protection. While this fear wasn't entirely rational, her brain interpreted it as a potential threat.

For our ancestors, maintaining status and acceptance within the group was essential for survival. Mistakes or perceived inadequacies could mean losing connection, safety, or resources. Noelle's brain carried forward these ancient fears, even though her modern world was far from life-threatening. Her brain wasn't trying to sabotage her, it was trying to keep her safe.

When she thought about her conservation project, her inner caveperson saw it as a potential threat. Sharing her ideas with the world felt risky because it opened her up to judgment and rejection. Her brain's fight-or-flight response kicked in. Instead of encouraging her to take action, her brain encouraged her to avoid the task entirely. This avoidance made her feel ashamed and confused, as if something were wrong with her. The more she avoided the project, the more her anxiety grew, and her belief in herself and her abilities began to fade.

Have you ever felt this way? You tell yourself you'll start tomorrow, but when tomorrow comes, the same hesitation is still there. You might even feel busy, caught up in endless preparation or research, but never actually start. And the longer you wait, the harder it becomes.

Noelle's struggle wasn't a sign of laziness or incompetence. It was a result of her brain working overtime to protect her from perceived danger. For her, procrastination wasn't about time management, it was about avoiding the discomfort of potential failure. Her brain had learned to see criticism and failure as threats to her survival. The more she avoided, the more those threats felt real.

What about you? Have you ever felt that internal tug-of-war between wanting to act and feeling stuck? Do you feel that knot in your stomach, that wave of anxiety, or the sudden urge to distract yourself? These are signals that your brain is trying to protect you, but you don't have to let them control you.

One way Noelle started to shift these responses was by separating herself from her inner caveperson. She practiced noticing when her brain sent out fear signals and paused to ask herself, "Is this a real threat, or is my brain overreacting?"

This simple question helped her create space between the fear and her reaction to it. You can try this too. The next time you feel fear or hesitation, pause and ask yourself if the threat is real or imagined.

This process isn't about silencing your inner caveperson. It's about understanding its voice and choosing how to respond. Our brains evolved to keep us alive, but many of the fears that once served our ancestors no longer apply. By recognizing these fears, you can begin to challenge them and take small, courageous steps forward.

Imagine what it would feel like to take that next small, but meaningful step toward reaching your goal, even if it's uncomfortable. By recognizing and quieting your inner caveperson, you can disarm fear and move forward. Understanding where these feelings come from will help you to reclaim control and to create a life of action and growth.

Where Procrastination Begins: The Stories That Shape Our Self-Doubt

One of the first things I tell clients is that thoughts are not facts, but we often treat them as truths. This habit can get us into trouble. The stories we tell ourselves shape not just our thoughts but also our feelings, our actions, and ultimately, our perceptions of the world. These internal narratives, built from childhood experiences, societal messages, and past failures, become the filter through which we judge our worth, abilities, and what we deserve.[8]

When you believe thoughts like *I'm not good enough* or *I'll never succeed* or *It has to be perfect*, they trigger emotional reactions that trap you in patterns of fear, self-doubt, and avoidance. These stories might feel like the truth, but often, they are just the voices of old experiences or distorted beliefs.

Your brain treats them like real threats, causing feelings of fear or shame so strong that they influence what you see and how you interpret your experiences in the world. These stories become your self-constructed reality.[9]

Noelle's journey did not stop at identifying her inner caveperson and understanding why she procrastinated. The next step was to trace the origins of her self-doubt and perfectionism and see how they had shaped her thoughts, emotions, and behaviors over time.

If you remember, Noelle's parents were caring but expected Noelle to perform at her best. She often mentioned that she could hear their voices in her head, reminding her that being the winner, getting a perfect score, and performing the best were all that mattered. Noelle absorbed the message that her best was not quite enough.

When it came time to apply to college, Noelle chose a university known for its strong environmental-science program. Her passion for conservation guided her decision, but it was not the prestigious institution her parents had envisioned. They did not hide their disappointment.

"Your cousin Sarah got into that top-tier school. You could have made a better choice," they said. In that moment, her brain registered her choice not as a thoughtful step toward her future but as a failure to meet expectations.

Her parents' words were not meant to hurt her, but they fed into a story that had already begun forming. The story told her she was falling short, that her choices were not good enough, and that she was not good enough. Her brain, trying to protect her from future disappointment, held on to these moments as evidence that taking risks was not worth it.

For a good decade or so of her adult life, perfectionism and the drive to be the best served her well. She excelled in academics, sports, even trivial pursuit with friends. She rigorously applied herself to everything, striving to be the best and to always be at the top of her field. This was all driven and supported by her narrative that she needed to be perfect to finally gain the approval of her parents. She kept hoping and trying and pushing herself.

But instead of fully acknowledging these successes, she focused on the few moments when she fell short. If she got a 95% on a test, she only remembered the professor's note saying, "Great job, but next time make this section a bit stronger." If she received praise in a performance review, her mind zeroed in on the one suggestion for improvement. Her brain magnified these moments, reinforcing the story that she was always just shy of being good enough. The underlying message remained: There was always something more she could have done.

These small moments, repeated over time, built a narrative of uncertainty and hesitation. Her inner caveperson, though not always at the forefront of her mind, was there in the background amplifying these stories. It magnified the fear of rejection and reminded her of the times she fell short. Though the threats were no longer real, her brain clung to these old narratives as though her survival depended on them.

Can you relate to this? Think back to your own childhood, your family's expectations, or those defining moments at school or work. Were there times when a single comment or experience planted a seed of doubt that grew into a story you still believe today? Perhaps your parents, teachers, or peers meant well, but their words left you feeling like you were not good enough or that failure was something to be avoided at all costs.

These stories do not just shape our thoughts. They influence our actions. If you believe you are destined to fail, you might avoid opportunities that could prove otherwise. If you think your work is not good enough, you might delay sharing it. The more these stories replay in your mind, the stronger they become, creating patterns that are difficult to break.

But the conservation project was different for Noelle. It wasn't just another task; it was tied to her identity and self-worth. Writing about conservation reflected who she was and what mattered most to her. If she failed at the project, it felt like she was failing herself. The story she told herself about the need to be perfect and the best to earn the approval of her parents, and her brain's ancient need to avoid failure and rejection collided. It created a sense of fear that was stronger than her desire to move forward. No amount of thinking, planning, or pressuring herself was enough to overcome this fear.

Noelle's story shows how powerful these narratives can be. They are built from layers of experience reinforced by repetition and amplified by the brain's instinct to protect us.[10] Once established, these patterns can shape how we see ourselves for years, even when the original circumstances that created them are long gone. Understanding where these stories come from allows us to recognize them for what they are: old beliefs, not absolute truths. By questioning them, we open the door to change, making space for a narrative built on self-compassion, courage, and the possibility of something new.

What stories do you carry with you? Are they based on facts and evidence, or are they echoes of a past you have outgrown? Remember, these stories are not fixed. By identifying and questioning them, you can begin to write a new narrative, one grounded in self-compassion, courage, and possibility.

Procrastination Loops: How Beliefs Keep Us Stuck

Stephen R. Covey wrote, "We see the world, not as it is, but as we are—or, as we are conditioned to see it." [11] This insight underscores how our perceptions shape our reality. Our beliefs influence how we see ourselves, approach challenges, and respond to opportunities. When those beliefs are negative, they can create patterns of behavior that keep us stuck, often without us realizing it.

By now, you might be thinking, *Oh great, we're talking about self-fulfilling prophecies again.* And you're right. But there's something more to examine here, how these scripts form and become ingrained over time. Self-fulfilling prophecies don't happen in isolation. As we've discussed, our survival instincts can be part of your brain's primitive survival mechanisms, warning you to avoid risk, failure, and discomfort. These automatic responses, meant to keep us safe, can unintentionally reinforce avoidance and self-doubt.

We are going to take a break from Noelle for a while and talk about Jake. His story shows how long-standing beliefs and survival-based thinking can trap us in cycles of procrastination. While Noelle hesitated due to perfectionism, Jake's procrastination stemmed from something else, a deep-seated self-doubt.

When Jake came to therapy, he was frustrated, exhausted, and weighed down by his constant procrastination. He had missed several key deadlines at work and was now on a Performance Improvement Plan. The more he tried to change, the more stuck he felt.

"I just feel like I can't do anything right," he admitted. "My doctor says I'm depressed, and it makes sense. But I have been on medication for four months, and nothing has helped. If I can just get over this depression, maybe things will finally get better."

Jake's belief that everything hinged on getting over his depression made him feel powerless. This was a form of all-or-nothing thinking. He believed he had to feel completely better before he could take action. Have you ever told yourself something similar? Maybe you have thought, *I will start that project when I am less stressed* or *I will get back to exercising when life calms down.*

This kind of thinking feeds into self-fulfilling prophecies. By waiting for the "perfect" moment, you reinforce the belief that you cannot move forward until everything aligns perfectly. Or worse, you start believing you will never be successful, good enough, or capable of change. And then you do not get that new job, you do not start the exercise routine, and you end up experiencing exactly what you believed to be true.

While I told him I understood that he felt depression was the problem, I asked, "What were things like before the depression took hold? What was going on?"

As we talked, the pieces of Jake's experience started to come together. He described moments of hesitation, missed opportunities, and a deep sense of self-doubt that had been there long before the depression. These narratives were not new. They were part of a larger story Jake had been telling himself for years, a story about his abilities, his worth, and his potential. It was as if his brain had built an internal script, one that kept replaying, regardless of his actual abilities.

Jake often felt overshadowed by his younger brother, who seemed to excel at everything. Even when Jake performed well, he could not shake the feeling that he would never quite measure up. "If we were on the same team, I might be first string, but he would always be the captain," Jake explained.

This dynamic left Jake feeling inadequate, even when he succeeded. Over time, he internalized the belief that no matter how hard he tried, he would never measure up. To protect himself from the pain of failing to meet expectations, Jake started procrastinating.

Have you ever put off trying something because you were afraid of falling short? Avoiding the task can feel safer than risking failure, but it often keeps you stuck in place.

"Looking back, I think I avoided trying altogether," Jake admitted. "If I waited until the last minute and things did not go well, I could tell myself it was not because I was not good enough. It was because I did not have enough time."

This pattern is known as self-handicapping. By delaying tasks, he gave himself a way to explain failure without confronting the possibility that he wasn't capable.[12] But as the deadline got closer, the scarcity of time woke up his inner caveperson, amplifying anxiety and fear. The pressure felt like a threat, making avoidance seem like the only option. This cycle—delay, pressure, avoidance—became deeply ingrained.

Certain cognitive biases reinforced Jake's avoidance. One of the strongest was something called "temporal discounting." His brain prioritized the short-term comfort of avoiding a task over the distant reward of completing it.[13] The immediate relief of avoidance felt more real than the long-term benefits of success.

His brain was also caught in filtering (another term for negativity bias). He focused only on his failures and struggles, ignoring any moments of progress or success. Each missed deadline or negative comment felt like undeniable proof that he was broken. Even when he completed tasks or received praise, his mind dismissed it as a fluke.

Then there was something called "catastrophizing." When Jake thought about starting a task, his brain leapt to the worst-case scenario. He imagined his boss being furious, his colleagues judging him, and his career falling apart. With each exaggeration, his avoidance felt more justified.

Jake paused, a flicker of understanding in his eyes. He took a deep breath and said, "So maybe it is not just about the depression. If my brain is creating these patterns, maybe I can start to change them." There was a hint of hope in his voice, a realization that he was not as trapped as he thought.

What about you? Have you ever assumed that change was out of reach because of an old belief? Are there beliefs that keep you delaying action or avoiding challenges? Do patterns like self-handicapping, temporal discounting, or catastrophizing make it feel impossible to move forward?

In the next section, we'll explore how your brain's wiring, specifically the Default Mode Network (DMN), keeps certain narratives alive, looping through thoughts that reinforce procrastination.[14]

Avoidance and the Brain: Why We Resist What We Need Most

Procrastination is something we have all encountered. At times, it feels like you are stuck in a cycle, knowing exactly what needs to be done yet somehow avoiding it. It can feel like an internal tug-of-war, where part of you wants to move forward, but another part pulls you away from the effort.

Maybe you've been here before: You sit down to tackle an important task, but instead of making progress, your mind pulls you in a dozen directions. You find yourself reliving past mistakes, worrying about what might go wrong, or imagining what others might think. Before you know it, you're organizing a drawer, eating a donut, or doing anything except the thing you set out to do.

At first, it might seem like procrastination is just a lack of discipline or motivation, but that's not what's happening. At its core, procrastination is about avoiding discomfort. Your brain isn't just putting things off for no reason. It's responding to stress, uncertainty, or the possibility of failure. Instead of pushing through, it steers you toward short-term relief, like a distraction that feels good in the moment.[15] This is where neuroscience gives us some important clues.

Noelle and Jake's struggles are good examples of how the brain fuels procrastination. Noelle's blog about conservation was not just another task. It was deeply personal. Writing about something she cared so much about made the stakes feel impossibly high. She worried that making mistakes or facing judgment would reflect on her as a person, not just as a writer. This fear paralyzed her, making avoidance feel like the only safe option.

Jake's procrastination looked different, but the root cause was similar. He felt overshadowed by his younger brother, believing he would never measure up. For him, avoiding tasks was a way to protect himself from disappointment and the fear of failure.

When it comes to these struggles, the brain plays a big role. Two key networks influence how we approach or avoid tasks: the Default Mode Network (DMN) and the Task-Positive Network (TPN). The DMN is active when you are at rest, daydreaming, or reflecting on yourself. This is where self-doubt and overthinking often take hold.

The TPN, on the other hand, activates when you focus on a specific task, make decisions, or solve problems. It helps you stay present and productive. Think of the DMN as your worry network and the TPN as your do-it-now network. These two networks operate like a switch, where only one can dominate at a time.[16]

For Noelle, sitting down to write triggered her DMN. Instead of focusing on her ideas, her mind wandered to thoughts of judgment, potential failure, and what others might think. Her fear of getting it wrong activated her brain's stress response, making it nearly impossible to engage her

TPN. The more she overthought, the more avoidance felt like the safest option.

This explains why tasks tied to identity or personal significance often feel the hardest to start. When something matters deeply to you, the stakes feel higher. Your brain interprets the task as risky, and the DMN takes over, pulling you into self-doubt and rumination instead of action.

Jake's experience added another layer to this. His procrastination had become a habit, something his brain had automated over years of avoiding tasks. As discussed in earlier chapters, the brain is incredibly efficient at creating patterns, and when you repeatedly avoid something, it strengthens the neural pathways that tell you to keep avoiding it.[17] Over time, this becomes the brain's default setting. This is why procrastination can feel so automatic. It is your brain following a well-worn path of least resistance.

As we've already explored, the brain's reward system also plays a role. When you avoid a task, you often turn to distractions that offer quick, easy relief, like checking social media, watching TV, or reorganizing your desk. These small distractions trigger a release of dopamine, the brain's feel-good chemical, which reinforces avoidance. Unfortunately, this relief is only temporary. The longer you avoid the task, the more the brain links procrastination with comfort, making it harder to break the cycle.

Stress and anxiety can amplify this pattern. When the brain is overloaded, the prefrontal cortex, the part responsible for focus and decision-making, struggles to function effectively. This can leave you feeling paralyzed, as though the simplest tasks are too much to handle.[18] For Jake, this often showed up as a mental fog that kept him stuck. For Noelle, it came as a wave of anxiety that made starting feel impossible.

The amygdala, the brain's fear center, adds another layer to this struggle. When the amygdala perceives a task as threatening, whether because of fear of failure, rejection, or criticism, it triggers the fight, flight, or freeze response. This stress response is designed to protect you, but in the modern world, it can keep you from taking action on important tasks. For Noelle, the amygdala amplified her fear of judgment. For Jake, it reinforced his belief that he was not capable of succeeding.

Overcoming these habits is challenging, but it is possible. It all begins with awareness. When you catch yourself procrastinating, pause and ask yourself, "What am I avoiding, and why?" Is it discomfort, fear of failure, or fear of judgment? Recognizing what is happening in your brain can help you take the next step.

For Noelle, breaking the cycle started with taking smaller, less intimidating steps. Instead of trying to write her entire blog in one sitting, she started with fifteen minutes of brainstorming or writing just one paragraph. These small actions helped lower her brain's resistance and gave her a sense of progress. For Jake, breaking his habit of avoidance meant working with his brain's natural rhythms. He identified the times of day when he felt most focused and scheduled his most challenging tasks during those hours. He also created a workspace that encouraged focus by removing distractions like his phone.

In both cases, progress came from focusing on small wins rather than perfection. Each step forward helped create new neural pathways, shifting their brains from avoidance to action. Over time, these new patterns made it easier to engage their TPN and quiet the DMN, reducing the grip of procrastination.

What about you? Have you noticed how certain tasks feel harder to start when the stakes feel high? Or how small distractions can pull you away from what matters most? Recognizing these patterns will help you take action. Procrastination is not a personal failing. It is your brain's way of trying to protect you. By understanding how your brain works, you can begin to take back control, one manageable step at a time.

Reclaiming Time: Breaking Free from Procrastination

Procrastination often feels like a thief, stealing our time and leaving us frustrated. Procrastination is not a permanent part of who you are. It is a habit, not a personality trait, and with intention and practice, it can be changed. By rewriting the stories that hold you back, you can reclaim your time and move toward a more productive and fulfilling life.

Noelle and Jake both struggled with procrastination but did not realize how much it was tied to deeper patterns of fear and self-doubt, and how their brains responded to stress. They saw themselves as people who simply put things off without recognizing the internal wiring that made certain tasks feel impossible to start. Through our work together, they discovered that breaking free from procrastination was not about forcing themselves to be more disciplined. It was about understanding why avoidance happened in the first place and taking small, intentional steps toward change.

For Noelle, avoiding her conservation project had nothing to do with laziness. Every time she tried to start, a wave of anxiety hit her. She worried about getting things wrong, about people judging her, about not being knowledgeable enough. The moment she sat down, her mind would tell her to do anything but write. The voice of her inner critic, which she later named Betty, told her, *This will never be good enough* or *You do not know enough to write this.*

Giving that voice a name helped her recognize it for what it was, just a thought, not the truth. Instead of letting Betty's warnings paralyze her, Noelle started responding with cognitive defusion, a technique I taught her to help her step back from negative self-talk. "Thanks for your input, Betty, but I am going to write anyway." The more she practiced this, the less power those critical thoughts had over her.

After addressing her inner critic, Noelle noticed something else. Procrastination was not just mental, it was physical. The act of sitting down to work triggered an anxious, restless feeling that made it hard to focus. We talked about how stress signals from the nervous system can make tasks feel overwhelming, causing the brain to seek immediate relief through distraction.[19]

To counter this, Noelle started using physiological state shifts, quick, simple actions that helped regulate her nervous system before starting a task. Instead of waiting until she felt ready, she built momentum through movement. A short walk, a few stretches, or even splashing cold water on her face helped reset her body's stress response, making it easier to sit down and focus.[20] She also used behavioral activation, setting small, low-pressure goals like brainstorming for ten minutes or writing one sentence. This prevented her from feeling paralyzed by the overwhelming nature of the project.

She also began using her brain's dopamine system to work for her instead of against her. Rather than relying on the quick dopamine hit that came from avoiding work, she trained her brain to expect dopamine from effort itself.[21] Instead of giving herself a reward before starting, she rewarded herself after completing a small task, reinforcing the connection between action and satisfaction. A cup of tea, a quick stretch, or stepping outside for fresh air became her post-task rewards. Over time, this small shift rewired her brain's motivation loop, making it easier to stay engaged.

She also found visualization helpful. Before starting, she would close her eyes and picture herself writing with ease, feeling the satisfaction of making progress. Instead of letting her brain anticipate failure, she trained it to expect success.

As she made these adjustments, Noelle started to feel a shift. "I still hear Betty sometimes," she told me. "But now I just acknowledge her and move forward anyway. I am not letting that voice be in charge anymore."

While Noelle's procrastination was fueled by perfectionism and fear of judgment, Jake's had a different root, fear of not measuring up. He had spent most of his life comparing himself to his younger brother, the overachiever of the family. No matter what Jake did, it never felt like enough, so at some point, he stopped trying. Procrastination became his safety net. If he avoided putting in full effort, then failure could not feel personal.

"I think I have always identified as a procrastinator," Jake admitted. "If I wait until the last minute, then I have an excuse if things go wrong."

One of the biggest challenges Jake faced was getting started. His brain had been wired to seek immediate relief through distractions, reinforcing the habit of procrastination. To counteract this, we focused on naturally boosting his baseline dopamine levels before engaging in tasks, a technique grounded in neuroscience.[22]

Instead of waiting for motivation to strike, Jake layered movement into his routine to help prime his brain for focus. Before sitting down to work, he did a short walk outside or a quick set of push-ups, activating dopamine production and increasing alertness. This small habit made it easier for him to transition into work mode instead of defaulting to avoidance.

Another strategy that worked for Jake was rewarding effort instead of results. In the past, he only felt accomplished when a task was fully completed, which made the act of starting feel overwhelming. To retrain his brain, he began breaking tasks into small milestones and celebrating progress rather than just the final outcome. Finishing a thirty-minute work session or drafting an outline became a dopamine hit in itself, reinforcing the habit of taking action instead of delaying.

Jake also tackled his habit of seeking instant gratification. The urge to check his phone or scroll through social media provided quick dopamine hits, reinforcing avoidance. Instead of completely banning distractions, which often led to binge-scrolling later, he implemented a technique called dopamine stacking.[23] He paired enjoyable activities with work, telling himself, "Once I complete forty-five minutes of work, I will listen to my favorite podcast for ten minutes." This created positive reinforcement, making it easier to stay engaged without feeling deprived.

As Jake integrated these strategies, procrastination started to lose its grip. He no longer relied on pressure or last-minute panic to get things done. Instead, he trained his brain to associate effort with reward, breaking free from the avoidance cycle and building sustainable motivation.

"I always thought procrastination was just part of who I am," Jake reflected. "But now I see that it is just a habit, not my identity. And habits can be changed."

Both Noelle and Jake discovered that procrastination was not a personal flaw. It was a learned response to discomfort, uncertainty, and self-doubt. The more they challenged their automatic thoughts, shifted their physical state before starting, and focused on small, consistent actions, the easier it became to stay engaged instead of avoiding tasks.

What about you? Have you ever put something off because it felt overwhelming? Do you avoid certain tasks because they bring up stress or doubt? Lasting change starts with self-awareness. From there, you can experiment with small shifts, detaching from negative self-talk, resetting your physical state, or setting small, achievable goals. You do not need to wait to feel ready. You just need to start.

Key Takeaways

Procrastination isn't just about putting things off; it's about how your brain responds to stress, fear, and discomfort. Understanding its roots can help you loosen its hold.

- **Procrastination is rooted in fear.** It often masks fear of failure, judgment, or rejection. Your brain perceives these risks as threats, activating its survival instincts to avoid discomfort, even when the danger isn't real.
- **Avoidance brings short-term relief but creates long-term stress.** Your brain rewards avoidance with a temporary sense of relief, reinforcing the habit. This cycle makes procrastination feel automatic, even though it increases stress and leaves tasks unfinished.
- **Taking action rewires your brain.** Every small step you take challenges your brain's avoidance patterns. By consistently acting, even in small ways, you create new neural pathways that shift your brain from avoidance to action, reducing procrastination over time.

Understanding procrastination as a survival mechanism helps you approach it with curiosity and compassion. With awareness and practice, you can step out of the cycle and build habits that support your goals.

Moving from Understanding to Action

Procrastination can feel like a constant uphill battle, but it's not about laziness or a lack of willpower. It is about how our brains are wired and how they respond to fear, discomfort, or feeling overwhelmed. By taking small, intentional actions, you can shift out of the procrastination loop and into a place of focus and productivity. Here are five actionable strategies to help you move forward today:

- **Start by resetting your physical and mental state.** If you feel stuck or overwhelmed, try engaging in something simple like taking a quick walk, stretching for a few minutes, or splashing cold water on your face. This shift in physical energy helps to disrupt procrastination patterns and to clear your mind so you can refocus on the task at hand.
- **Break the task down into the smallest possible step.** When a project feels overwhelming, focus on just one tiny action, like opening a document, writing down one sentence, or brainstorming a single idea. These small wins help reduce the fear of starting and create momentum toward finishing the larger goal.
- **Work in short, focused intervals with built-in rewards.** Set a timer for twenty-five minutes to focus fully on your task, then give yourself a short five-minute break to do something enjoyable. This structure, known as the Pomodoro Technique, helps reduce overwhelming feelings while providing consistent motivation through small, manageable steps.
- **Set up your environment to support your focus.** Before starting, take a few minutes to remove distractions, like silencing your phone or clearing clutter from your workspace. A calm, distraction-free space can make it easier for your brain to stay present and engaged with the task.
- **Practice responding to discomfort with action.** When you feel resistance or self-doubt creeping in, pause and remind yourself that discomfort is

temporary. Give that inner critic a name if it helps and respond with compassion. For example, say, "I hear you, but I'm choosing to take this one step anyway." Then immediately act on something small, like writing one sentence or organizing your materials.

Procrastination isn't a character flaw or a reflection of your abilities. It is simply a habit that can be reshaped with intention and practice. Each small action you take builds confidence and rewires your brain for focus and forward movement. Over time, these small steps lead to bigger changes. You've got this.

8

Feeling Invisible: Breaking Free and Rebuilding Self-Worth

"To be yourself in a world that is constantly trying to make you something else is the greatest accomplishment."

—Ralph Waldo Emerson,
poet and transcendentalist thinker

Have you ever felt lost, like you don't know who you are or what your purpose is? Or maybe you've caught yourself doubting your own worth or abilities, wondering if you'll ever feel good enough.

You are not alone. These feelings are far more common than you might think. Like everything else we've been discussing, they often stem from a mix of survival instincts passed down through generations, early experiences with caregivers, and the way our brains adapt to the world around us.

Self-esteem, our belief in our own worth, starts forming in our earliest relationships. As we explored in chapter 6, when caregivers respond to a child's needs with warmth, love, and attention, the child learns that they are valued. This creates a foundation for confidence and self-worth that can last a lifetime.

But if a child's emotional needs are ignored, dismissed, or unmet, a different story begins to form. The child may start to believe that they are not enough. To cope, they might hide parts of themselves or take on roles that earn approval, like being the "good" or "helpful" one. Over time, these strategies can lead to a deep sense of invisibility. They may start to believe that their worth depends only on meeting others' expectations.

Our ancient survival instincts can reinforce this sense of invisibility. Our inner caveperson, which is designed to keep us safe, constantly looks for signs of rejection or failure and tells us to stay quiet, avoid risks, and blend in. Long ago, this helped our ancestors survive. But today, these same instincts can trap us in self-doubt and stop us from expressing who we really are.

When we suppress ourselves to stay safe, it doesn't just affect how we feel. It can actually change our brains. Long-term stress from feeling invisible or unheard can overstimulate the amygdala, the part of the brain that processes fear and threats. This makes us more anxious and sensitive to rejection. At the same time, the prefrontal cortex, which helps us make decisions and manage our emotions, becomes less effective. This makes it harder to think clearly, stay calm, or see our own potential.[1]

The world around us can reinforce this conditioning. Societal expectations, biases, and the roles we play in our families, workplaces, or communities can make us feel overlooked.[2] The constant pressure to meet other people's needs or to present a perfect version of ourselves online can add to the feeling that our true selves do not matter.

Thanks to neuroplasticity—the brain's ability to form new connections—these dynamics are not fixed. It is possible to heal and rebuild our self-esteem. Practices like self-compassion, mindfulness, and healthy relationships can help us change how we respond to stress and help us reconnect with our sense of worth.

Breaking free from the grip of invisibility begins with understanding where these feelings come from. In the next sections, we'll explore how survival instincts, early experiences, and repeated patterns shape this sense of being unseen. We'll uncover the psychological roots of invisibility, the toll it takes on the brain and body, and how these patterns keep us stuck. Most importantly, you'll learn practical ways to challenge these beliefs, reconnect with your true self, and step back into the light of your own life.

You are not meant to stay hidden. You are worthy of being seen.

Your Inner Caveperson: How Survival Instincts Shape Our Self-Concept

By now, you're familiar with your inner caveperson, that part of your brain that urges you to stay safe, avoid risks, and blend in. You've seen how these ancient instincts can keep you trapped in patterns of self-doubt and hiding. When your inner caveperson is always scanning for danger or rejection, it's easy to believe that staying quiet, hidden, or invisible is the safest option. But survival instincts don't just influence what you do; they shape how you see yourself.

The idea of survival instincts shaping your sense of self might seem abstract. But seeing it play out in real life makes it easier to understand. Charlie's journey offers a powerful example of how these ancient patterns can lead to feeling invisible and disconnected. Through his experience, you'll see how these survival instincts can reinforce the belief that your needs and identity don't really matter. By understanding how this conditioning takes hold, you can start to recognize them in your own life. And once you see them clearly, you can begin to challenge these old beliefs and embrace who you truly are.

Charlie, a kind and thoughtful fifty-two-year-old man, came to therapy after the devastating loss of his twin brother. The loss left him feeling untethered. It wasn't just the pain of losing his brother; it was the deeper sense of not knowing who he was without the role he had built around caring for him. While the initial focus of therapy was his grief, it soon became clear that Charlie's struggle ran deeper. His pain was rooted in a lifelong feeling of invisibility and a lack of purpose.

"Charlie, how did you cope with your parents' attention to your brother while you were growing up?" I asked during one of our sessions.

"I guess I just kept quiet," he said. "I didn't want to cause any trouble or stress. The few times I asked for anything, they acted pretty stressed, so I just stopped asking."

Charlie's twin brother had intellectual and physical disabilities that required constant care and frequent medical attention. Their parents, though loving, were stretched thin, leaving little emotional bandwidth for Charlie. Over time, Charlie learned that expressing his needs often resulted in rejection or additional stress for his parents. To avoid upsetting them, he internalized the belief that his needs were selfish and unimportant.

For our ancestors, maintaining social harmony was essential for survival. The cohesion of the group ensured safety and increased chances of survival. Any behavior that disrupted this balance, like drawing too much attention to oneself, could result in exclusion or rejection. Charlie's inner caveperson, driven by this primal need for acceptance and harmony, urged him to suppress his emotions and prioritize the needs of others.

"Charlie, do you remember a time when you expressed your feelings and got a response that made you feel small?" I asked.

He thought for a moment and shared this memory from childhood. One day, he came home from school upset about something that had happened. He tried to tell his mother about it, but she cut him off, saying, "I know you can handle this, Charlie. Just be strong and don't make a fuss, okay? We've had a hard week with your brother."

Charlie admitted that after that moment, he stopped trying to share his feelings with his parents. "It just felt easier to keep things to myself. I didn't want to add to their stress," he said.

I explained to Charlie that moments like these leave a mark, shaping how we view ourselves and the world around us. When a child perceives that expressing emotions leads to rejection or disconnection, their brain adjusts to protect them from that pain. Over time, the inner caveperson raises the emotional-threat level, discouraging them from speaking up in order to avoid rejection. This creates a pattern of silence and self-suppression, reinforced by repeated experiences of being dismissed or overlooked.

Charlie's hypervigilance to the needs of others, while initially a survival mechanism, had become a barrier to his self-expression. His constant focus on others' emotions and reactions had led to decades of self-neglect.

"Have you ever thought about what you want or need in your daily life, Charlie?" I asked one day.

He paused before responding. "Sometimes I think about it, like when I'm hungry and want to eat lunch. But it's hard to think beyond small things like that."

"What happens when you think about expressing a need or sharing an opinion?" I asked.

He hesitated, then said, "I get this tight feeling in my gut, like I'm about to do something wrong. I can hear my dad's voice in my head telling me, 'Just go along, Charlie. Don't make things more difficult.' "

We reflected on how his inner caveperson had taken over during moments like these, warning him to stay silent to maintain harmony and avoid conflict. While this strategy helped him navigate his family dynamics as a child, it was no longer serving him as an adult.

Charlie's story highlights how deeply ingrained survival mechanisms, rooted in ancestral wiring, can shape our behaviors and beliefs. Many of us carry similar patterns, learned in childhood, into our adult lives. We say yes to requests even when overwhelmed, avoid conflict because it feels too uncomfortable, or hold back our true feelings to keep the peace.

Do you find yourself constantly checking for approval in conversations or seeking reassurance from others? Maybe you overapologize or second-guess your decisions in an effort to align with what you think others expect. These behaviors often stem from the same survival instincts Charlie experienced, an overactive drive to maintain harmony and connection.

While these behaviors may have kept us safe in the past, they can lead to feelings of invisibility and a lack of identity in adulthood. When we prioritize the needs of others to the exclusion of our own, we neglect our own growth and self-discovery. Over time, this can leave us feeling empty, directionless, and unsure of who we are.

Reflect on your own experiences. Can you recall moments when you felt dismissed or invisible? How have those moments shaped how you navigate relationships or view your own needs? By recognizing these patterns, shaped by survival instincts and childhood experiences, we can begin to challenge and change them.

Where Self-Worth Begins: The Stories that Shape How We See Ourselves

As we've discussed in earlier chapters, the stories we tell ourselves often begin long before we're even aware of them. These narratives are shaped by our childhood experiences, family dynamics, and early environments. Over time, they define how we see ourselves and interact with the world. Sometimes these stories support us, but other times, they hold us back, keeping us stuck in patterns that no longer serve us.

Charlie's earliest story was that his needs didn't matter and that taking up space was a burden. Growing up as the twin brother of a sibling with significant intellectual and physical disabilities, Charlie learned early on to suppress his own emotions and wants. He learned to ignore his own needs and to keep his opinions to himself. His role, he believed, was to accommodate, not assert. The narrative that formed for him was one of invisibility.

As Charlie grew older, this belief shaped many areas of his life. He started to see his role as helping others and never asking for anything in return. To keep the peace, he avoided speaking up, always agreeing with others and making sure their needs were met, even when it meant putting himself last.

At work, this meant Charlie was a dependable team member but never someone who pushed for leadership roles. "I thought if I kept my head down and did my job, people would appreciate me," he said. But his reluctance to speak up or advocate for himself often left him unnoticed for promotions. He took this as proof that his only value was in supporting others, not in standing out or being recognized.

In his marriage, this story showed up in similar ways. Early in their relationship, Charlie's wife appreciated his attentiveness and willingness to go along with her preferences. But over time, his lack of engagement started to frustrate her.

"You never tell me what you want, Charlie," she said during one couples-therapy session. "I feel like I'm the only one making decisions. I just want you to share what you're thinking."

But Charlie had spent so many years suppressing his own desires that he didn't even know how to answer her. "It's just easier to let her decide," he told me. "I didn't think it was a problem. I thought I was being a good husband." When his wife eventually asked for a divorce, Charlie was devastated. He thought he had done everything right. He avoided conflict; he was agreeable; he put her first. But in doing so, he had erased himself from the relationship.

Carrie, another client, held a different story, but the core belief was remarkably similar. Growing up with parents who prioritized their careers over family time, Carrie learned to equate love with achievement. She believed that if she could just be perfect enough, she would finally earn her parents' attention and approval.

"I always thought, *This time they'll notice*," she told me. "If I just accomplish this one thing, they'll finally be proud of me."

As an adult, this belief fueled Carrie's drive to excel in her career. She earned multiple degrees, spoke several languages, and landed a lucrative job in tech. Despite these achievements, however, she often felt invisible and undervalued.

"No matter how hard I work, it's like no one notices me," she said during one session.

Carrie's feelings of invisibility were reinforced by her role as a contractor, which often kept her on the periphery of her workplace. She wasn't excluded because she lacked skills or talent, but because of her temporary position. Yet she internalized it as proof that she didn't belong.

"It just feels like I'm always on the outside looking in," she explained.

Both Charlie and Carrie filtered their experiences through the lens of their childhood stories, interpreting neutral or circumstantial events as proof of their deepest insecurities. For Charlie, every time his voice went unheard (or unspoken), it reinforced his belief that his needs didn't matter. For Carrie, every instance of feeling excluded affirmed her fear that she wasn't good enough.

When they started to recognize the stories they'd been telling themselves, they were able to challenge them. For Charlie, this meant understanding that expressing his needs wasn't selfish. For Carrie, it meant seeing her worth beyond her achievements and recognizing that her invisibility was more about her role than her value.

What stories are you telling yourself that are holding you back? Once you identify them, you can start to rewrite them in a way that serves your growth and well-being.

When Self-Doubt Becomes a Script: How Invisibility Becomes a Self-Fulfilling Prophecy

We've now talked about how the stories you learned in childhood shape the way you see yourself and your self-worth. You've also seen how these stories can operate beneath the surface, driven by your inner caveperson, that part of your brain wired for survival and belonging. In this section, we're going to take a closer look at how these stories about your identity and value are amplified and reinforced by the brain's automatic processes. The way you remember events as they relate to your self-worth, the judgments you make about your value and contribution, and the conclusions you draw about how others see you are all influenced by heuristics, cognitive biases, and distortions. These mental shortcuts bring your old beliefs to life, making them feel real and true and causing you to fall into the same patterns over and over again.

We'll explore how this works through Charlie's and Carrie's stories, not just as abstract ideas, but as experiences that are happening in real life. By looking closely at their stories, you'll have a better chance of spotting these patterns when they show up in your own life. The more familiar you are with these cycles, the more power you have to step beyond them and rewrite the narratives that no longer serve you.

Charlie's story is a perfect example of how self-fulfilling prophecies are maintained by unconscious processes. One of the earliest narratives he learned as a child was "My needs don't matter." This belief took root because most of his parents' attention and energy were directed toward his brother, who had significant medical and emotional needs.

"I remember working so hard on a school project in middle school," Charlie said during one session. "I was really proud of it and couldn't wait to show my parents. But when I got home, my brother was having another meltdown, and my mom barely even glanced at my work. I thought, *Why even bother? They never have time for me anyway.*

This experience, and others like it, became the foundation for Charlie's belief that his contributions didn't matter. His brain, trying to protect him, clung to these negative moments. You have already seen how negativity bias, the tendency to focus more on negative experiences than positive ones, can reinforce these beliefs. For Charlie, each ignored effort felt like undeniable proof that his needs were unimportant, while moments of acknowledgment faded away or did not seem to count.

As Charlie grew older, his belief shaped his behavior. He avoided advocating for himself, stayed silent about his needs, and focused on helping others instead. The Spotlight Effect, the tendency to believe that others are paying more attention to you than they actually are, made this fear even more intense. Whenever he considered expressing his needs, it felt as if a glaring spotlight was on him, amplifying the fear that everyone would notice and become stressed or annoyed. He worried that speaking up would burden others or create trouble, just as it had seemed to do for his parents.

This fear of scrutiny, combined with memories of his parents' exhaustion and frustration, convinced him that staying quiet was the safest option. Even in situations where people were willing to listen, Charlie's brain clung to the belief that his needs would only cause trouble. This reinforced his instinct to stay small and invisible.

Charlie's self-fulfilling prophecy kept him trapped. Each time he stayed silent, his needs were overlooked, reinforcing the belief that speaking up was pointless. His brain filtered out any evidence to the contrary, keeping him stuck in a loop of invisibility and self-doubt.

But not everyone responds to these early experiences in the same way. For some, the need to be seen and valued drives them to work harder, achieve more, and prove themselves at every turn. This was Carrie's story. "I always thought, *This time they'll see me*," Carrie said, reflecting on her childhood. "But even when I brought home straight A's or excelled at sports, I'd just hear, 'That's good, but can you do even better next time?' " As an adult, despite all her accomplishments, she felt invisible and unappreciated. Her drive to succeed was relentless, but it never seemed to be enough.

Just like Charlie, Carrie was trapped in a self-fulfilling prophecy from her childhood. "If I can just do better or achieve more, they'll notice me." Carrie's brain reinforced this belief through confirmation bias, the tendency to search for and interpret information in a way that confirms existing beliefs. When her ideas weren't acknowledged in meetings, she didn't consider external factors like her role as a contractor. Instead, her mind filtered the experience as proof that she wasn't good enough.

"It's like I'm invisible," Carrie told me. "No matter what I do, no one notices or cares."

Carrie's self-fulfilling prophecy pushed her to overwork, trying to prove her worth. Her brain's reliance on overgeneralization caused her to interpret each overlooked moment as evidence that she would always be unseen. No matter how much she achieved, it felt like the goalposts were constantly moving.

Her mind also relied on something called "the false-consensus effect," a cognitive bias that makes people assume their thoughts and feelings are more widely shared than they actually are. Because Carrie saw herself as inadequate, she automatically assumed others saw her that way too. When her manager praised her presentation, her first thought was, *He doesn't really mean it.* Her belief that she was invisible wouldn't allow her to fully accept the compliment. Instead, she rationalized it away, convinced it didn't align with the negative story she told herself.

Just like Charlie, Carrie's brain filtered out the positive moments and clung to the negative ones. This survival mechanism, meant to protect her from rejection, instead kept her trapped in a cycle of exhaustion and frustration.

This is how self-fulfilling prophecies work. Beliefs shape behaviors. Behaviors create situations. Situations reinforce the original beliefs. And over time, behaviors become automatic, repeating themselves without conscious thought.

Charlie once told me, "I guess I stopped trying a long time ago. What's the point if nothing changes?" His inner caveperson was working hard to protect him, whispering that it was safer not to try than to risk rejection or failure.

Carrie, on the other hand, kept pushing herself harder and harder, trying to prove her worth. But no matter how much she achieved, her belief that she wasn't enough caused her to focus only on moments of rejection or invisibility, ignoring her successes. Her brain's tendency to filter out the positive ensured she only saw the evidence that confirmed her fears.

Both Charlie and Carrie were stuck in cycles shaped by their early experiences, their beliefs, and the automatic processes of their brains. Thankfully, these patterns can be interrupted. Recognizing self-fulfilling prophecies and the biases that maintain them makes breaking free possible. Charlie and Carrie learned that their beliefs weren't facts; they were stories they had been telling themselves for years. And like all stories, they could be rewritten. By starting small, challenging their thoughts, and acknowledging positive experiences when they happened, they began to disrupt the cycles that had kept them stuck.

Think about your own life for a moment. What stories do you tell yourself that feel like absolute truths? Do you believe you're not good enough, that your voice doesn't matter, or that you'll always be overlooked? How do these stories shape the way you act? And how might your actions be creating situations that reinforce those stories? What might happen if you began to rewrite them?

Seeing Yourself Clearly: The Mental Barriers That Keep You Hidden

As we explore why we stay stuck in patterns of invisibility, you may recognize some ideas we have touched on before. That is because these truths are foundational. They shape so much of how we navigate the world. But this is not just a recap. In this section, we will approach these ideas from different angles, using new stories and perspectives to illustrate them in a fresh light.

We will also dig deeper into the ways your brain's wiring, chemistry, and natural processes work behind the scenes to keep these dynamics alive. These mechanisms are shaped by your early experiences and your brain's drive to keep you safe. They often operate automatically, reinforcing old beliefs and behaviors even when you want to change. By understanding how these processes work, you will be better equipped to recognize them in your own life and begin the journey toward seeing yourself more clearly.

We have seen how Charlie's belief that his needs did not matter led him to stay silent, and how Carrie's drive to prove her worth left her overworked and exhausted. These patterns, rooted in their early experiences, created behaviors that seemed to confirm their beliefs. Even though these situations are familiar by now, it is worth looking at from a different angle why they are so hard to break.

The answer lies deep within our brains. The very structure of our minds has been shaped by our experiences, like paths in a garden. The more we walk a particular path—think a specific thought or exhibit a specific behavior—the clearer and easier it becomes. For Charlie, the path of staying quiet had been walked so often that it was the only one he saw. For

Carrie, the path of relentless effort and achievement was well-trodden, making it difficult for her to step away and rest.

Your brain prefers to follow these familiar paths because it is designed to conserve energy. When a behavior or thought is repeated often enough, your brain shifts into autopilot mode, reacting in a way that feels automatic, as if you didn't choose it.

For Charlie, staying quiet was not a conscious decision. His brain defaulted to silence because that path required less effort. For Carrie, pushing herself to exhaustion became a reflexive habit. Her brain followed the path of achievement without stopping to question it. Even when they wanted to change, their default responses pulled them back.

These automatic patterns are reinforced by implicit beliefs, which operate beneath the surface. Many of us carry these hidden beliefs. Maybe you have felt like speaking up is too risky or that slowing down means you are not doing enough.

Charlie's brain had internalized the belief that expressing his needs would lead to rejection, triggering anxiety whenever he considered speaking up. Carrie's brain processed the idea of rest as a threat to her worthiness, making her feel guilty whenever she tried to slow down. Even though these responses felt safe, they kept them trapped.

When Charlie or Carrie tried to change, they ran into something called "limbic friction." This is that frustrating internal resistance we feel when we know what we should do but struggle to take action.[3] The efficiency of our brains, as you already know, means they resist change in favor of what feels safe and familiar. This creates a push-and-pull between what we want to do and what feels easier in the moment.

You've probably felt this before. You set a goal and genuinely want to follow through, but when the moment comes to act, something inside pushes back. You plan to have a tough conversation but suddenly convince yourself now isn't the right time. You want to eat healthier, but the stress of the day makes that bag of chips impossible to resist. You know you need to start a project, but somehow, you find yourself deep in a scroll hole on social media instead. That's *limbic friction*, the gap between logical intention and emotional impulse. The limbic system, which controls emotional responses like fear, anxiety, and motivation, reacts to change as if it were a threat, even when that change is positive.[4] At the same time, your prefrontal cortex, the part of the brain responsible for decision-making and long-term planning, tries to push you forward. The result? You feel stuck.

It is no wonder change feels hard. Our brains are working to protect us, even if it is keeping us stuck. For Charlie, the idea of speaking up triggered anxiety and avoidance. For Carrie, resting brought up fear and guilt. Their struggle wasn't just about breaking a habit; it was reinforced by years of conditioning, deeply held beliefs, and the emotional weight of past experiences. Their prefrontal cortex, responsible for conscious decision-making, had to work harder to override the emotional resistance of old patterns. This effort felt exhausting, making the familiar path of their old habits seem like the easier option.

At the same time, your brain is constantly reshaping itself through something called "synaptic pruning." Think of your brain as a garden. The paths you walk most often stay clear, while the neglected ones get overgrown.

If Charlie rarely expressed his needs, the neural connections for speaking up grew weaker. If Carrie seldom allowed herself to rest, the pathways for relaxation faded. This pruning process helps the brain stay efficient by strengthening frequently used connections and eliminating unused ones. While this allows us to adapt and learn, it can also reinforce habits that no longer serve us, making old patterns feel like the only options.[5] This process is useful for learning and adapting, but it can also make old habits feel inescapable.

But while pruning clears away unused pathways, your brain is always capable of growing new ones. Each small step in a new direction helps these pathways take root and strengthen. At first, the new path may feel unfamiliar, but the more you use it, the clearer and easier it becomes. It is like planting seeds in your mental garden. With care and repetition, those seeds develop roots, expand, and eventually create entirely new pathways that reshape your patterns of thinking and behavior.

Glial cells, the brain's support network, play a critical role in maintaining and repairing new pathways, by acting like gardeners. They clear out debris from old, unused pathways while supporting the growth of new ones. But chronic stress can disrupt this system, making glial cells less effective. When this happens, the brain struggles to form new connections or repair existing ones, making change feel even harder.[6]

This can leave you feeling stuck, as if change is just out of reach. But knowing this can help you be more patient with yourself. Your brain is not broken. It just needs time, support, and consistent effort to grow new pathways.

When stress is ongoing, the amygdala, the part of your brain that detects threats, becomes hyper-sensitive, reacting to even minor challenges as if they were major dangers. For Charlie, the thought of expressing his needs triggered anxiety, making him avoid speaking up even more. The more he avoided speaking up, the more his brain associated self-expression with risk, deepening the cycle of fear.

Carrie's constant overworking kept her amygdala on high alert, flooding her system with stress hormones and leaving her emotionally drained. Even when healthier alternatives were available, her brain, wired for survival, pushed her to keep going, mistaking rest for failure.

Chronic stress can also shrink the hippocampus, which helps you distinguish between past and present.[7] When this happens, old fears and reactions feel just as real and immediate as they did years ago, even when your circumstances have changed. This made it hard for both Charlie and Carrie to recognize that their current situations were not the same as their childhood experiences.

Additionally, your brain's Default Mode Network (DMN), which is most active when your mind is at rest, can reinforce these patterns. It's designed to help you process memories and reflect, but when stuck in negative loops, it replays past fears like a broken record, making it harder to move forward.[8] When Charlie and Carrie reflected on their experiences, their DMNs strengthened the same neural loops of self-doubt and fear.

Have you ever found your thoughts circling back to the same worries or regrets? That is your DMN at work, keeping old thought patterns alive and making change feel just out of reach. But like any habit, these loops can be disrupted with intention and awareness.

These reactions, shaped by autopilot, implicit beliefs, emotional conditioning, limbic friction, synaptic pruning, glial cell function, and chronic stress, might feel hardwired, but they aren't.

Thanks to neuroplasticity, your brain can form new pathways throughout your life. Each time you make a different choice, even a small one, you begin to tend to a new part of your mental garden. It might feel awkward or difficult at first, like clearing away tangled weeds. But the more you use that new path, the stronger and clearer it becomes.

Think about areas in your own life where you feel stuck. Are there habits or beliefs that have become so automatic you barely question them? Do you notice how these patterns reinforce themselves, keeping you in the same loop?

Recognizing these cycles and understanding how your brain supports them is another step toward change. You are not failing, broken, or unworthy. Your brain is simply following the paths it knows best. But now, you have the power to start creating new ones.

From Overlooked to Empowered: Rewriting Your Story

In the last several chapters, you have explored ways to challenge and rewrite your narratives and befriend your inner caveperson, and you have learned how to have your brain work for you instead of against you. For Charlie and Carrie, it was no different. Their journeys started with understanding how and why their behavior, thought, and emotional patterns had developed in the first place.

Rewriting the internal narratives that keep us stuck takes time and practice, but the results can be life changing. For both Charlie and Carrie, the journey began by uncovering the beliefs they had held on to for years. These beliefs shaped their behaviors and reinforced the stories they told themselves about their worth and place in the world. Once they understood where these patterns came from, they could begin making small, intentional changes to create new stories that aligned with who they truly were.

For Charlie, it began with recognizing that his habit of suppressing his needs was not a personal failing. It was a survival mechanism he had developed as a child. His brain had learned to prioritize others as a way to maintain peace in a household dominated by his brother's needs. With this awareness, Charlie started questioning his automatic responses of "It doesn't matter" or "I'll just go along."

What automatic responses might you be holding on to? Do you ever silence yourself out of habit, without realizing it?

To help Charlie reconnect with his preferences, we started small. He practiced noticing and acting on simple thoughts like *I feel like having a sandwich for lunch* or *I want to go for a walk this afternoon*. These everyday decisions gave Charlie a chance to acknowledge his desires without fear of rejection or conflict. Over time, he began to see that tuning into his needs was not selfish. It was a crucial step toward reclaiming his sense of self.

Expressing his preferences with others was a harder challenge, so we took gradual steps. Charlie practiced stating his opinion about which movie to watch with a friend or choosing a restaurant when asked. Each time he did this, his brain formed a new experience. He was reinforcing the idea that his needs mattered and could be heard without negative consequences.

What small preferences could you begin to express in your own life? Even a tiny step can start to build a new path.

For Carrie, the work was more emotionally complex. Her story was deeply tied to the belief that she had to achieve perfection to gain love and recognition. We explored how this belief took root in her childhood, when she often felt overlooked by her parents. I asked Carrie to think back to moments when she felt invisible or dismissed and to imagine what her younger self might have needed in those moments.

One day in session, Carrie described a memory of being six years old, waiting by the front door with a drawing she had worked on all day. When her parents came home, her father went straight to his office. Her mother gave her a quick pat on the head before heading into the kitchen to start dinner. Carrie remembered feeling crushed but never said anything.

I asked her, "What would you say to that six-year-old version of yourself if you could talk to her now?"

Carrie hesitated, then said softly, "I'd tell her that her drawing is beautiful and that she worked so hard on it. I'd tell her that she is loved and doesn't have to do anything special to earn it."

This exercise brought tears to her eyes, but it also helped her recognize how much love and reassurance she had been missing as a child.

Can you think of a moment from your own childhood when you needed comfort or validation? What would you say to your younger self now?

Over time, we worked on helping Carrie connect with her inner child through journaling and guided visualization. One exercise involved writing letters to her younger self. In these letters, she acknowledged her feelings of being overlooked and offered the encouragement and love she had needed. She began to rewrite the narrative of her worth, reminding herself and her inner child that she was enough, exactly as she was.

During a guided visualization, I asked Carrie to picture that six-year-old girl sitting in front of her. "What does she look like?" I asked.

"She's holding her drawing, but she looks really unsure of herself, like she's hoping someone will notice," Carrie said.

"Now imagine yourself walking into that memory," I said. "What would you say to her?"

Carrie paused for a moment and then said, "I'd kneel down next to her and tell her how proud I am of her drawing. I'd tell her that I see her, that she's important, and that her work matters."

This exercise was transformative for Carrie. It allowed her to access emotions she had suppressed for years and gave her a new way to comfort herself. By repeatedly engaging with her inner child, Carrie began to understand that her feelings of invisibility were not a reflection of her worth. They were the result of unmet emotional needs in her childhood.

As Carrie started offering herself the love and validation she had been seeking from others, she felt less driven to over-achieve. This shift allowed her to rediscover activities that brought her joy, like painting. Through creative expression, she reconnected with her authentic self, free from the pressure to perform for others.

Both Charlie and Carrie learned the importance of self-compassion. For Charlie, this meant recognizing that his habit of self-neglect was not a failure. It was a coping strategy that had helped him survive a challenging environment. For Carrie, it meant forgiving herself for the times she had over-worked or felt inadequate, and realizing that her worth was not tied to her accomplishments.

Mindfulness was another critical tool for both of them. By practicing mindfulness, Charlie became more aware of the automatic thoughts that led him to suppress his needs. Carrie learned to notice when her inner critic was pushing her too hard. These moments of awareness gave them the opportunity to pause and choose a different response.

Charlie also found hope in learning about neuroplasticity, the brain's ability to change and form new connections at any age. Each time he acted differently, he was creating new path-ways in his brain. This motivated him to keep expressing his needs and making decisions for himself.

Carrie's understanding of neuroplasticity helped her see that the feelings of invisibility she experienced at work could shift in time. By speaking up in meetings and asserting her ideas, she reinforced the belief that her voice mattered.

Both Charlie and Carrie discovered the freedom that comes with rewriting their internal scripts. Charlie learned that expressing his needs did not jeopardize his relationships; it actually strengthened them. Carrie realized that when she stopped overworking for recognition, she had more time for the things that truly brought her joy and fulfillment.

For both of them, the journey was not about becoming someone new. It was about discovering who they had always been beneath the layers of self-doubt and learned behaviors.

Their stories are reminders that it is never too late to rewrite the narratives that shape your life. Remember, every time you make a choice that aligns with your true self, you are building a new story, one that is uniquely yours.

Key Takeaways

Understanding how the feeling of invisibility takes root can help you begin to emerge from it. By exploring these roots, you can begin to rewrite the story of your self-worth and step into the light of your own life.

- **Explore where the story about yourself began.** Your self-worth begins to form in childhood based on how your emotional needs were met. When caregivers dismiss or overlook your feelings, your brain adapts to protect you by hiding parts of yourself. This can lead to a deep-seated belief that you are not enough, even as an adult. Recognizing this origin helps you understand that invisibility is not your fault but rather a learned survival mechanism.
- **See the instinct for what it is.** Your brain's ancient wiring reinforces feelings of invisibility by prioritizing survival over self-expression. For instance, your inner caveperson sees rejection as a threat, encouraging you to stay quiet or blend in. While this instinct kept your ancestors safe, it holds you back today by keeping you small and unseen. Becoming aware of this instinct allows you to question its relevance in your current life.
- **Feelings of invisibility are not permanent.** Thanks to the brain's ability to rewire itself through neuro-plasticity, you can create new pathways that reinforce self-worth. By practicing small acts of self-expression, engaging in self-compassion, and reframing limiting beliefs, you can rebuild your confidence and begin to see yourself as worthy of being seen.

Healing the feeling of invisibility takes time, and it progresses with small steps. By understanding the roots of your patterns and taking action to nurture your true self, you can reclaim your voice and create deeper, more authentic connections with yourself and others.

Moving from Understanding to Action

Feeling invisible can leave you unsure of where to begin, but each small action you take works toward rewriting the story of your worth. These steps are designed to help you move past the belief that you must hide, allowing you to express yourself and reconnect with your needs in manageable, practical ways.

- **Start a daily "visibility journal."** Each day, write down one way you advocated for your needs, whether it was saying no to something you didn't want to do or sharing your opinion during a conversation. This simple practice builds self-awareness and helps you recognize your progress in breaking old patterns.
- **Ask yourself for what you need.** Set a timer for five minutes and reflect on what you want right now without judgment. This exercise helps you practice identifying your needs and desires without dismissing them as unimportant. Over time, this builds a stronger connection to your inner voice and encourages you to honor your preferences.
- **Let yourself be seen.** Choose one relationship where you feel unseen and commit to sharing something personal with that person. It could be as simple as expressing how you feel about a movie you watched

together or letting them know you had a difficult day. Sharing your inner world, even in small ways, reminds you that your thoughts and feelings deserve to be heard.

- **Celebrate small wins.** Create a "truthful compliments" habit by giving yourself credit for small wins throughout the day. For example, you might say, "I'm proud of myself for speaking up in that meeting" or "I'm doing a great job by taking care of myself today." This reinforces positive beliefs about your worth and quiets the inner critic that often reinforces invisibility.

- **Anchor into self-recognition.** Try a mindfulness exercise where you place your hand on your chest and repeat, "I see myself, I hear myself, I am enough." This grounding practice helps you reconnect with your presence and reminds you that you do not need external validation to know your value. Practicing this daily creates a foundation of self-worth that can grow stronger over time.

Breaking free from invisibility is a process that starts with small, intentional choices. Each time you honor your voice, express your needs, or remind yourself of your worth, you are taking steps toward reclaiming your sense of self. With time and consistency, these actions will help you move from feeling unseen to fully embracing who you are.

9

Struggling with Boundaries: Building Strength and Restoring Balance

"Daring to set boundaries is about having the courage to love ourselves, even when we risk disappointing others."
—Brené Brown,
author and expert on courage and empathy

Think about the last time you felt completely overwhelmed because you couldn't say no. Maybe a friend asked for a favor when you were already swamped, or a colleague kept piling on tasks until you felt like you were drowning. Perhaps you said yes to something you didn't want to do just to avoid conflict or keep someone happy. Or maybe you snapped over something small, damaging a relationship in the process because you had stretched yourself too thin.

Sound familiar? These situations often boil down to one thing: boundaries.

Boundaries are the invisible lines that let people know what is and isn't okay for you. They protect your time, energy, and emotions, and they help you have healthier relationships. For example, boundaries might look like telling a friend, "I need some time to myself today, can we talk tomorrow?" or letting a coworker know, "I can't take on another project right now." Boundaries aren't about shutting people out. They're about taking care of yourself and communicating your needs in a way that's clear and respectful.

Boundaries are like a personal perimeter of safety. Just as you instinctively create physical space between yourself and others in a crowd, emotional boundaries help you define how much emotional space you need. When your perimeter is clear and firm, you protect yourself from being overwhelmed or drained. This perimeter allows you to engage with others without losing sight of your own needs.

One thing that's often overlooked is that boundaries don't just protect you, they protect the people around you too. Imagine coming home after a stressful day. If you don't carve out some time to decompress, you might snap at a loved one or take your stress out on them without meaning to. Healthy boundaries help you avoid this by giving you the space you need to recharge, so you can show up as your best self.

But what if setting boundaries doesn't feel safe?

For many of us, the thought of saying no or speaking up about what we need can feel scary. That fear often comes from past experiences, especially if you grew up in an environment where boundaries weren't respected. If as a child your needs were dismissed or ignored, your brain might have learned that setting boundaries leads to conflict, rejection, or punishment.

As adults, we might carry these same fears. Maybe you freeze when someone asks for something, because you don't know how to say no. Maybe you immediately say yes to avoid upsetting anyone. Or maybe you've convinced yourself it's just easier to give in than to risk conflict. These responses, whether freezing, fawning, or staying silent, were ways your brain learned to keep you safe in the past, but they can make setting boundaries feel impossible in the present.

It's important to understand that these behaviors aren't personal flaws. They're survival instincts your brain developed to protect you. While they might have helped you in the past, they don't need to control your life now.

So why do boundaries feel so hard to set and stick to?

1. **Childhood shaped your view of boundaries.** If your parents or caregivers dismissed your needs or didn't allow you to say no, you might have learned that speaking up wasn't safe. Maybe you were told "Don't be selfish" or "Don't make a fuss" when you tried to express your preferences. Over time, you might have started to believe that your needs didn't matter, which makes it hard to advocate for yourself now.

2. **Cultural and societal messages reinforce self-sacrifice.** Many of us grow up believing that being liked or accepted means putting others first. Saying no can feel selfish, or you might feel pressure to meet everyone's needs to avoid being seen as difficult. These messages can make it hard to prioritize yourself without guilt.

3. **Codependency complicates boundaries.** If your self-worth is tied to pleasing others, you might feel responsible for their happiness. This can make it feel impossible to say no, even when it's exhausting or harmful for you. The need to keep people happy can overshadow your ability to protect your own energy and well-being.

4. **Trauma impacts how we approach boundaries.** Past experiences of neglect, abuse, or rejection can make setting boundaries feel unsafe. If asserting yourself in the past led to conflict or punishment, your brain might treat boundaries as dangerous. For example,

someone who was criticized for saying no might avoid it altogether to prevent tension.

5. **Your brain reacts to stress.** When you feel stressed or overwhelmed, your brain's natural fight, flight, or freeze responses kick in, making it harder to think clearly or assert yourself. You might freeze up when someone asks for a favor, say yes to avoid conflict, or lash out in frustration because you feel cornered. These responses are your brain's way of protecting you, but they can keep you stuck in patterns that don't serve you.

6. **Your inner caveperson avoids risk.** From an evolutionary standpoint, keeping the peace in your group was essential for survival. Being rejected or cast out could mean danger, so our brains became wired to avoid conflict at all costs. This ancient survival instinct still shows up today as thoughts like *If I say no, they won't like me*, or *If I speak up, I'll cause a problem.* While these fears aren't as relevant now as they were for our ancestors, they still influence how we approach boundaries.

What about you?

- Have you ever agreed to something you didn't want to do just to avoid upsetting someone?
- Do you feel like you're always putting others' needs ahead of your own, even when it leaves you exhausted?
- Have you stayed quiet instead of speaking up because you were afraid of someone's reaction?

If any of this sounds familiar, you're not alone. Struggling with boundaries is common, and it's often tied to the way we were raised or the experiences we've had.

Like any skill, boundaries can be learned and strengthened with time and effort.[1] It might feel uncomfortable at first, but every small step you take helps you move toward healthier relationships and a greater sense of well-being. Boundaries aren't about shutting people out. They're about creating space for connection, respect, and balance.

With time and practice, you can learn to honor your own needs without sacrificing your relationships. And the best part? The healthier your boundaries become, the better your relationships will be, not just with others, but with yourself.

Your Inner Caveperson: Understanding Boundaries Through the Lens of Ancestral Voices

By now, from reading this book, I'm sure you know what I'm going to say. Our struggles with boundaries are tied to our ancient survival instincts. Boundaries are not just modern concepts; they reflect our brain's old drive to balance safety, connection, and autonomy. In early human societies, staying part of the group was essential for survival. Asserting your needs at the wrong time or pushing too hard for space could lead to exclusion or conflict, which often meant danger.

These survival strategies still show up in how we navigate boundaries today. When we overextend ourselves to please others, can't say no, or lash out when our space is violated, these are often ancient instincts kicking in. Understanding these patterns can help us see that these responses are not personal flaws. They are protective mechanisms that may have helped us survive in the past but are no longer serving us.

Alyx (they/them) came to therapy because their partner and their employer had both given them the same ultimatum: get their anger under control or risk losing their relationships.

Alyx had a serious problem with blowing up over the smallest things. But beneath their outward aggression was a deep need to be liked and accepted. Alyx felt unworthy of attention and care, which only fueled their frustration.

At first, anger might not seem connected to a lack of boundaries. Anger can feel like a hard, protective wall. But in reality, it is often a last-ditch effort to protect ourselves when our boundaries are ignored or disrespected. For Alyx, their anger was not so much a shield as it was a flare. It signaled frustration, unmet needs, and a fear of being invalidated or overlooked.

Have you ever felt like you needed to "get big" or lash out to be noticed or respected? What was happening in that moment? Did you feel like your needs didn't matter?

Alyx grew up in a chaotic household where boundaries did not exist. Their parents often invaded their personal space, making Alyx feel like their feelings and needs were unimportant. Speaking up never led to safety or validation. On top of that, Alyx was bullied in school, which reinforced their belief that they had to fend for themselves. As an adult, Alyx lashed out quickly and avoided showing vulnerability. Their inner story became "If I don't stand up for myself aggressively, I will be overlooked and invalidated."

During one of our sessions, I asked Alyx, "What did it feel like to be you as a kid? Can you describe three things?"

They thought for a moment and said, "I had no space. A closed door seemed to mean 'come in.' Sometimes there was no room for me emotionally. The only way to get space was to get really big. And it was lonely."

This constant invasion of boundaries left Alyx's brain in a heightened state of alertness and reactivity. Their nervous system perceived even small slights as major threats. The parts of their brain responsible for rational thinking, emotional control, and self-soothing were overshadowed by the need to stay on guard. Alyx's brain and body were stuck in survival mode, interpreting almost every interaction as a potential danger.

Have you ever reacted strongly to something small, only to realize later that it reminded you of something bigger or older? How often do those past patterns influence your responses today?

As we explored further, we identified several inner survival voices, or inner cavepeople, driving Alyx's behavior. The Defender lashed out to protect against perceived threats. The Isolator pushed others away to avoid being hurt. The People Pleaser wanted acceptance so badly that it led Alyx to over-accommodate others. The Hypervigilant Scout kept Alyx constantly on edge, scanning for boundary violations.

When I asked Alyx what their anger was protecting them from, they paused before answering. "I guess . . . I would feel small. I would feel like I didn't matter, like no one would hear me unless I got big and loud."

Have you ever thought about what your anger might be trying to protect you from? What fear or need is hiding underneath it?

This insight helped Alyx see that their anger was not the core problem. It was a symptom of unmet needs and unspoken boundaries. Their inner cavepeople were doing their best to protect them, but these old strategies were now pushing people away.

Michael came to therapy with a different struggle. He needed to maintain control and authority in his relationships. To avoid vulnerability, he worked hard to appear self-sufficient, rarely shared his problems, and refused to ask for help. His need for control often led him to cross other people's boundaries, leaving them feeling frustrated and untrusted. But while Michael could ignore others' boundaries, he kept his own walls rigid and impermeable. He was closed off, keeping others at a distance to protect himself. "Show no weakness" was his motto.

In one session, Michael admitted, "I always feel like I have to be in control, especially with the people closest to me. I hear this voice in my head saying, 'Show no weakness' every time I feel emotional."

I asked Michael to sit with that voice and try to identify its source. After a moment, he said, "It's my dad. He always told me to toughen up, to stop crying, to stop being weak."

Michael's father had demanded strength and self-reliance. As a child, Michael learned that vulnerability was dangerous. This belief followed him into adulthood, shaping how he connected with others. His inner cavepeople, the Protector, the Perfectionist, the Isolator, and the Silent Sufferer, worked hard to shield him from weakness.

In both his personal and professional life, Michael struggled to delegate. "If I don't do it myself, it won't be done right," he said. This belief was rooted in perfectionism and the fear of failure. In ancient times, precision in tasks like building shelter or preparing food could mean the difference between survival and danger. But in Michael's modern life, this drive for control only caused stress and strained his relationships.

When I asked Michael what happened when he considered delegating or showing vulnerability, he said, "I feel this intense anxiety, like everything will fall apart. I see my dad scowling at me, like I've already failed."

"This anxiety is your inner cavepeople trying to keep you safe," I explained. "They don't realize that letting go and trusting others can actually build connection."

Michael nodded. "So it's about teaching my brain that letting go won't lead to disaster?"

"Exactly," I said. "Each small step you take to let go and trust others helps create a new story."

Both Alyx and Michael's struggles with boundaries were shaped by early experiences and reinforced by inner survival mechanisms. Their inner cavepeople were trying to protect them, but those old strategies were no longer helpful. Recognizing these protective strategies was the key to learning healthier, more balanced ways to connect with others.

Boundaries are not about shutting people out. They are about knowing where you end and others begin. By understanding the ways your brain's ancient instincts influence your boundaries, you can start to respond differently. Small steps toward self-awareness, honesty, and vulnerability can help you build boundaries that protect your well-being and strengthen your connections with others.

What would it look like to set a boundary that protects your peace without shutting others out? How might you begin to view boundaries not as a form of rejection but as a way to build deeper trust with others? Each time you take a small step toward healthier boundaries, you are teaching your brain a new story, one where you can honor your needs, connect authentically, and still feel safe.

Boundaries are not barriers. They are pathways to stronger, healthier relationships, both with others and with yourself. You deserve to feel seen, respected, and valued.

Rewriting the Stories: Exploring Boundaries and Beliefs and Understanding the Past

By now, you've seen this pattern emerge again and again, our beliefs are shaped by past experiences, whether we're aware of it or not. We've explored this idea in different ways.

The way we navigate boundaries, what we consider acceptable, what feels safe, and how we maintain connections with others are all shaped long before we're even aware of them. These beliefs develop from our personal experiences, family dynamics, cultural messages, and the stories we absorb throughout our lives.

The narratives we carry influence how we see ourselves, what we believe we can achieve, and whether we feel safe asserting our needs. Often, these stories operate in the background, guiding our decisions, shaping our relationships, and reinforcing patterns that can either support us or keep us stuck.

We've also seen how easy it is to mistake these narratives for absolute truths. When we experience rejection, conflict, or criticism, our minds filter those experiences in ways that strengthen our existing beliefs. If we've learned that speaking up leads to rejection, we may hesitate to assert ourselves. If we've been told that success is the key to acceptance, we might push ourselves to exhaustion to prove our worth. These mental models, once established, can become so automatic that we don't even question them.

Our relationship with boundaries is shaped much in the same way. Some of us learned that setting boundaries led to conflict, while others were taught that prioritizing personal needs was selfish. Over time, these lessons shape whether we feel confident enforcing limits or whether we struggle with guilt, anxiety, or fear when trying to protect our space and well-being.

So how do these ingrained beliefs play out in real life?

Let's take a closer look at Alyx and Michael, two people whose experiences highlight the ways in which these internalized stories shape the boundaries we set, the ones we struggle with, and the ones we never learned to form at all.

It was no surprise, given their childhood experiences, that for Alyx, boundaries had always felt like something to defend, something to enforce through force rather than express with clarity. Growing up in a chaotic home where personal space was frequently ignored, they learned that speaking up rarely led to validation. When they tried to express their needs, they were met with indifference or dismissal. Outside of the home, things weren't much better. In school, relentless teasing and bullying reinforced the idea that vulnerability was dangerous. The message, over and over again, was that their emotions were not important, their voice did not matter, and the only way to protect themselves was to become loud, forceful, and unmovable.

How did your earliest experiences shape the way you express your needs? Did you learn that speaking up led to conflict? That saying no made you unlikable? Or did you absorb the idea that setting boundaries was a sign of selfishness?

Anger, for Alyx, became a tool of survival. It wasn't just about responding to the present, it was about pushing back against years of being ignored, overlooked, or diminished. Their defensiveness in relationships and at work wasn't a conscious choice. It was a learned instinct, built from past experiences that had repeatedly told them that setting gentle boundaries wouldn't be enough. I explained to Alyx that they learned to wield anger to protect themself as a child, and now, as an adult, the same behavior is not protecting him as it once did.

Michael's relationship with boundaries was different but just as deeply shaped by early experiences. In his family, control and self-sufficiency were everything. Vulnerability was not an option. His father frequently reminded him that "toughness" was what mattered, and his years playing competitive sports reinforced the message. Coaches praised resilience and discipline, pushing him to keep going no matter what. Strength, Michael learned, was about pushing through discomfort, not about acknowledging it.

Can you think of moments in your life when you were rewarded for not showing emotion? Were you ever encouraged to "toughen up" rather than express what you were feeling?

An anchor moment in Michael's story came early in his career. He had taken on a high-profile project and poured everything into it. But when things didn't go as planned, his boss publicly criticized his leadership. The experience confirmed what he had feared all along, any loss of control meant failure. From that moment on, he doubled down. He avoided collaboration, took on more than he could handle, and refused to let anyone else take the reins. If he didn't let anyone in, they couldn't let him down.

These personal experiences weren't the only influences shaping and reinforcing the stories he was telling himself. Cultural messaging reinforced them too. Action heroes and strong, silent male figures in movies reinforced the idea of masculinity as toughness. One of Michael's favorite actors was Sylvester Stallone, whose characters embodied resilience and control. These portrayals, along with early experiences with authority figures like coaches and teachers, cemented Michael's belief that strength was everything and vulnerability was failure. These portrayals of self-reliance and control made it even harder for him to see vulnerability as strength.

Boundaries, for Michael, weren't about protection but about maintaining an illusion of strength. It was as if he had this narrative running all the time: *If I stay independent and keep people at a distance, I can protect myself from getting hurt. People let you down, and I don't want to risk feeling disappointed or vulnerable. It's easier to just rely on myself; no one can mess that up, and I won't have to deal with the pain of expecting too much from others.* In his career, this meant avoiding delegation because trusting others felt too risky. In relationships, it meant keeping emotions tightly controlled, convinced that showing too much need or vulnerability would weaken him in the eyes of others.

What about you? Was there a moment in your life when a single event seemed to confirm what you already feared? A time when failure, rejection, or criticism cemented a belief that was already lingering beneath the surface?

Both Alyx and Michael were responding to unspoken lessons absorbed in their earliest relationships. The ways they engaged with others, whether by being forceful and aggressive in their boundaries or avoiding them altogether, were not conscious choices, but deeply ingrained patterns that operated on autopilot, beneath conscious awareness.

As we saw with Michael's example, these expectations don't just come from personal experience but also from the world around us. Many messages about boundaries, whether they should be firm or flexible and whether prioritizing yourself is selfish or necessary, are reinforced by movies, television, and cultural narratives that influence how we think about independence, strength, and connection.

Recognizing these influences doesn't mean rejecting them entirely. Instead, it allows us to step back and ask important questions: Where did our beliefs about boundaries come from? Are they truly serving us, or are they keeping us in patterns that no longer fit?

Some people, like Michael, might find that their instincts around control and independence prevent them from forming the close relationships they want. Others, like Alyx, may begin to see how their defensiveness has made it difficult to express their needs in a way that feels calm and sustainable.

Boundaries are not just about saying yes or no. They are about understanding how we've learned to relate to others, how we protect ourselves, and how we navigate connection and autonomy. When used mindfully and with compassion for yourself and others, they inform others about how to be in a relationship with us.[2] The more we examine these relational habits, the more room we have to shift them, not through force, but through awareness and choice.

What messages have shaped your own approach to boundaries? Are they aligned with what you need today, or are they echoes of a past that no longer fits?

Trapped in the Loop: How Boundary Struggles Reinforce Themselves

At this point, we've talked about self-fulfilling prophecies enough that you might be tempted to skim past this section, thinking, *Yeah, yeah, I get it, beliefs shape behavior, behavior reinforces beliefs, and the cycle continues.* And you'd be right, but stay with me. Boundaries bring a whole new layer to the conversation.

Unlike internal beliefs that mostly impact how we see ourselves, boundary-related self-fulfilling prophecies shape how we interact with others and how they respond to us in return. When you believe that people will ignore your needs, that belief changes how you express yourself, how you react to being overlooked, and even how others learn to treat you. If you expect that asserting a boundary will make people angry or push them away, you may communicate it with hesitation, frustration, or defensiveness, making it more likely that the response you fear is exactly what you get.

This is the tricky thing about self-fulfilling prophecies. We don't think we're making them come true, but our brains, in their endless quest for predictability, subtly nudge us toward familiar outcomes. It's like walking into a conversation convinced the other person won't listen, so you speak a little less clearly, shrink back slightly, or come off more defensive than intended. The other person picks up on those cues, and suddenly, your worst expectation is playing out in real time.

So, if you've ever thought, *No one respects my boundaries* or *People always push me to do things I don't want to do*, it's worth asking, What patterns keep repeating? What if the way you're approaching boundaries, whether through avoidance, over-explaining, or going straight to defensiveness, is reinforcing the very cycle you want to escape?

To see how this plays out, let's step into Alyx's and Michael's stories. Each of them developed beliefs about boundaries early on, and without realizing it, they lived into those beliefs again and again. Their brains filtered reality in a way that reinforced their expectations, making it harder to break the cycle, until they learned to see the patterns for what they were.

Alyx and Michael didn't just believe their struggles with boundaries were inevitable, they unknowingly acted in ways that made them feel true. Their behaviors reinforced their fears, keeping them stuck in cycles they didn't know how to escape. This is the trap of self-fulfilling prophecies: We respond to a belief as if it's fact, and in doing so, we create the very outcomes we fear.

For Alyx, the belief was simple: People won't respect me unless I make them. Their childhood taught them that being small, quiet, or vulnerable meant being overlooked or dismissed. As an adult, their brain filtered every experience through this expectation, this is called an expectation bias. They anticipated being dismissed, so they braced for rejection before it even happened. If a friend didn't text back immediately, their brain didn't consider that the person might be busy. Instead, Alyx jumped straight to *See? They don't really care.* This expectation shaped their interactions. Frustration simmered beneath the surface, making them quicker to lash out. That reaction, in turn, made people hesitate to engage, unintentionally confirming Alyx's belief that no one truly valued them.

Alyx's confirmation bias—the mental shortcut that makes the brain seek out evidence that reinforces existing beliefs—ensured they only noticed moments when their boundaries were dismissed and ignored the times people listened. The availability heuristic, which causes the brain to rely on the most easily recalled examples when making decisions, made past moments of disrespect and invalidation feel like undeniable proof that they always had to fight to be heard. These unconscious processes distorted reality, keeping Alyx convinced that the only way to get respect was to demand it.

Michael's self-fulfilling prophecy worked in the opposite direction. He believed that letting go of control would lead to chaos and failure, so he avoided it at all costs. If a project at work required teamwork, Michael took over. If his partner wanted to make a decision, he second-guessed it. And when people eventually stopped offering input, deferring to him just to keep the peace, Michael took it as proof that he had been right all along: No one else could be trusted to handle things.

Michael's struggle with control was fueled by egocentric bias, emphasis on *ego*. He was convinced his colleagues were watching his every move, dissecting his decisions like forensic analysts, and whispering behind his back, "Did you see that? He hesitated for a full second before responding!" In reality, his colleagues were too busy overanalyzing their last email or wondering if they left their laundry in the washer too long. Egocentric bias has a way of making you think people are paying way more attention to you than they actually are.[3] But

Michael's fear of looking weak made him double down on control. The more he micromanaged, the more people disengaged, not because they were incapable, but because they were tired of being treated like they couldn't handle anything on their own. And as they backed off, Michael took it as further proof that no one else could be trusted to get things done.

Both Alyx and Michael also fell into attentional bias, a mental shortcut that causes the brain to focus on information that supports existing beliefs while ignoring evidence to the contrary. Alyx noticed every moment they felt overlooked, every time someone cut them off mid-sentence. But when a friend checked in, or when someone genuinely listened, those moments didn't carry the same weight. Similarly, Michael could recall every single time delegating had backfired, but when things went smoothly, his brain didn't bother to store those moments as proof that trust was possible.

And just to make sure these beliefs stayed locked in place, their brains also relied on memory distortion, specifically "consistency bias," the tendency to misremember the past in a way that aligns with current beliefs. When Alyx thought back to childhood, they didn't just recall isolated moments of being dismissed. Their brain had rewritten the past into a single, cohesive story: No one ever listened to me. The same was true for Michael. His mind replayed every criticism from his father, every moment he felt like he had to be the strong one, solidifying the belief that if he wasn't in control, he was failing.

These biases weren't just reinforcing old fears, they were amplifying the voice of their inner caveperson. Alyx's brain, wired for survival, was trying to protect them from rejection by staying hyperaware of potential slights, whether real or imagined. Michael's brain, convinced that safety depended on control, filtered out any proof that letting go might actually strengthen his relationships. Both were stuck in loops that felt impossible to escape, not because change was impossible, but because their brains were so good at keeping things *predictable*.

But the predictability that once felt like safety had become a trap. And the only way out was to start questioning the beliefs that felt like absolute truth. And that is exactly what we did.

Why We Stay Stuck: Understanding the Brain's Role in Boundary Struggles

At this point, you might not be surprised to hear that your brain has a lot to do with your struggles around boundaries. We have explored the brain's wiring in previous chapters, but it is worth revisiting because these ingrained responses are foundational, and they are often the reason change feels so hard. Even when you know what you need to do, your brain tends to default to old habits, especially when those habits were designed to keep you safe. Understanding these mechanisms does not just explain why you feel stuck; it also gives you the power to start shifting those patterns.

When Alyx and Michael came to therapy, their boundary struggles were not just surface-level behaviors. They were deeply embedded habits shaped by years of repetition, survival instincts, and brain chemistry. These responses developed over time, and breaking free from them was not about willpower alone. It required understanding how their brains were wired to protect them, even when that protection came at a cost.

For Alyx, saying yes when they wanted to say no had become automatic. Each time they overcommitted or prioritized others, their brain reinforced the belief that saying yes would keep them safe from rejection. Similarly, Michael's need for control had become deeply ingrained. Every time he micromanaged a project or avoided delegating, his brain rewarded him with a brief sense of security. These behaviors, practiced over and over, strengthened the neural pathways that made these behaviors feel natural.

These patterns, practiced over and over, strengthened the neural pathways that made these behaviors feel natural. Every time we repeat a behavior, we strengthen the connections between the brain cells involved in that action. You might recall from an earlier chapter that it's called Hebbian learning: "Cells that fire together, wire together." Alyx and Michael had practiced their patterns so many times that these behaviors became second nature, even when they caused problems or conflict.

But repetition is not the only thing keeping Alyx and Michael stuck. Their brains also rewarded these behaviors with short-term relief. For Alyx, saying yes helped them avoid the immediate anxiety of disappointing someone. For Michael, micromanaging gave him the fleeting satisfaction of feeling in control. These quick, unconscious rewards reinforced their patterns, making it hard to change, even when the long-term consequences were draining or damaging.

Do you ever find yourself slipping into old patterns even though you know they are not helpful? Maybe you keep saying yes when you want to say no, or you insist on doing everything yourself. It is frustrating, but it does not mean you are failing. It means your brain is simply following the pathways it knows best.

Emotional responses also play a big role. For Alyx, anger was not just frustration; it was a way to avoid feeling vulnerable or rejected. For Michael, perfectionism masked his anxiety, giving him something concrete to control while avoiding his fear of failure. When we do not process these deeper emotions, they do not just go away. They surface in other ways, like lashing out or clinging to control, keeping us stuck in patterns that sabotage our boundaries.

We have touched on implicit memories before, but it is worth recognizing how powerful they are. These are the memories stored deep in the brain that shape your automatic reactions without your realizing it. Alyx's brain held on to memories of being praised for helping others, which pushed them to overcommit. Michael's brain clung to memories of his father's harsh criticism, making him avoid vulnerability at all costs. These memories operate like invisible strings, pulling you back into familiar behaviors.

And let us not forget the brain's negativity bias, another concept we have explored previously. This ancient survival mechanism makes you focus more on threats and failures than on successes. Alyx remembered every time someone ignored their boundaries but struggled to recall moments when their needs were respected. Michael fixated on the rare occasions delegating went wrong, ignoring all the times things went smoothly. This bias keeps you stuck in fear and self-doubt, even when there is plenty of evidence that things can go right.

When your brain is at rest, the Default Mode Network (DMN) often kicks in, leading to rumination and over-thinking.[4] Alyx replayed conversations, worrying they had let someone down. Michael lay awake at night, anticipating every possible problem. Sound familiar? That is your DMN in action, keeping you stuck in cycles of worry.

Even empathy can complicate boundary struggles. Alyx's mirror neurons made them feel others' distress so intensely that they could not separate their own needs from someone else's. Michael's mirror neurons worked differently. He interpreted others' actions as challenges to his authority, which triggered his need to assert control.

Finally, chronic stress played a significant role. We have discussed how ongoing stress keeps the brain's amygdala on high alert, flooding the body with cortisol. This makes it harder to regulate emotions or think clearly. Stress also weakens the hippocampus, which helps with memory, and the prefrontal cortex, which supports decision-making. No wonder it feels so hard to change old patterns when you are stressed.

When Alyx and Michael understood how their brains were working, they realized their struggles were not personal flaws. Their brains were just trying to keep them safe. And recognizing this gave them hope. If their brains had learned these responses, they could also unlearn them.

What if you saw your own struggles with boundaries not as failures, but as old wiring that you can change? What small steps could you take today to start rewiring your brain for the life you want?

Rewriting the Script: Building Healthy Boundaries and Connections

You've seen this throughout the book: Change begins with understanding. For Alyx and Michael, rewriting their scripts required more than identifying their stories. It meant digging deeper into the web of survival instincts, cognitive biases, mental shortcuts, neural pathways, and learned behaviors that created and reinforced their patterns. This understanding was key to interrupting their automatic responses and creating space for better choices.

Alyx's story, "If I don't say yes, I'll be rejected," wasn't just a simple belief. It was tied to their inner caveperson's fear of being cast out of the group. The overgeneralization bias convinced them that setting any boundary would lead to rejection. Their People Pleaser urged them to keep everyone happy, while the Hypervigilant Scout stayed on high alert for signs of disapproval. Combined with deeply ingrained neural pathways that made saying yes feel automatic, these default reactions trapped Alyx in a cycle of overcommitment, resentment, and anger.

Michael's script, "If I lose control, I'll be seen as weak," was similarly layered. His Protector, driven by the fear of losing safety or status, compelled him to cling to perfection and control. His Perfectionist reinforced black-and-white thinking, where delegating tasks meant risking failure. Years of practicing these habits had strengthened neural pathways that made these behaviors feel automatic. As a result, Michael struggled to trust others or show vulnerability, even when this behavior harmed his relationships.

For Alyx and Michael, the key was recognizing that these automatic responses came from their inner survival instincts. These instincts were designed to protect them but were no longer useful. By giving their inner cavepeople distinct identities, Alyx and Michael were able to step back and see these voices not as their true selves but as outdated strategies. For Alyx, the People Pleaser and Hypervigilant Scout were working to prevent rejection. For Michael, the Protector and Perfectionist were trying to shield him from failure. Naming these voices helped them approach their behaviors with curiosity instead of judgment.

For Alyx, this meant pausing before automatically saying yes and asking, "Is this my People Pleaser talking? What is it afraid of? What would happen if I said no instead?" For Michael, it meant recognizing the voice of his Perfectionist and questioning, "What's the worst that could happen if I let go of control? Is it really as dangerous as it feels?"

To help with this process, I introduced them to a technique I put together called the "insert-here" strategy. It's my own combination of ideas from Adam Grant's book *Think Again* and Byron Katie's book *The Work*, especially her question, "Is that really true?" The goal is to create a mental pause, just long enough to interrupt automatic reactions and rethink the story before it runs the show. When Alyx or Michael felt fear or vulnerability take over, I asked them to imagine inserting a mental card with a question like "What if this isn't true?" or "Can I see this differently?" This simple prompt interrupted their habitual responses and opened the door for new perspectives.

For Alyx, the "insert here" card might say, "What if saying no doesn't lead to rejection but earns me respect?" For Michael, it could be "What if letting go of control helps me build trust with others?" Practicing this technique gave them a chance to pause, question their fears, and make different choices.

This process wasn't about rejecting their inner voices. These voices had a purpose. The goal was to understand why they were there and to choose when to listen. Alyx and Michael realized that their automatic patterns were rooted in old fears and began to separate themselves from those behaviors.

Alyx practiced setting small, manageable boundaries to retrain their brain. Instead of automatically saying yes, they started experimenting with saying no to requests that weren't urgent. Each time they did, they created new neural pathways, showing their brain that boundaries could be safe, and relationships could remain intact. And when they'd report back in a session, we'd laugh and say together, "And I/you didn't die!!" because for a brain wired to people please, saying no can feel about as risky as locking eyes with a T. rex and hoping it doesn't see you.

Michael's work involved letting go of control in small, safe ways. He started by delegating a single task to a colleague, observing the outcome, and building trust in the process. "Each time you delegate or let go of control," I told him, "you are teaching your brain a new story, that trust is possible and letting go doesn't mean failure."

Mindfulness played a key role for both Alyx and Michael. They began to notice when their automatic responses were triggered. For Alyx, this might look like catching the wave of anxiety that came with setting a boundary. For Michael, it was noticing the urge to micromanage when something didn't go perfectly. Mindfulness gave them the space to pause and choose a different response.

We have touched on mindfulness in previous chapters because it is foundational to slowing down enough to question ourselves. Without this pause, it's easy to stay on autopilot, repeating old patterns. Mindfulness allows you to step back, observe your reactions, use the insert-here technique and ask, "What else might be true here?"

To make these changes stick, we had to rewire their brains to stop treating boundaries like life-or-death situations. That meant practicing in small doses. This is known as *graded exposure* in neuroscience, so their nervous systems could adjust without going into full panic mode. Alyx started with easy noes before working up to bigger ones. Michael tested the waters by handing off minor responsibilities before tackling the bigger challenge of letting go.

Since their brains were wired to freak out over change, we also worked on physiological state shifts to help calm their nervous systems. That meant deep breaths when the anxiety kicked in, movement to shake off stress, and sometimes just splashing cold water on their face, whatever helped reset their body's reaction to discomfort.

We also talked about reframing discomfort as progress instead of failure. Every time Alyx and Michael felt that knot of anxiety after setting a boundary, we reminded them, "This means your brain is learning something new, not that you did something wrong." With time, they started to see that resilience wasn't about never feeling uncomfortable; it was about knowing they could handle the discomfort without crumbling.

Another key part of their journey was self-compassion. Alyx and Michael had spent years being harsh critics of themselves. Alyx's inner voice told them they weren't enough unless they were constantly helping others. Michael's inner critic insisted that any mistake would lead to failure. By learning to treat themselves with kindness, they softened these critical voices and gave themselves permission to grow.

As Alyx and Michael continued rewriting their scripts, they began to see changes in their lives. Alyx learned that saying no didn't ruin relationships. In fact, it gave them more energy to connect authentically with the people they cared about. Michael discovered that letting go of control didn't weaken his relationships. It strengthened them by building trust and mutual respect.

Rewriting the script isn't just about changing behaviors. It's about understanding the beliefs, instincts, and patterns that drive those behaviors and making conscious choices to change them. It's about creating space between stimulus and response, where you can pause and ask, "Is this really serving me?"

What about you? What scripts have you been living by? Maybe you've told yourself that saying no will push people away or that showing vulnerability makes you weak. What would happen if you challenged those beliefs?

Every time you set a boundary, delegate a task, or take a moment to pause, you are creating new neural pathways. With practice, these new behaviors will become second nature, replacing the old, automatic ones that no longer serve you.

It's never too late to change your story. Growth takes patience, courage, and persistence, but every small step brings you closer to a more authentic, fulfilling life. So what's one step you can take today?

Key Takeaways

Boundaries aren't just about saying no. They help you recognize what you need and communicate it with confidence. If setting boundaries feels hard, it's often because of past experiences, survival instincts, or fear of rejection. With practice, you can strengthen your boundary skills.

- **Your brain may treat boundaries like a threat, but that doesn't mean they are.** If setting boundaries makes you feel anxious, guilty, or afraid of conflict, that's just your nervous system reacting to past experiences. With practice, your brain can learn that boundaries are not dangerous. They are necessary for healthy relationships and emotional well-being.
- **Small boundary-setting moments create big changes over time.** The key to strengthening boundaries is to start small. Practicing in low-stakes situations helps your brain adjust, making it easier to advocate for yourself in bigger moments. Each time you hold a boundary, you reinforce new neural pathways that make it feel safer and more natural.
- **Boundaries help you build relationships rooted in mutual respect.** They aren't about controlling others but about honoring your own needs and communicating them clearly. As you practice setting boundaries, your relationships become more balanced, supportive, and fulfilling.

Setting boundaries isn't about pushing people away. It's about creating space for healthier relationships and honoring what you need. The more you practice, the easier it gets, and over time, boundaries become a natural part of how you show up for yourself and others.

Moving from Understanding to Action

Setting boundaries can feel overwhelming at first, but small, intentional steps make a big difference. The goal isn't to get it perfect; it's to practice. The more you reinforce your boundaries, the more natural they become. Here are some things you can do to start:

- **Practice saying no in simple situations.** Start with low-stakes situations, like declining an extra task at work or saying no to plans you don't want to attend. This helps your brain adjust to boundary-setting without triggering overwhelming fear.
- **Pause before automatically saying yes.** When someone asks for your time or energy, give yourself a moment to check in. Ask yourself, *Do I actually want to do this? Do I have the capacity?* A short pause can help you respond intentionally instead of out of habit.
- **Notice where resentment builds.** Feeling drained or frustrated is often a sign that a boundary is needed. Pay attention to when you feel overextended and consider where you might need to set clearer limits.
- **Use clear, simple language.** Boundaries don't need long explanations. Try phrases like, "I can't take that on right now" or "That doesn't work for me." The more direct you are, the less room there is for negotiation.
- **Expect discomfort, but remind yourself you're safe.** If saying no makes you anxious, that's just your brain reacting to old patterns. Take a breath, remind

yourself that boundaries are healthy, and push through the discomfort. It will get easier with time.

The more you practice, the more confident you'll become in advocating for yourself. Boundaries aren't about keeping people out; they're about making space for healthier, more fulfilling connections.

10

The Inner Work of Professional Growth: Moving Beyond Self-Limiting Patterns

*"We cannot become what we want
by remaining what we are."*

—Max De Pree,
leadership expert and author

Have you ever felt stuck in your career, despite doing everything "right"? Do you find yourself constantly overlooked for promotions or opportunities, even though you know you have the skills, knowledge, and experience to succeed? If so, you are not alone. Professional stagnation is a common challenge, and it can feel deeply frustrating when your hard work does not seem to lead to the growth or recognition you deserve.

The roots of career stagnation go deeper than just technical ability or intelligence. Often, it stems from internal beliefs, learned behaviors, and workplace dynamics that unconsciously hold us back.[1] Maybe you carry self-limiting thoughts like *I'm not cut out for leadership* or *I have to be perfect to succeed.* These beliefs, shaped by childhood experiences or past failures, quietly influence your choices and behaviors.

Over time, they create cycles of self-doubt and hesitation that undermine your progress before you even begin.

But it is not just self-doubt. Perfectionism can trap you in endless refinement and overwork, leaving no space for strategic thinking or risk-taking. Both of these are necessary for growth. On the other hand, overconfidence or a lack of meaningful feedback can blind you to areas where improvement is needed. Workplace culture adds another layer of complexity. In some environments, factors like seniority, visibility, or soft skills are valued more than technical expertise, making it difficult to advance without understanding these hidden dynamics.

Much of what happens in the workplace is shaped by unconscious motivations, biases, and emotional triggers.[2] Often, we are unaware of how subtle factors influence our behavior. The tone of a conversation, the mood in a room, or someone's nonverbal cues can all impact how we respond. Without realizing it, these signals prime us to react in ways that may not align with our intentions.

Think of a time when a colleague's feedback made you feel defensive. You may have thought it was just the content of their words, but the real trigger might have been their tone or expression. Perhaps their demeanor reminded you of a critical parent or past authority figure. Similarly, walking into a tense meeting can unconsciously push you to stay quiet or avoid conflict, even if you planned to speak up for yourself.

These automatic reactions are not flaws. They are survival strategies shaped by your inner caveperson, the part of your brain wired to keep you safe by avoiding perceived risks. While these instincts helped our ancestors survive dangerous situations[3], they can complicate modern professional life. Constructive feedback can feel like a threat, advocating for yourself might feel risky, and leadership opportunities can seem too daunting to pursue.

And remember, it is not just you. Everyone in the workplace brings their own unconscious patterns, triggers, and beliefs. Every colleague, manager, or client you interact with is dealing with their own mix of insecurities and past experiences. Understanding this dynamic can help you approach conflicts with empathy and realize that other people's reactions are often more about them than about you.

Professional stagnation is not just about external factors or technical skills. It is about the internal stories you carry, the unconscious patterns you follow, and the unspoken dynamics at play. By becoming aware of these hidden influences and challenging the beliefs that hold you back, you can begin to rewrite your professional narrative. Growth is not just about doing more or working harder. It is about doing the inner work to align your efforts with your potential.[4] Recognizing these forces, both internal and external, is crucial for moving from stagnation to a career defined by intention, confidence, and purpose.

Your Inner Caveperson: How Survival Instincts Shape Professional Growth

Why is it that some people seem to rise effortlessly in their careers, while others, who work just as hard or harder, find themselves stuck and unable to move forward? Why do promotions, recognition, and opportunities feel just out of reach no matter how much effort we put in?

I know what you are thinking. I am about to tell you that your career frustrations are tied to your inner caveperson. You are absolutely right. Unfortunately, our caveperson is a bit of a mixed bag. On the bright side, it is the reason you are here today. Its finely tuned survival instincts helped your ancestors avoid saber-toothed tigers and navigate all kinds of danger. The downside? That same caveperson is still calling the shots in situations it does not fully understand, like navigating workplace dynamics. It means well, but it is just a little outdated.

Take Julia, for example. Julia has spent over ten years at the same company, consistently exceeding expectations. She hits every deadline, goes above and beyond for her team, and earns glowing feedback from her peers. Yet she cannot seem to move up the ladder.

"Why is my hard work not being recognized?" she asked me during one of our sessions.

When I asked Julia what she usually does after being passed over for a promotion, she shrugged and said, "I just keep my head down and move on. I do not want to stir up any trouble or seem ungrateful."

To Julia's inner caveperson, this response makes perfect sense. In ancient times, blending in with the group was critical for survival. Standing out too much, challenging authority, or stirring conflict could lead to ostracism, which was as good as a death sentence. While this instinct once protected us, in today's workplace it can backfire. Promotions and opportunities often go to those who confidently advocate for themselves, a behavior that can make your caveperson break out in a cold sweat.

And it is not just about staying quiet. Julia once decided to share a big success during a team meeting. She had completed a major project ahead of schedule and under budget, so she thought, *Why not let people know?*

Instead of the praise she expected, her manager pointed out a minor issue in the report. The feedback was constructive, but Julia walked away feeling embarrassed and exposed. Her caveperson immediately filed the experience under "never do that again" and set the self-promotion alarm to "dangerous."

Have you ever felt that flash of discomfort when you tried to share an accomplishment or speak up in a meeting? Maybe you have told yourself that hard work should "speak for itself" or that drawing attention to your achievements feels risky. That is your caveperson whispering, or shouting, *Stay safe, do not rock the boat.* It is not trying to sabotage you. It genuinely thinks it is protecting you.

Mark's story highlights another way the caveperson can get in the way. Mark is a talented engineer who excels at delivering flawless work. He has built a reputation for solving tough problems and producing high-quality results, yet his career feels like it is at a standstill.

"I always thought my work would speak for itself," Mark said during one session. "But no matter how much I accomplish, I am still in the same role."

Mark's inner caveperson pushed him to take full responsibility for his projects, convinced that if he did not oversee every detail, something would go wrong. "If I do not handle everything myself, it could fail, and then it is on me," he explained. This need for control, rooted in a survival instinct to ensure safety and maintain status, kept him stuck in the weeds, unable to step back and demonstrate leadership skills like delegation and strategic thinking.

For our ancestors, maintaining control over their environment was a matter of survival. Guarding the fire, protecting the group, or securing food were responsibilities that could not be left to chance. In Mark's professional life, this instinct translated into micromanaging and avoiding collaboration. The very behaviors that once ensured survival were now preventing him from advancing in his career.

Have you ever felt like the success of a project or team depended entirely on you? Have you hesitated to let go of control because it felt too risky? That is your inner caveperson at work again, urging you to cling tightly to responsibility to "survive" in your professional tribe.

This instinct to control can be compounded by another caveperson tendency: the drive to conserve energy. As you already know, in primitive times, expending mental or physical effort unnecessarily could be dangerous. In today's workplace, this drive to avoid emotional and mental strain can show up in unexpected ways. For Julia, it meant avoiding asking for feedback, because it felt draining. For Mark, it meant skipping networking opportunities, dismissing them as distractions from "real work." Their caveperson brains nudged them toward the safer, easier path, even though it limited their growth.

Our inner caveperson is not trying to sabotage us. It simply has not gotten the memo that we are no longer living on the savanna. Recognizing these outdated instincts is essential to overcoming them. Julia and Mark both had to challenge their caveperson thinking to disrupt survival-based loops.

For Julia, this meant speaking up in meetings, sharing her accomplishments, and asking for feedback, even when it felt uncomfortable. For Mark, it meant loosening his grip on control, trusting his team, and stepping into opportunities that required him to delegate and build relationships.

What would stepping outside your comfort zone look like for you? Maybe it is sharing an idea in a meeting, advocating for your accomplishments, or letting go of perfection and trusting your colleagues. Small, intentional steps can help quiet your inner caveperson and move you closer to the growth and success you are capable of achieving.

Rewriting the Stories That Shape Professional Growth

We've explored how ancient instincts can hold us back, but there's another powerful force at play: the stories we tell ourselves. These narratives, shaped by our upbringing, experiences, and environments, quietly dictate how we approach our careers and whether we step into or shrink away from opportunities. Sometimes these stories push us forward. Other times, they keep us stuck.

If you've ever thought, *I'm not ready* or *I shouldn't draw attention to myself* or *If they really knew me, I wouldn't be good enough*, you're not alone. These internal stories, often running on autopilot, can limit how we show up at work and how we advocate for our growth.

Let's look at how these stories played out for Julia and Mark and how recognizing them was the next step toward change.

When Julia came to therapy, she was exhausted and frustrated. "Every time a promotion passes me by, I feel resentful, but I also start doubting myself," she admitted. "What if I fail if I push for more?"

Her words stopped me. Julia was doing all the right things, yet still holding herself back. "What does 'enough' look like to you?" I asked.

Julia hesitated. "I don't know. I see my coworkers staying late, working weekends, always 'on.' It feels like they're doing so much more than me, but I don't even know if I could keep up with that."

Does any of this sound familiar to you? Have you ever felt like your hard work should be enough, but somehow it isn't? Like Julia, you might wonder if you are doing something wrong or if there is something wrong with you.

As Julia and I talked, a bigger picture emerged. Her beliefs about work and success were not just about her job. They were rooted in her upbringing. Julia's parents, a nurse and a mechanic, were models of quiet diligence. They worked hard, avoided conflict, and never spoke about advocating for themselves or climbing the ladder. Success, in Julia's family, was about keeping your head down and letting your work speak for itself.

"It was just an unspoken rule," Julia told me. "My mom used to say, 'If you do your best, people will notice.' So I've always thought that if I just keep working hard, someone will recognize it."

But what happens when no one does?

Julia's inner narrative, shaped by her family's silent work ethic, was only part of the story. The other part came from the world around her, workplace culture, societal expectations, and double standards that many women and minorities face. Julia admitted that the few times she had tried speaking up, she felt self-conscious, as though her confidence was being misinterpreted.

"I once brought up my accomplishments in a meeting, and instead of praise, my manager pointed out something I could have done better," she said. "It wasn't even a big deal, but it felt so humiliating. I've never done it again."

Julia's experience is not uncommon. For many women and minorities, self-promotion can feel like walking a tightrope. While advocating for yourself might be encouraged for some, others may fear being labeled as too aggressive, pushy, or emotional. Even though as I write this it is 2025, these double standards persist, making it difficult to speak up without second-guessing yourself.

Can you relate? Have you ever hesitated to share your achievements or ideas because you worried about how others might perceive you? Have you told yourself that if you work hard enough, your efforts will eventually be noticed, only to find yourself stuck and overlooked?

These moments are not just about workplace dynamics. They are tied to survival instincts. Back in ancient times, standing out could be risky. Challenging authority or stepping out of line might have led to exile, which could mean life or death. Our brains still hold onto this wiring, telling us to avoid rocking the boat. Julia's hesitation to promote herself wasn't just a personal choice; it was her brain trying to protect her from a perceived threat.

Mark's story reflects how internal narratives can shape our careers in subtle yet powerful ways. A skilled engineer, Mark took pride in his technical expertise and the flawless results he delivered. He believed that if he simply did his job well, success would follow naturally. Yet despite his consistent performance, he found himself stuck in the same role. "I've always believed that if I just do my job well, everything else will fall into place," he explained, illustrating how his reliance on technical mastery alone without considering leadership or self-promotion had kept him from advancing.

Mark's belief made sense. Growing up in a family of engineers, he often heard his father say, "Get every detail right, and success will follow." This was more than just advice. It was the family code. For Mark, hard work and technical mastery were the keys to advancement. But while these traits made him excellent at his job, they left little room for leadership, networking, or visibility.

"What if it's not just about doing the work?" I asked him. "What if success also depends on letting others see what you bring to the table?"

Mark looked uncomfortable. "I don't know. . . . I've always thought my work should speak for itself."

His perfectionism, another relic of his upbringing, made it even harder to step back and see the bigger picture. "I was so focused on getting every detail right that I didn't make time for collaboration or leadership," he admitted. "I thought I was doing what I was supposed to, but maybe I've been holding myself back."

Have you ever told yourself that the work you do is enough, that you don't need to promote it because people should notice? This mindset, while comforting, can keep you from recognizing the importance of relationships, trust, and visibility in today's workplace.

Mark also felt an enormous sense of responsibility. "Sometimes it feels like everything depends on me," he said. "If I don't handle every detail myself, something will go wrong, and it'll be on me."

This belief is another survival instinct at work. For our ancestors, control was crucial. Knowing every detail about food supplies, weather patterns, and predator behavior often meant the difference between life and death. In Mark's case, this need for control became a habit, leaving him hesitant to delegate or collaborate. His inner narrative was telling him, "Better safe than sorry," but it was holding him back from the trust and strategic thinking required for leadership roles.

Interestingly, both Julia and Mark's stories could have turned out differently with a few key experiences. For Julia, what if her parents had modeled self-advocacy alongside hard work? For Mark, what if his family had emphasized the value of teamwork and leadership?

What about your own story? What moments in your past have shaped how you see yourself today? Perhaps a teacher's comment, a peer's reaction, or a cultural message taught you that it was safer to stay quiet, avoid conflict, or focus solely on "the work."

While these stories are powerful, they can change and evolve. By recognizing the narratives we carry and the survival instincts they reinforce, we can begin to rewrite them. For Julia, this meant taking small steps to share her ambitions and ask for feedback. For Mark, it meant loosening his grip on perfectionism and focusing on building relationships.

What would rewriting your story look like for you? Maybe it is sharing an idea in a meeting, speaking up about your accomplishments, or letting go of the belief that you have to do everything yourself. Perhaps it is asking yourself, "What am I really afraid of?" and challenging the voice that says, *Stay safe*.

Our stories have the power to challenge or affirm our survival instincts. They can either reinforce the fears of our inner caveperson or help us rise above them. By choosing to rewrite these stories, you are not just changing how you see yourself. You are creating space for growth, confidence, and opportunity.

The Cycle of Belief and Behavior: How Self-Fulfilling Prophecies Keep Us Stuck

We've got our inner caveperson, our origin stories, and the narratives we carry from life experiences all working together against us. And if that's not bad enough, we also have the mental shortcuts we use daily, the same ones that shape how we interact with the world and interpret the interactions we have.

To complicate matters further, self-fulfilling prophecies come in two forms: self-imposed and other-imposed. Self-imposed prophecies occur when your expectations about yourself shape your behavior. Other-imposed prophecies happen when you internalize someone else's expectations because you hold their opinion in high regard.[5] We will see how both types play out in the lives of Julia and Mark.

All of these pieces weave together to create powerful cycles. Beliefs shape behaviors, behaviors create outcomes, and outcomes reinforce beliefs. Over time, this cycle becomes so automatic that we don't even realize it's happening.

Take Julia, for example. She is a capable, hardworking professional who consistently exceeds expectations. Yet she feels overlooked and undervalued at work. Julia believes that hard work alone should lead to recognition, and she's frustrated when promotions continue to pass her by. Deep down, she wrestles with a fear of failure, which keeps her from speaking up or advocating for herself. Instead, she tells herself, "If I just keep my head down and work harder, someone will notice."

This belief creates a self-imposed prophecy. Julia's fear of speaking up leads her to stay silent, reinforcing the outcome she dreads: invisibility. When she's passed over for promotions, it seems to confirm that she doesn't deserve recognition, even though her silence played a role in the outcome.

Julia's story also includes an other-imposed prophecy. Growing up, she deeply respected her parents' values of humility and hard work. Her mother's advice, "If you do your best, people will notice," shaped Julia's actions. Because she held her mother's opinion in such high regard, she adopted this belief as her own. But in today's workplace, this mindset holds her back. The belief that quiet diligence will be rewarded keeps Julia from promoting herself or asking for feedback.

Cognitive biases reinforce these self-fulfilling prophecies. Confirmation bias makes Julia focus on instances of criticism, like the time her manager pointed out a small mistake, while overlooking moments of praise. The availability heuristic amplifies her fears by bringing emotionally charged memories, like a colleague being dismissed for speaking up, to the forefront of her mind. Meanwhile, negativity bias ensures that the sting of critical feedback lingers far longer than any compliments she receives.

What about you? Have you ever downplayed a compliment because it didn't align with your self-doubt? Or avoided advocating for yourself because you focused on what could go wrong instead of what might go right? These mental shortcuts aren't flaws, they're natural processes. But when left unchecked, they can trap us in cycles of self-fulfilling prophecies.

Mark's story offers another perspective. Mark is a talented engineer who prides himself on his technical expertise. Growing up, he admired his father's belief that mastery of one's craft was the key to success. This other-imposed prophecy led Mark to think, "If I keep delivering excellent work, everything else will fall into place." Yet his career has plateaued.

Mark's additional self-imposed prophecy reinforces this stagnation. He believes that stepping away from the technical details to focus on leadership or networking will compromise his work quality. This belief keeps him stuck, micromanaging tasks instead of delegating them.

Several cognitive biases, not yet covered, play a role in Mark's behavior and contribute to his professional stagnation. One of these is the "endowment effect," a tendency to overvalue things simply because we've invested time or effort into them. In Mark's case, this bias causes him to place too much emphasis on his technical expertise, as he has spent years perfecting it. Another bias at play is the "Zeigarnik effect," which suggests that people are more likely to fixate on unfinished tasks because they create a sense of mental tension. For Mark, this means he becomes preoccupied with small, incomplete details, preventing him from shifting his focus to more strategic, high-level responsibilities. Finally, "cognitive inertia" refers to the tendency to stick to familiar ways of thinking, even when they no longer serve us. For Mark, this means clinging to old patterns of behavior that limit his growth and prevent him from embracing new challenges.

Mark's experience also highlights "projection bias." He assumes that others value technical expertise as much as he does. This assumption prevents him from promoting his achievements or seeking mentorship, which could help him advance.

These self-fulfilling prophecies, shaped by cognitive biases and survival instincts, keep both Julia and Mark stuck. Julia's fear of visibility reinforces her invisibility. Mark's need for control keeps him tethered to technical tasks, preventing growth. In both cases, their beliefs shape behaviors that lead to the very outcomes they fear.

So how do we break these cycles? By identifying the biases, shortcuts, and prophecies at play and then challenging them. Julia started by sharing her accomplishments in team meetings, reframing self-promotion as contributing to her team's success. Mark began delegating tasks to his colleagues, creating space to develop his leadership skills.

What about you? What beliefs or biases are keeping you stuck? Do you avoid taking risks because they feel unsafe, or focus so much on one area that you neglect others? By questioning these internal rules and stepping outside your comfort zone, you can begin rewriting your narrative.

Breaking free from self-fulfilling prophecies isn't easy, but it is possible. Julia and Mark discovered that the stories they told themselves weren't facts, they were just stories. And like any story, they could be rewritten. You have that same power.

What story will you choose to tell yourself?

The Inner Work of Professional Growth: Moving Beyond Self-Limiting Patterns

By now, you understand how our experiences, beliefs, emotions, and behaviors all tie together. You've seen how our survival instincts and the stories we tell ourselves shape our actions, even when those actions hold us back. Being human is hard. In life, there's always tension between what we want, what we think we should do, and what we actually end up doing.

Changing old habits is tough. Stepping out of your comfort zone can feel uncomfortable or even scary. But curiosity and understanding how your brain works can make change feel a little easier and more possible.

In this section, we'll dive into the neuroscience behind why we feel stagnant in our careers. We'll revisit some familiar ideas, like habit loops and reward systems, and introduce new insights into how your brain operates. The good news? These patterns can be updated. Once you understand what's going on in your brain, you can start to initiate change and create new pathways for growth and success.

Let's go back to Julia. Julia works harder than almost anyone else in her office. She is reliable, diligent, and consistently takes on extra projects. But no matter how much she accomplishes, she still feels invisible. Deep down, she doubts her worth and fears that her contributions aren't truly valuable.

In one of our sessions, she shared, "I know I'm doing good work, but sometimes I wonder if it even matters. Maybe I'm just not cut out for more."

Her brain had settled into a pattern of self-doubt. Every time she avoided speaking up or promoting herself, her brain gave her a small sense of relief. This relief came from a dopamine loop. When she sidestepped the risk of advocating for herself, her brain released dopamine, reinforcing the belief that staying quiet was safer.[6]

When I asked her, "What happens when you think about sharing your accomplishments?"

She paused and said, "I feel this tightness in my throat, and my heart races. It's like my whole body is telling me to stay quiet."

This physical reaction came from her brain processing her internal emotional state. Her brain interpreted these sensations as signs of danger, reinforcing her belief that speaking up was risky. It was as if her brain was saying, *Don't do it. You might get it wrong, and it's safer to stay invisible.*

Julia's brain also relied on past experiences to predict what would happen. Since she had been overlooked or criticized before, her brain expected the same outcome each time she considered speaking up. These predictions kept her in a cycle of silence. To interrupt that cycle, Julia needed to create new experiences that would contest those predictions. If she experienced a positive outcome, like getting a good response when sharing an idea, her brain could form new pathways, making it easier to advocate for herself in the future.

Mark's story shows another way our brains keep us stuck. Mark is a skilled engineer known for his technical expertise. He believes that if he delivers flawless work, success will naturally follow. But despite his abilities, his career feels stagnant.

Mark's brain had also settled into a pattern. He avoided tasks like networking, leadership, or anything involving soft skills because they felt unfamiliar and unpredictable. Instead, he focused on technical work, where he felt confident and in control. This kind of professional stagnation affected his brain's ability to stay flexible and creative. By avoiding new challenges, he missed out on strengthening his brain's neural connections. Just like a muscle that weakens without exercise, his brain became less adaptable.

Mark's avoidance also affected his motivation. Since he wasn't achieving new or different goals, his brain didn't get the dopamine boost that comes from novelty and success. Without this boost, he felt less motivated and more inclined to stick with what he knew.

When Mark thought about delegating tasks or stepping into a leadership role, his body would tense up. "I feel a knot in my stomach," he said. This was his brain signaling discomfort, pushing him back toward familiar work. His brain predicted success with technical tasks and uncertainty with leadership. To change this, Mark needed to create new experiences that would challenge those predictions. When he delegated successfully and his team performed well, his brain registered a positive surprise, helping him see that leadership wasn't as risky as he thought.

Both Julia and Mark were dealing with neural pathways that prioritized safety over growth. Thankfully for us—and for them—the brain is not fixed. It can change. Because of neuroplasticity, new patterns can form with effort and practice.

When Julia shares her accomplishments or when Mark takes on leadership tasks, they are teaching their brains that these new behaviors lead to good outcomes. At first, it may feel uncomfortable. But each small win makes the new patterns stronger.

What about you? What are the patterns keeping you stuck? Maybe you avoid advocating for yourself because it feels uncomfortable, or you stick to familiar tasks because they're easier than trying something new. What is one small step you could take today to challenge those patterns?

Julia's and Mark's stories remind us that we aren't stuck with the habits we've formed. By understanding how our brains work and taking small, deliberate steps, we can rewrite our pathways. When we do, we create a future shaped not by our past limitations but by new possibilities.

Breaking Patterns: Taking Control of Your Professional Growth

Mark and Julia came to therapy feeling stuck in their careers. Both were hardworking professionals, but despite their efforts, they weren't advancing. The issue wasn't their abilities, but the habits and beliefs they had developed over time. These routines, though comfortable, were limiting their growth.

Mark had relied on his technical skills, believing that doing good work would naturally lead to success. However, as he pursued leadership roles, his perfectionism, micromanagement, and reluctance to collaborate began to hold him back. Julia faced a different challenge: She believed that hard work and staying quiet would earn recognition. Yet she felt invisible and unsure how to break the cycle.

In therapy, the focus was on helping them identify the stories they had been telling themselves. Mark needed to challenge the belief that technical skills alone would suffice, while Julia had to reframe her fear of self-promotion. She began to see that sharing her accomplishments wasn't bragging but was a way to communicate her value to others.

One of the most important tools we used for both Mark and Julia was self-reflection. I encouraged them to slow down and notice when they were slipping into old habits. Mark started to pause when he felt the urge to micromanage, asking himself, "Am I helping my team grow, or just repeating what feels safe?" Julia practiced catching herself in meetings when she hesitated to speak up. She learned to ask, "What's the worst that could happen if I share this idea?" These moments of awareness helped them step off autopilot and make more deliberate choices.

We also tried behavioral experiments, small and manageable steps to test new ways of thinking and acting. For Mark, this meant delegating one noncritical task to a teammate. At first, he worried something might go wrong. But when the task was completed successfully, it gave him evidence that he could trust others without needing to oversee every detail. For Julia, it was speaking up in one meeting or casually sharing a recent accomplishment with her manager. Each time she tried, she realized her fears of being judged or dismissed were often exaggerated. These experiments helped both Mark and Julia take small steps toward new patterns of behavior.

To manage the discomfort that came with stepping out of their comfort zones, we worked on calming techniques. Growth rarely feels easy, and both Mark and Julia had to learn how to handle the stress that came with change. For Mark, this meant recognizing the anxiety that surfaced when he let go of control. I taught him a simple grounding exercise: take a deep breath, focus on the bigger picture, and remind yourself why you are making this change. For Julia, we practiced role-playing scenarios to help her feel more prepared and confident before speaking up.

Over time, these small shifts started to add up. Mark began attending networking events, building relationships with colleagues, and practicing active listening in meetings. He let go of his need to control every detail and focused on empowering his team instead.

As a result, Mark wasn't just seen as the technical expert anymore. He was becoming a leader.

Julia made progress too. She started voicing her ambitions and sharing her ideas. She scheduled regular check-ins with her supervisor to discuss her goals and found a mentor who gave her guidance and support. Slowly but steadily, Julia began to feel seen, appreciated, and in control of her career.

This process wasn't about making dramatic changes overnight. For both Mark and Julia, it was about taking small, intentional steps to challenge their old patterns. It started with awareness, recognizing when their habits weren't helping them, and trying something different, even when it felt uncomfortable.

Each time they made a new choice, they reinforced new habits. Mark's efforts helped him become the leader he had always wanted to be. Julia stopped waiting for recognition and started creating opportunities for herself.

What about you? Have you noticed patterns that might be holding you back? Maybe you avoid risks because staying in your comfort zone feels safer. Maybe you've convinced yourself that hard work will eventually get noticed, or you hesitate to speak up because you fear judgment.

These instincts aren't failures. They are habits your brain created to protect you. But they can be changed.

Breaking free starts with small steps. Mark learned to pause and question his actions instead of defaulting to what felt comfortable. Julia practiced sharing her accomplishments one conversation at a time. Each step moved them closer to their goals.

You can do the same. By taking deliberate action, testing new behaviors, and rewriting the stories you tell yourself, you can create new habits that support your growth. Change doesn't have to happen all at once. Each small step builds momentum.

The road to growth isn't always easy, but it's worth it. By stepping off autopilot and making intentional choices, you can take control of your career and create a future that reflects your true potential.

Key Takeaways

Here are some steps you can take to move past career stagnation and step into professional growth. Recognizing the beliefs, habits, and survival instincts that keep you stuck is the first step. By making small but meaningful shifts, you can change how you show up at work and advocate for yourself with confidence.

- **Your survival instincts influence your career more than you realize.** Your brain is wired for safety, not success, which means it often keeps you in patterns that feel comfortable but hold you back. The fear of standing out, the hesitation to self-promote, or the instinct to control every detail are not personality traits, they are outdated survival mechanisms that can be rewired.

- **The stories you tell yourself shape your professional reality.** Thoughts like *I have to be perfect to succeed* or *If I just work hard, people will notice* may feel true, but they are often unconscious scripts learned from past experiences. Recognizing and rewriting these narratives is essential for breaking cycles of hesitation, invisibility, and perfectionism.

- **Cognitive biases reinforce career stagnation.** Your brain naturally focuses on past failures more than successes, making you underestimate your abilities and avoid risks. Biases like confirmation bias and negativity bias make it easy to stay stuck in limiting patterns. Awareness of these mental shortcuts can help you challenge them and make more strategic career decisions.

- **Growth requires intentional discomfort.** Your brain prefers familiarity, but progress comes from stepping into uncertainty. Whether it's sharing an idea, delegating responsibilities, or asking for a raise, small risks train your brain to tolerate discomfort and expand your professional opportunities.

Breaking free from career stagnation starts with recognizing the unconscious patterns holding you back and taking small, intentional steps toward growth.

Moving from Understanding to Action

Breaking free from career stagnation means moving beyond self-awareness and taking deliberate actions that align with your growth goals. Here are five practical steps to help you shift old patterns, showcase your value, and open doors to new opportunities.

- **Reflect on your internal narratives and how they may be holding you back.** Ask yourself if you believe hard work alone should lead to recognition or if you avoid advocating for yourself because it feels uncomfortable. Write down the beliefs you want to challenge and practice reframing them into positive, growth-oriented statements.
- **Focus on developing soft skills alongside technical ones.** Take a course, attend a workshop, or read a book on skills like emotional intelligence, communication, or conflict resolution. These abilities demonstrate leadership and are often what organizations value most for promotions and advancement.
- **Start practicing self-promotion in small, authentic ways.** Share your accomplishments as part of team

discussions, progress updates, or casual conversations with colleagues. Reframe self-promotion as a way of contributing to your team's success rather than bragging.

- **Proactively seek feedback from your manager or trusted colleagues.** Use this opportunity to ask about areas for growth and how to align your work with the organization's goals. Feedback is a valuable tool for identifying blind spots and demonstrating your commitment to development.

- **Volunteer for opportunities that challenge you to step outside your comfort zone.** Offer to lead a project, represent your team in a meeting, or tackle a stretch assignment. These actions not only help you grow but also increase your visibility as someone who takes initiative and delivers results.

Taking action can feel uncomfortable, but it's in that discomfort where growth happens. By developing soft skills, seeking feedback, and taking deliberate steps outside your comfort zone, you can begin to shift patterns, build momentum, and position yourself for career advancement.

11

Resilience: The Foundation for Lasting Change

"The human capacity for burden is like bamboo; far more flexible than you'd ever believe at first glance."

—Jodi Picoult,
novelist and author of *My Sister's Keeper*

As I reflect on the many clients I have worked with over the years, there is one thing they have all had in common. No matter what brought them into my office, whether it was self-doubt, out-of-control inner caveperson, relationship struggles, procrastination, fear, or difficulties setting boundaries, resilience has always been at the hearts of their journeys.

Some walked in feeling like they had no resilience at all. They felt overwhelmed by their emotions, reactive to every stressor, and stuck in patterns they could not seem to break. Others believed they were resilient because they had survived tough circumstances, but their resilience often came at a cost. Rigidity, fragility, or emotional reactivity made it hard for them to adapt, trust, or grow.

And maybe you can relate. Have you ever felt like your emotions are running the show, leading you to impulsive reactions or decisions you regret later? Perhaps you have been called "overly sensitive" or "too reactive," and it stung, because deep down, you wondered if it might be true.

Or maybe you do not recognize yourself in those descriptions at all. Maybe your struggle is quieter, a sense of anxiety or unease that bubbles up in new situations. Do you find yourself feeling overwhelmed when life throws you something unexpected? Do you wake up at night replaying the day's events, unable to stop the worry from spiraling?

If any of this sounds familiar, you are not alone. Every challenge we have explored in this book, whether it is self-doubt, procrastination, boundary issues, or fear, is, at its core, tied to resilience. Resilience is the ability to navigate life's ups and downs, to bounce back from setbacks, and to stay steady when emotions run high. Without it, it is easy to feel overwhelmed, stuck, or powerless to change.

But resilience is only part of the picture. Emotional balance is its essential partner. Emotional balance is what helps us regulate our responses to life's ups and downs so that we can respond thoughtfully rather than react impulsively.[1] This ability comes down to a powerful part of your brain: the prefrontal cortex. It acts as the CEO of your emotions, helping you regulate impulses, consider consequences, and make intentional choices instead of defaulting to old survival patterns.[2] When resilience is strong, the prefrontal cortex keeps emotional reactions in check, allowing you to pause, reflect, and respond in a way that aligns with your values instead of reacting out of fear or frustration. Together, resilience and emotional balance form the foundation for everything else we have talked about in this book. They are the skills that allow us to integrate the lessons we have learned, take action, and move forward with clarity and courage.

The opposites of resilience and emotional balance are rigidity, fragility, and emotional reactivity, which can keep us stuck in old patterns.

- Rigidity shows up when we cling to familiar routines or beliefs, unable to adjust to new circumstances. That little inner voice might whisper, *Stick to what you know; it is safer.* While this can feel comforting, it can also prevent us from embracing new opportunities or learning from change.
- Fragility leaves us feeling vulnerable to stress, as if even small challenges or setbacks are too much to bear. In those moments, our inner voice might warn, *This is not safe!* This response can make us feel overwhelmed, as if we lack the resources to handle adversity.
- Emotional reactivity leads to heightened responses that can escalate conflict, strain relationships, or leave us feeling out of control. Instead of pausing to reflect, we may lash out or react impulsively, only to regret it later.

The good news? These responses, while challenging, are not fixed. Resilience is a skill, not an inherent trait, and like any skill, it can be built with practice. Emotional balance, too, is something we can strengthen, allowing us to approach life with greater calm and flexibility. And here's why that matters: Your brain is designed to adapt. Thanks to neuroplasticity, every time you push back against an old habit, whether that's choosing to reframe a setback instead of spiraling or pausing before snapping at someone, your brain lays down new pathways that make resilience feel easier next time.[3] Think of it like upgrading your mental operating system. The more you practice, the stronger those pathways get, making resilience not just a choice, but a default way of responding to life's challenges.

In this chapter, we will explore how resilience and emotional balance can help us step out of old cycles, face challenges with confidence, and adapt to whatever life throws our way. We will look at how our brains, bodies, and past experiences influence our ability to stay steady in the face of adversity and how we can continue to rewrite the narratives that keep us stuck.

The truth is resilience is not about avoiding difficulty. It is about learning to navigate it. And while it may seem like some people are born with more resilience than others, it is not something you either have or do not have. It is something you can cultivate.

So let's explore how you can build the resilience and emotional balance you need in order to bring everything you have learned in this book to life.

Your Inner Caveperson: How Survival Instincts Shape Resilience

Have you ever felt that a minor disruption, such as a canceled plan or a missed deadline, sent you spiraling into stress or frustration? What about when a project you were working on didn't go as planned? Maybe you have found yourself shutting down in response to a challenge that, logically, seemed manageable. These moments can feel confusing, even overwhelming, but they are not random. They are ancient survival instincts kicking in; your inner caveperson is stepping in to take control.

By now, you probably have a good understanding of how our ancient survival traits shape the way we navigate the world. The role of this inner caveperson is simple: to keep us alive, conserve our body's resources, both physical and mental, and protect us from danger. So it might not surprise you to learn that this same part of your brain also plays a significant role in your ability to handle challenges and disruptions.

When resilience is low, this same part of your brain takes over completely, amplifying fear and avoidance.

Resilience is about how we respond to life's challenges, but when the inner caveperson has too much influence, it can leave us feeling stuck, reactive, or overwhelmed.[4] Instead of helping us bounce back, these survival instincts can hold us back. In this chapter, we will look at how the inner caveperson affects our resilience and how understanding these drives can help us respond to life's disruptions with more balance and intention. Through the stories of Tessa and Davis, we will explore how ancient instincts shape modern struggles and what you can do to create a new sense of control when life feels overwhelming.

Tessa had spent much of her life moving from one temporary job to another, clinging tightly to routines she had built to keep her world in order. Her childhood had been marked by neglect and instability, leaving her in a constant battle to create control in a life that often felt out of her hands. Yet when anything disrupted her carefully constructed plans, her inner caveperson took over, flooding her with anxiety and triggering emotional outbursts that left her feeling frustrated and ashamed.

"Every time something unexpected happens, I just lose it," she admitted during one of our sessions. "I can't seem to control myself."

Tessa's struggles were not just a personality trait or a quirk. They reflected survival instincts that were deeply ingrained and passed down through generations. Our ancestors relied on these instincts to respond quickly and decisively to the unexpected. While that wiring once helped them escape predators or navigate sudden dangers, instead of helping Tessa, these instincts were working against her, leaving her reactive and overwhelmed.

While Tessa's world looks very different from the one her ancestors navigated, her brain did not know that. To her inner caveperson, the unpredictability of a missed meeting or a canceled dinner plan still registered as a potential threat.

"If something disrupts my routine," she explained, "it's like my brain just shuts off, and all I can feel is panic."

That panic was not about the disruption itself. It was about what the disruption represented. For Tessa, it was tied to her childhood experiences of instability, where unpredictability often meant danger or emotional chaos. As a child, she had learned to react strongly to regain some semblance of control in an unpredictable world.

What about you? Have you ever felt your reaction to a minor inconvenience was far stronger than the situation called for? Maybe your inner voice started spiraling, telling you, *This is too much*, even though, logically, you knew it was not a big deal. That is your inner caveperson at work, trying to keep you safe, even if the danger is not real.

Tessa's journey toward resilience and emotional balance involved creating space between her immediate response and her reality. She began learning how to step back from the edge of panic and see situations for what they really were. Recognizing these reactions helped move her toward calming those ancient survival instincts and finding a sense of balance when life felt overwhelming.

Davis, another client of mine, faced his own battle with those ancestral instincts after a close family member died in a tragic accident. Davis's childhood and adolescence had been marked by struggles with depression and anxiety, but through therapy and concerted effort, he built a life in which he managed both well and no longer considered himself a person who struggled with either. He was a successful software engineer who had learned how to maintain stability and balance in his daily life.

After the trauma of his loss, however, Davis felt like he was back where he had started. He described feeling fragile, depressed, and anxious in ways he thought he had left behind.

"Since the accident, I feel like I can't handle anything," he confessed during one of our sessions. "Even small problems at work make me want to shut down."

Why does trauma leave us feeling so vulnerable, even to minor stressors? It's because trauma doesn't just create emotional pain. I believe it wakes up the inner caveperson, making it louder and more dominant than ever.

For our ancestors, stress was often tied to physical threats, and survival depended on reacting quickly to danger. In an earlier chapter, we explored how the brain, especially the amygdala and hippocampus, processes stress and perceives threats. When stress is prolonged, these systems can become overactive, making even minor challenges feel like major dangers.

After a traumatic event, the brain would stay on high alert, ready for the next threat. This is exactly what happened to Davis. His inner caveperson, formerly a quiet, background presence, became the dominant force in his life, scanning for danger as if it were still just around the corner.

This heightened state drained Davis's emotional and physical resources, leaving him unable to return to a place of calm. Everyday tasks, like responding to emails or collaborating with his team, felt impossible because his brain was still locked in survival mode, treating them as life-or-death situations.

Have you ever felt this way after a loss or a traumatic experience? Like your brain could not settle down, even when you knew, logically, that you were safe? That is your inner caveperson doing its best to protect you, sending signals to keep you alert long after the actual danger has passed.

For both Tessa and Davis, the key to change was recognizing that their inner caveperson was not trying to sabotage them. It was simply trying to keep them safe. But what their brains did not realize was that the threats they were reacting to were no longer relevant.

Tessa learned to pause when her routines were disrupted, asking herself, "Is this truly dangerous, or is my brain just reacting to the unexpected?" Davis began practicing grounding techniques to help his nervous system settle, slowly teaching his brain that it was safe to relax.

These steps may seem small, but they are powerful. Each time Tessa and Davis chose to respond rather than react, they were creating new patterns in their brains, patterns that supported resilience and balance rather than reactivity and fear.

The same is possible for you. What might happen if you started recognizing your inner caveperson's voice and challenging its assumptions? How might your life change if you could step back from those automatic reactions and make choices that align with who you want to be?

Rewriting the Stories That Shape Our Emotional Reactions

By now, we have explored how the stories we carry shape how we navigate the world. These narratives, often formed in childhood, influence the way we interpret challenges, make decisions, and view ourselves. But let's shift our focus for a moment to how these stories play out in our emotional world. What happens when life throws you one curveball after another or when a seemingly small disruption feels like it is unraveling everything?

The stories we tell ourselves do more than guide our choices; they also influence how we process stress, handle conflict, and bounce back when things go wrong. They determine how we respond when our emotions are tested, when the unexpected throws us off course, or when stressors pile up and leave us feeling overwhelmed. Sometimes, these narratives become the reason we shut down or react in ways we don't understand.

In this section, we'll take a closer look at how the stories we carry influence our emotional responses to life's inevitable disruptions. Through Tessa's and Davis's stories, we'll explore how old narratives can shape our reactions and how rewriting those narratives can open the door to greater resilience and emotional balance.

For Tessa, structure became her lifeline. Growing up in a home marked by neglect and instability, she learned early on that routines were the only way to feel safe. Her parents were often absent, both physically and emotionally, leaving her to create her own sense of stability in a world that felt unpredictable. As a child, unpredictability often meant danger or emotional chaos, and disruptions made her feel like the ground was shifting beneath her feet.

School provided some structure, which helped Tessa feel a bit more grounded, but it wasn't always enough. When things became overwhelming, her emotions would erupt. "If I got sent to the principal's office, I wasn't scared," she admitted. "It felt like a relief. I didn't have to deal with the classroom, and everyone just left me alone."

What Tessa didn't realize then was that her brain had developed a survival strategy. Her emotional outbursts gave her what she needed: space, distance, and a break from the chaos. This reinforced a pattern where, when things felt overwhelming, losing control became a way to regain it.

As Tessa grew older, this need for structure followed her into adulthood. She clung tightly to routines, believing they would keep her life manageable and safe. However, these rigid systems started to backfire. If a colleague missed a deadline, a friend canceled plans, or a meeting ran late, Tessa felt like her carefully built world was crumbling. Her anxiety would spike, and her emotions would take over.

Her reactions weren't just about the inconveniences themselves. They were deeply rooted in the story her brain had absorbed as a child: The world is unsafe, and maintaining control is the only way to feel secure. Beneath that story, though, was an even deeper belief, the fear that she couldn't handle the unpredictability of life itself. This belief, though understandable given her early experiences, kept her locked in a cycle where her need for control became both her armor and her greatest vulnerability.

Tessa's story is not unique. Many of us carry narratives like this, shaped by our past, that influence how we handle stress and change. These stories might not always feel obvious, but they show up in how we react to disruptions, setbacks, and challenges.

Davis carried a different story that shaped his emotional responses. Growing up in a household where vulnerability was rarely acknowledged, Davis learned to equate emotional expression with weakness. His parents, though loving, believed in staying strong and pushing through challenges.

"When I got upset or scared, they'd tell me to push through it," Davis shared during one of our sessions. "I thought showing emotion meant I was weak."

As a child, Davis absorbed the message that emotions were something to be avoided, a sign that you were not tough enough to handle life's challenges. By adolescence, he had started to view his own sensitivity as a personal flaw. If he felt anxious about a test, nervous before a game, or over-whelmed by stress, he kept it to himself. On the rare occasions he opened up, his college buddies chided him, telling him he needed to toughen up.

Through therapy and effort in his early adulthood, Davis found ways to manage his anxiety and build a steady, fulfilling life. He no longer thought of himself as someone who strug-gled emotionally. But after the sudden loss of his close family member, that stability was shaken.

"Since the accident, I feel like I've lost control," Davis confessed. "My thoughts are racing, and I'm always on the verge of tears. I'm either angry, panicked, or wishing I could just disappear. Nothing I usually do to manage my emotions is working."

For Davis, the accident tapped into old patterns of self-doubt and fragility that he thought he had left behind. His brain's story about not being strong enough resurfaced, rein-forcing the belief that he couldn't handle life's challenges.

The stories we tell ourselves act like filters, shaping how we interpret challenges and influencing how we respond. For Tessa, her narrative of needing control made even small disruptions feel overwhelming. For Davis, his belief in needing to suppress emotions turned setbacks into personal failures. Beneath both of these narratives lay an even deeper story, the fear that they couldn't handle the world around them. These perceptions, rooted in their inner narratives, affected their ability to adapt and respond.

Recognizing the stories we carry helps us work toward rewriting them. For Tessa, understanding how her past shaped her reactions helped her step back and see her outbursts for what they were: a response to an outdated story, not the current situation. She began to ask herself, "Is this disruption really dangerous, or am I just reacting to old fears?"

For Davis, it was about challenging his belief that vulnerability equaled weakness. By exploring the roots of his story, he began to understand that asking for help or expressing his emotions didn't make him fragile. It made him human.

You may notice similar patterns in your own life. Perhaps you see yourself overreacting to disruptions, holding on to rigid routines, or suppressing your emotions because of what you learned growing up. These reactions may feel like they define you, but they don't have to.

Psychologists have found that people who create narratives that emphasize personal growth and redemption tend to feel more satisfied with life and have better mental health. By learning to rewrite their stories, Tessa and Davis shifted their focus from fear and doubt to growth and possibility. This didn't just change how they felt in the moment. It helped them build the emotional resilience to face future challenges.

Our stories are not written in stone. With reflection, self-awareness, and a willingness to challenge the narratives we have carried for years, we can rewrite them into something that supports our growth and resilience. You are not bound by the past. You have the power to shape the story that defines your future.

Resilience and Self-Fulfilling Prophecies: How Our Beliefs Shape Our Ability to Bounce Back

So here we are again, talking about the beliefs we hold about ourselves, others, and the world that shape how we respond to challenges. These beliefs influence the way we act, often in ways that make them come true. Throughout this book, we've seen how self-fulfilling prophecies shape our lives. Whether these beliefs come from stories we tell ourselves or messages we've absorbed from others, they guide our actions and create the outcomes we fear or expect.

What makes self-fulfilling prophecies so powerful is how they rely on mental shortcuts and unconscious processes. Cognitive biases, heuristics, and distortions simplify the way we see the world, but they also trap us in cycles of reinforcing the same beliefs over and over.[5]

You might already see this in your own life. Have you ever believed you weren't strong enough to handle something, only to find yourself avoiding the challenge and then feeling like you proved yourself right? Or maybe you've told yourself that things never get better, and as a result, you've stopped looking for ways to improve your situation. These loops aren't just frustrating; they actively shape our reality and can make us feel stuck, even when we want to move forward.

Let's take a closer look at Tessa and Davis to better understand the mechanisms that shape their resilience or lack of it and to see how self-fulfilling prophecies don't just keep us stuck; they create the very conditions we are trying to avoid.

You'll remember that Tessa grew up in a world where unpredictability felt really scary. Her parents were either absent or volatile, and as a child, she learned that stability wasn't something she could rely on. To cope, Tessa created strict routines, believing that control over her environment was the only way to feel safe. But when life disrupted those routines, whether it was a canceled meeting, a missed deadline, or a last-minute change, she didn't just experience frustration. She experienced proof.

Her emotional reasoning told her that because she felt overwhelmed, the situation must be overwhelming. Emotional reasoning is a cognitive distortion where we assume our emotions reflect objective reality; if we feel anxious, we assume something is dangerous; if we feel inadequate, we assume we are incapable. Tessa's brain didn't question whether the situation was actually a threat. Instead, it took her panic as proof that she was in danger.

Her caveperson piped up, flooding her with anxiety, and she responded with emotional outbursts. Her brain, wired to detect threats, interpreted small disruptions as confirmation that unpredictability was dangerous.

And here's where the self-fulfilling prophecy took hold.

Her brain expected unpredictability to mean chaos, so she reacted with panic and control-seeking behaviors. The more she tried to control her environment, the more reactive she became when things didn't go according to plan. Her emotional reasoning told her that her reactions were justified, reinforcing the belief that unpredictability was a serious threat.

The availability heuristic made this even more powerful. The availability heuristic is a mental shortcut in which the brain relies on the most easily recalled memories to predict a present moment situation. Instead of evaluating each event on its own, her brain automatically pulled from past experiences, especially emotionally intense ones, to make sense of what was happening.

Because her childhood memories of emotional chaos and instability were so vivid and deeply stored, her brain treated present disruptions as if they carried the same risks she faced as a child. When a colleague didn't meet a deadline or a meeting ran late, her brain didn't just see it as a minor inconvenience, it retrieved memories of past instability and treated the current situation as equally threatening.

Over time, Tessa's emotional outbursts became her way of coping with stress. They gave her short-term relief, helping her create distance from the situation and giving her a momentary sense of control. Her brain prioritized immediate emotional release over long-term problem-solving, a pattern known as "short-term relief bias." This happens when the brain chooses whatever will bring quick comfort, even if it does not actually fix the problem. The reaction feels necessary in the moment, but in the long run, it only reinforces the belief that there is no other way to cope.

For Tessa, these outbursts did not just happen; they became proof. Each time she lost control, she reinforced the idea that she was not capable of handling disruptions any other way. The more she reacted with frustration and panic, the more her brain associated unpredictability with danger. It was a loop she could not see at the time. Her emotions would explode, giving her a brief sense of relief, but then the fallout would make her world feel even more unstable. Instead of solving the problem, her reactions created more of what she feared.

Because she expected herself to struggle with unpredictability, she also struggled with confirmation bias. She noticed only the moments that supported her belief that she could not handle uncertainty. When she managed a disruption calmly, she dismissed it as luck. But when her emotions took over, it felt like undeniable proof that she was incapable of staying in control. Her brain filtered out anything that contradicted her fear, making it impossible for her to see growth, even when it was happening.

Her self-fulfilling prophecy was already in motion. Her emotional outbursts made her world feel unstable, which confirmed her belief that unpredictability was dangerous. The more she reacted this way, the more automatic it became. Each time she lost control, she was not just experiencing an emotion. She was reinforcing the idea that she was right to fear instability.

This pattern didn't just affect Tessa emotionally; it also shaped her career. She moved from one temporary job to another, often leaving positions when things felt overwhelming or being asked to leave after her emotional outbursts disrupted her work environment. Her self-fulfilling prophecy told her, *The world is unsafe, and I can't handle unpredictability.* And through her actions, she made that belief feel true.

Now let's look at Davis again.

Davis had spent years building a stable, predictable life. He thrived in his career, maintained a healthy routine, and considered himself someone who had left his struggles with emotional turbulence in the past. For a long time, it worked. Davis believed he had proven to himself and others that he was strong and capable.

But when Davis's brother passed away unexpectedly, everything changed. The routines that had kept him grounded felt meaningless, and the grief felt too heavy to bear. Slowly, the beliefs he thought he had left behind came flooding back.

"I don't think I'm strong enough to handle this," he admitted during one of our sessions. "I keep trying to pull myself together, but it feels like I'm failing at everything."

The loss triggered Davis's old belief that he wasn't resilient enough to handle life's challenges. Each time he tried to suppress his emotions only to feel them surge back, it reinforced the idea that his feelings were proof of his weakness. Instead of allowing himself to grieve, he withdrew from his routines, skipped workouts, and began avoiding friends and colleagues. Avoidance brought him a brief sense of relief, but each time he pulled away, his belief that he couldn't cope grew stronger.

His hindsight bias made it even worse. Hindsight bias is a cognitive distortion where the brain looks back on an event and convinces itself that the outcome was predictable. Davis told himself he should have seen the loss coming, that he should have done something to prevent it. Even though there was nothing he could have done, his brain distorted the past, making it seem like he had failed. These thoughts deepened his sense of helplessness, making the pain feel personal, as if it was not just grief but proof that he was incapable.

At work, Davis couldn't help but compare himself to colleagues who seemed to manage their own challenges with ease. *Why can't I just get through this like they would?* he wondered. This was an example of social comparison, a psychological process where we evaluate ourselves based on how we measure up to others. Instead of recognizing that grief affects everyone differently, Davis assumed that his struggles meant he was weak. The more he compared himself, the more convinced he became that he was different, weaker, and incapable of handling adversity. He did not consider that his colleagues might be struggling too. Instead, he only focused on the ways they seemed to be managing, which reinforced his belief that something was wrong with him.

Social comparison made him feel like an outsider, like someone who just wasn't built to handle hardship. The more he believed it, the more isolated he felt, and the harder it became to ask for help.

Over time, Davis fell into learned helplessness, a psychological state where a person stops trying to change their circumstances because past experiences have convinced them that their efforts will not make a difference. Learned helplessness develops when someone repeatedly faces situations where they feel powerless, and over time, they stop believing they have any control, even when opportunities for change exist.

Davis had always believed that his routines kept him stable, so when they no longer worked the way they once did, he felt like nothing would. After trying his usual methods to calm himself—exercising, journaling, or sticking to his routine—he felt defeated when nothing seemed to work. "I've done everything I can," he told himself, "and it's still not enough."

The more he tried and failed to feel better, the more convinced he became that no effort would make a difference.

Instead of seeking new strategies, he gave up, pulling further back from the world. His withdrawal deepened his self-fulfilling prophecy. He believed he was not capable of handling his emotions, and because he stopped trying, he never gave himself the opportunity to prove otherwise.

Tessa's and Davis's stories reveal how the beliefs we carry can shape the way we respond to challenges, creating loops that feel hard to escape. Recognizing these patterns and understanding the mental shortcuts that reinforce them is necessary to breaking free.

What about you? Have you ever told yourself you couldn't handle something, only to act in ways that made that belief feel true? These loops may feel automatic, but they're not unchangeable. With awareness and practice, you can begin to rewrite the beliefs that hold you back and create new patterns that support your growth and resilience.

Wired for Change: Understanding the Neuroscience Behind Staying Stuck and Breaking Free

And here we are again, looking at the wiring in our brain that either keeps us stuck in habits, patterns, and emotional reactivity or allows for growth, change, and breaking free. We are talking about how we are wired as it relates to our thinking, acting, and reacting patterns.

Do you ever wish there was a manual explaining why our brains get stuck in emotional or behavioral patterns? Looking through the lens of neuroscience gives us that manual, helping us understand how our brains are wired and why it's so difficult to change old habits and reactions.

Let's revisit Tessa's relationships, for example. She grew up in an unstable environment, so her brain learned to see unpredictability as dangerous. So when her partner was late or canceled plans, her brain didn't just register it as a simple inconvenience; it reinforced her existing belief that unpredictability meant risk. Her amygdala, the brain's built-in alarm system, detected the change as a potential threat. Since the amygdala processes emotions faster than the rational prefrontal cortex, her emotional response kicked in before she even had a chance to logically assess the situation.

Her amygdala fired off an alarm, treating the moment as if it were a serious threat, flooding her system with the same emotions she felt as a child when chaos meant something bad was about to happen. Her brain had wired itself for vigilance, interpreting even neutral disruptions as a sign of instability, and instability had always meant danger. Because the prefrontal cortex, responsible for logical reasoning, takes longer to process situations than the amygdala, her brain defaulted to the quickest, most familiar response: panic and control-seeking behaviors. Tessa's brain had strengthened neural pathways for emotional reactivity, making her responses feel automatic.

Throughout this book, we've explored how the brain rewires itself through neuroplasticity, the ability to create new pathways and change old ones. One of the ways this happens is through long-term potentiation (LTP), where neurons that repeatedly fire together wire together, reinforcing specific thought patterns and reactions.[6] Each time Tessa reacted with anger or anxiety, her brain reinforced those neural connections, making it easier to default to the same response next time.

Tessa's emotional response became ingrained because her brain kept strengthening the neural pathways associated with that reaction. Think of these pathways as well-worn roads in her brain, getting more and more traveled each time she reacted in that way. Each repetition reinforced the pattern, making it feel automatic, even when it no longer served her. Her neural circuits for reactivity had formed over time, shaped by her past experiences and emotional memories stored in the brain. This is how Tessa's reactions were hardwired, and it made it challenging for her to respond differently, even if she consciously wanted to. Her prefrontal cortex, which is responsible for emotional regulation, was effectively being sidelined, allowing her limbic system to take over and dictate her response.

This pattern in Tessa's brain also tied into dopamine and the reward system, something you have seen at play many times throughout this book. Her brain had learned that certain patterns of control, even if they did not lead to real growth, would give her short-term relief from anxiety. Each time she sought control over a situation and momentarily felt better, her brain rewarded her with dopamine, reinforcing the behavior. Even though her control strategies were no longer working for her, they still gave her just enough relief to keep her using them. The brain does not prioritize what is helpful in the long run. It prioritizes what feels good right now.

So while Tessa's coping mechanisms were not helping her move forward, they were keeping her stuck in a cycle that felt impossible to break.

Now, let's look at Davis again. Like Tessa, Davis's childhood experiences shaped his beliefs about himself. He grew up with the belief that he was too sensitive, too fragile to handle life's difficulties. This belief became deeply ingrained in his neural pathways over time. When facing emotional distress, Davis's brain would automatically trigger a fear response, activating his amygdala and other areas related to stress and survival. His brain had learned to associate emotional vulnerability with danger, so it defaulted to avoidance or withdrawal, reinforcing the idea that emotional discomfort was unsafe.

Davis's dopamine system also played a role. When he avoided discomfort, his brain released dopamine as a form of short-term relief. The brain's reward system gave him a quick emotional payoff for avoiding the pain, reinforcing the avoidance behavior and making it feel not just like a habit but like the only option. Each time Davis avoided his emotions, his brain learned that withdrawal was an effective way to relieve stress, strengthening the neural pathways for avoidance and making it harder for him to confront discomfort in the future.

This cycle of avoidance was further fueled by cognitive dissonance. Davis's brain had a strong need to resolve the discomfort of the conflicting beliefs: his belief that he couldn't handle emotions versus the reality of needing to face them. You've probably heard the term *cognitive dissonance* before, it's been making the rounds in news and social media. It's that uncomfortable mental tug-of-war when we hold two conflicting beliefs, and our brain scrambles to smooth things over, sometimes in ways that keep us stuck. One key player in this process is the anterior cingulate cortex (ACC), the part of the brain responsible for detecting these contradictions. The ACC works to dial down the discomfort, often by convincing us that avoidance is the best option, even when it's not actually helping.[7]

When Davis faced a loss, his brain once again activated these automatic responses, reinforcing the neural pathways that linked emotional distress with fear and avoidance. Each time he avoided the pain, he reinforced the neural pathways that told him he wasn't strong enough to handle it, keeping him trapped in the same cycle.

Both Tessa and Davis were experiencing a state where their brains defaulted to old survival patterns under stress, resulting in emotional rigidity and stress responses. When faced with uncertainty or discomfort, the brain often shifts into survival mode, prioritizing emotional reactions over thoughtful responses. The limbic system, responsible for fight-or-flight responses, takes over, while the prefrontal cortex, the part of the brain that handles reasoning, planning, and flexible thinking, gets sidelined. This combination of emotional rigidity and stress responses made it harder for them to step outside their familiar patterns, even when those patterns were holding them back.

On a deeper level, their deep-seated implicit beliefs, the subconscious stories they carried about themselves and the world, kept reinforcing these cycles.

Tessa's belief that unpredictability was dangerous and Davis's belief that he was too fragile were not just thoughts; they were ingrained fast-brain responses. As we explored in Chapter 4, this fast-brain system, which neuroscientists call 'the low road,' is the brain's quick and instinctive reaction system. It is designed for speed rather than accuracy. It operates on past experiences and reacts automatically rather than pausing to assess the present moment. Because these beliefs were shaped early on, they operated beneath their conscious awareness, making change feel nearly impossible. [8]

Finally, memory reconsolidation plays a key role in shaping our emotional responses. We've discussed how old emotional patterns can be rewired, but why do some memories remain so deeply ingrained? When difficult experiences occur, especially in childhood, the brain encodes them in ways that influence future reactions. Rather than storing memories like a static file, the brain revisits and reshapes them each time they are recalled. However, if emotional memories are repeatedly retrieved without reinterpretation, they can strengthen rather than fade. The hippocampus and amygdala work together to store and retrieve emotional memories, making it harder to override ingrained responses, unless intentional effort is made to update them. And that is what I asked Tessa and David to do.

So what does all of this mean? It means that the way our brains are wired by our past experiences, emotions, and even our survival instincts is fluid, not fixed. The circuits that keep us stuck can also be rewired. Our brains are doing exactly what they were designed to do: protect us, conserve energy, and avoid pain. But sometimes, this old wiring holds us back from growing.

Take a moment to think about your own life. Which old patterns or beliefs are you holding on to because they once helped you, but now they're keeping you stuck? Each time you choose a new response, you activate new neural circuits, gradually weakening the old ones and strengthening alternative pathways. This process, one of the fundamental principles of neuroplasticity, proves that lasting change is always possible. It won't be easy, but just like Tessa and Davis, you have the ability to outgrow these old habits and create new, healthier patterns of thinking and behaving.

Resilience as a Choice: Rewriting Your Narrative for Growth

We've come full circle, looking at the wiring in our brain that keeps us stuck in patterns, habits, and emotional reactivity. But we've also seen that this same wiring allows for growth, change, and ultimately, the ability to transform. Neuroplasticity, the brain's ability to rewire itself, means that every time you challenge an old story or choose a different response, you are actively reshaping your brain. Understanding how we are wired, how our thinking, acting, and reacting patterns have formed over time, helps us realize that we have the power to rewrite our stories.

Through therapy, Tessa began recognizing how her behaviors and choices were driven by old patterns, survival instincts, and biases. What once helped her navigate chaos was now holding her back from true stability and happiness. She saw that her brain, in its attempt to protect her, had reinforced fear and control, keeping her stuck in a cycle she was ready to break.

For Davis, his journey was about recognizing that his belief that he was fragile or too sensitive had shaped his responses to emotional challenges. This belief had served him as a child, but as an adult, it kept him from fully engaging in life. In therapy, he began to see how his brain's survival instincts of emotional avoidance were not making him stronger but rather keeping him stuck in a cycle of self-doubt. He came to understand that resilience isn't about feeling fearless; it's about facing discomfort rather than retreating into old patterns.

What about you? What stories have you developed in childhood that might still be influencing your life today? Have you noticed how your brain might be keeping you in familiar patterns, even when they're no longer serving you? The key to rewriting those stories lies in recognizing the patterns, understanding their origin, and consciously choosing new ways to respond. And each time you do, you reinforce the neural pathways that make resilience easier next time. This is where emotional balance and resilience come in. The more we understand how our brains work, the more we realize we can choose how we want to respond to challenges, even when it feels uncomfortable.

Tessa learned that stepping into the unknown didn't have to be terrifying, it could lead to new opportunities and growth. Davis discovered that emotional vulnerability didn't make him weak, it made him human, and that strength came from facing his emotions head-on. For both of them, therapy helped them rewrite the scripts they had been living by. Tessa learned to embrace unpredictability, while Davis learned to face discomfort with more courage.

Their journeys are a powerful reminder that while our brains are wired for survival, those same instincts can sometimes hold us back from the growth we need. The key is recognizing these survival defaults and choosing to step forward, even when it feels uncomfortable. This is how we shift from the automatic, reactive patterns of the low road to the more deliberate and conscious processing of the high road. When we understand that emotional resilience is not about avoiding discomfort but about learning to face it and grow stronger, we unlock the power to live in a way that serves our highest selves.

So here's the truth: You have a 100% success rate in getting through tough things even if it wasn't always graceful; you still did it. And you will continue to do it. That is what it is to be human: to adapt, to face challenges, and to choose growth over fear. Resilience isn't about avoiding pain or difficulty, but about embracing it, learning from it, and growing stronger with each experience. That is the hallmark of emotional balance.

As you move forward in life, remember that you have the strength to face whatever comes your way. You've done it before, and you'll do it again. The only thing that can truly hold you back is the belief that you can't. So take a moment to reflect on what you've learned through all of this, and remember: You have the power to rewrite your story. What will your next chapter look like?

Key Takeaways

Resilience and emotional balance, as explored in this chapter, form the bedrock of navigating life's inevitable challenges. Here are three unique takeaways designed to stand apart from prior chapters while remaining aligned with the themes of this chapter.

- **Grow your resilience.** Resilience is a skill, not a trait, and it grows through intentional practice.[9] While some people seem naturally resilient, research and life experience show that resilience can be cultivated by building specific habits and mindsets. Like learning any new skill, it requires time, effort, and repetition.
- **Be flexible, not rigid.** Rigid responses to life's challenges can block growth, but flexibility enables lasting change. Resilience does not mean "powering through" or holding fast to routines at all costs. Instead, it involves adapting to circumstances with curiosity and openness, allowing you to learn and grow even when plans go awry.
- **Interrupt the reactivity cycle.** Emotional balance begins with recognizing and interrupting reactive patterns. Many of the emotional responses that keep you stuck, like anxiety, anger, or avoidance, are based on outdated survival instincts. By pausing to notice these automatic reactions, you can begin to respond with greater thoughtfulness and control, building emotional resilience in the process.

Resilience is not about never falling; it is about learning to rise with greater strength and adaptability. By treating it as a skill to be developed rather than an innate quality, you empower yourself to grow through life's challenges rather than being defined by them.

Moving from Understanding to Action

Building resilience and emotional balance requires consistent, intentional action. Below are five steps that directly connect to the themes of this chapter while offering new and original approaches to cultivating these essential skills.

- **Track your resilience habits.** Keep a daily journal of situations where you practiced resilience, whether it was staying calm during a disagreement, trying something new, or handling a setback without giving up. Reflecting on these moments helps you recognize your capacity for resilience and identify areas where you can continue to grow.
- **Explore uncertainty with curiosity.** Choose one area of your life where you tend to cling to rigid routines or plans. Experiment with introducing a small amount of unpredictability, such as trying a new activity, exploring a different perspective, or allowing yourself to be flexible in the moment. This practice builds emotional flexibility and reduces fear of the unknown.
- **Learn to soothe your stress response.** When your body enters "fight or flight" mode in reaction to a challenge, practice techniques like progressive muscle relaxation or mindful body scanning. These strategies help deactivate your survival instincts, making it easier to approach challenges with calm and clarity.
- **Reframe your inner narrative about failure.** The next time you experience a setback, pause and ask

yourself: "What is this experience teaching me about resilience?" Write down one positive lesson or skill you can take from the situation. By focusing on growth rather than loss, you create space for emotional recovery and renewal.

- **Develop an emotional check-in routine.** At the end of each day, take five minutes to reflect on your emotional highs and lows. What triggered these responses, and how did you handle them? Over time, this practice increases your awareness of emotional patterns and allows you to develop a more balanced approach to life's challenges.

Resilience is built one step at a time, through small but deliberate actions. By incorporating these practices into your daily life, you create a foundation for navigating adversity with grace, adaptability, and self-awareness.

You're Ready. Now What?

If something shifted while reading this book, if you're seeing your patterns more clearly and you're ready to move, this is your next step.

I've created a video training that walks you through how to remove the prehistoric tendencies from your brain so you can finally achieve the goals you've been circling for years. Watch the training, and if it makes sense for you, book a call with me to discuss mentorship opportunities.

Start here: **calendly.com/prehistoricbrain**

Space is limited. This is personal work, and you'll be supported the whole way through.

12

Moving Forward: Rewriting Your Story with Intention

"Incredible change happens in your life when you decide to take control of what you do have power over instead of craving control over what you don't."

—Steve Maraboli,
motivational speaker and author

If you've made it this far, you've already taken an important step. You've explored the ways your brain, your past experiences, and the narratives you've absorbed have shaped how you navigate the world. You've recognized how your inner caveperson urges you to stay small and safe, how your brain favors familiar patterns over change, and how past wounds can quietly steer your present decisions. But awareness alone isn't enough. Change happens when you take that awareness and do something with it.

This book has given you insights, but now, it's time to take action.

Taking the First Small Action Step

The next step doesn't have to be a massive overhaul. It doesn't mean rewriting every belief in one night or expecting yourself to suddenly master the art of boundary setting, self-compassion, or resilience. It starts with one choice, one moment where you catch yourself in an old pattern and decide to do something different. Maybe it's pausing before saying yes to something you don't want. Maybe it's speaking up when you'd normally stay silent. Maybe it's recognizing that fear isn't a stop sign, but a signal that you're growing.

Your brain, and inner caveperson, will resist at first. It will try to pull you back into old comfort zones, whispering that change is too hard or too risky. That voice is not the truth, it's just the echo of past conditioning, a reflexive attempt to keep you from discomfort; but discomfort is not danger. Discomfort is often the sign that you are stepping into something new, something bigger than the story you've been living. Every time you push forward anyway, you're proving to yourself that you are capable of more than you've believed.

Growth Happens in the Micromoments

Change is not a straight path. Some days you'll feel strong and confident, and other days, you'll slip back into old patterns. That's not failure, it's part of the process. Every time you recognize an old habit and choose differently, even in the smallest way, you are rewriting your story in real time. Growth happens in the micromoments, in the spaces where you decide to challenge what you've always believed about yourself and what's possible for you.

Think back to the people we've met in these pages: Alyx, who learned to step out of defensiveness and into self-trust, and Michael, who redefined strength by allowing vulnerability. But they weren't the only ones on this journey. Carrie, who once believed her worth was tied to achievement, began to realize that she didn't need to prove herself to be seen. Jake, who struggled with procrastination, discovered that his avoidance wasn't laziness but fear masquerading as self-protection. Each of them had a moment, the moment where they realized they didn't have to stay stuck in the same loops. And neither do you.

Your Brain Will Make Excuses– Don't Listen

Now, let's be real for a moment. Your brain is going to come up with excuses. It'll say that now isn't the right time, that you'll start tomorrow, or that you need to read five more books before you're "ready." That's just your inner caveperson clinging to the illusion of safety. But here's the truth, readiness is a myth. You won't wake up one day suddenly feeling prepared, because change is inherently uncomfortable. And yet change still happens when you take the necessary step.

I can't even tell you how many times I had to force myself to sit down and write this book or how often my own inner caveperson tried to convince me that staying quiet was safer. Even though I teach this work every day, I still struggle with the same voices that try to hold me back. The difference is, I don't let them drive anymore. And neither do you have to.

The Science of Why Action Matters

Remember the Zeigarnik Effect from chapter 10? Your brain is wired to keep unfinished business at the forefront of your mind. That's why the things you avoid, like setting boundaries, having difficult conversations, or challenging long-held beliefs, continue to weigh on you. The good news? Taking action, even in the smallest way, disrupts that loop. When you finally address something your brain has been keeping open, you create a sense of closure that frees up mental energy for something new.

Speaking of mental energy, have you ever noticed how exhausting change feels? That's because of something called "Cognitive Load Theory." Your brain can only handle so much at once. When you're trying to break old habits while also managing work, relationships, and daily stress, it can feel overwhelming. This is why people often stick to what is familiar. It is not about willpower. Their brain is already overloaded.

Imagine deciding to start a workout routine, but instead of easing in, you demand yourself to hit the gym for an hour every day. By day three, your brain and body rebel, and you revert to doing nothing at all. The same thing happens when you try to overhaul your entire mindset overnight. The key is to introduce change gradually, in ways that don't overload your mental bandwidth.

Breaking the Cycle of Inaction

Let's say you decide you're going to start working out. You plan to wake up early, put on your gym clothes, and go for a run. But morning comes, and suddenly, your brain has a lot of opinions. You're too tired. You'll start tomorrow. You don't have the right shoes. The Zeigarnik Effect kicks in, making you dwell on the fact that you *should* be working out but aren't. Cognitive load piles up because you're trying to do too much at once, wake up early, push through discomfort, and commit to an entirely new habit. The result? You give up before you start, reinforcing the story that change is too hard.

I always joke with my husband about this because his approach to change is the exact opposite of mine. The man goes balls to the wall with everything. If he decides to exercise, he's running five miles on day one. If he wants to start eating healthier, suddenly he's meal-prepping like a professional athlete. And you can probably guess what happens. His body or brain gives out because it was *too much* all at once. It's not a lack of willpower; it's science.

So how do you avoid this trap? You make it easier for your brain. Instead of setting the bar impossibly high, you start with the smallest possible action. Maybe you just put on your running shoes. Maybe you do five minutes of stretching. By making the action so small that it's impossible to fail, you trick your brain into getting started, and once you're in motion, it's easier to keep going. That is exactly how I began the process of writing this book (after thinking about it and thinking about it and thinking about it until I stopped thinking and I took action instead). The same principle applies to boundaries, self-worth, confidence, any change. The key is to start small and let momentum build.

You Are Rewiring Your Brain

Neuroscience tells us that your brain is adaptable, constantly forming and pruning connections based on what you repeatedly do. Remember Hebbian Learning, summed up by the phrase "neurons that fire together, wire together." Every time you challenge an old belief, set a new boundary, or take an action that aligns with your future self, you're literally rewiring your brain. It's not just a motivational phrase; your thoughts and actions physically reshape you. The more you practice a new behavior, the stronger those neural pathways become, making change feel easier over time.

Your Future Self Is Waiting

Speaking of your future self, imagine that person for a moment—the version of you who has done this work, who has set boundaries with confidence, who no longer carries the weight of outdated fears, who moves through life with greater ease and clarity. What would that version of you tell you right now? What encouragement would they offer? What wisdom have they gained from the steps you're about to take? Let their voice be louder than the fear that tells you to stay the same.

Your Next Chapter Starts Now

Transformation is not about fixing yourself—because you were never broken. It's about stepping into the fullest version of yourself, the one that isn't weighed down by outdated narratives. The one who sees possibilities where fear once lived. The one who realizes that growth isn't about erasing the past but about choosing your future.

So where do you go from here?

Start small. What is one shift, one new belief, one new behavior, one new boundary that you can begin practicing today? Don't wait for the perfect moment. Don't wait until you feel ready. Change happens in the doing, not just the knowing.

And you don't have to do it alone.

If you want to take this work deeper, I invite you to stay connected. You can find me online by searching my name or visiting my website for future offerings and resources. Whether you're looking to move beyond self-doubt, set healthier boundaries, or step into a more confident, empowered version of yourself, the tools and insights you've explored here can help you create real, lasting change.

Your next chapter is waiting to be written. How will you choose to write it?

Keep Your Momentum Going

If what you've read here makes sense and you're ready to take this work further, I've created a free training that walks you through the next steps for removing the prehistoric tendencies from your brain and creating a new level of success in your life.

Watch the training, and if it resonates, we can talk about working together to turn these insights into lasting change.

Start here: **instincttointention.prehistoricbrain.com**

Bibliography

Ainslie, George. *Breakdown of Will*. Cambridge University Press, 2001.

Ariely, Dan. *Predictably Irrational: The Hidden Forces That Shape Our Decisions*. HarperCollins, 2008.

Arnsten AF. Stress signalling pathways that impair prefrontal cortex structure and function. Nat Rev Neurosci. 2009 Jun;10(6):410-22. doi: 10.1038/nrn2648. PMID: 19455173; PMCID: PMC2907136.

Bandura, Albert. *Self-Efficacy: The Exercise of Control*. W.H. Freeman and Company, 1997.

Barrett, Lisa Feldman. *How Emotions Are Made: The Secret Life of the Brain*. Houghton Mifflin Harcourt, 2017.

Baumeister, Roy F., and John Tierney. *Willpower: Rediscovering the Greatest Human Strength*. Penguin Press, 2011.

Bowlby, John. *Attachment and Loss: Vol. 1. Attachment*. Basic Books, 1969.

Brown, Brene. *Braving the Wilderness: The Quest for True Belonging and the Courage to Stand Alone*. Random House, 2017.

Brown, Brene. *Dare to Lead: Brave Work. Tough Conversations. Whole Hearts*. Random House, 2018.

Brown, Brene. *Daring Greatly: How the Courage to Be Vulnerable Transforms the Way We Live, Love, Parent, and Lead*. Avery, 2012.

Carter, C. S. "Neuroendocrine Perspectives on Social Attachment and Love." *Psychoneuroendocrinology*, 238 (1998): 779–818.

Choi, J. N., and A. Y. P. Chu. "The Motivational Dynamics of Unproductive Work Behavior: A Study of Procrastination." *Journal of Organizational Behavior*, 265 (2005): 485–507.

Clear, J. *Atomic Habits: An Easy & Proven Way to Build Good Habits & Break Bad Ones*. Avery, 2018.

Covey, Stephen R. *The 7 Habits of Highly Effective People: Powerful Lessons in Personal Change*. Free Press, 1989, p. 28

Cozolino, Louis. *The Neuroscience of Human Relationships: Attachment and the Developing Social Brain*. W.W. Norton & Company, 2014.

Cozolino, Louis. *The Neuroscience of Psychotherapy: Healing the Social Brain*. W.W. Norton & Company, 2017.

Curtis, Valerie. *Don't Look, Don't Touch, Don't Eat: The Science Behind Revulsion*. University of Chicago Press, 2013.

Davidson, R. J., and S. Begley. *The Emotional Life of Your Brain*. Penguin Books, 2012.

Dispenza, J. *Breaking the Habit of Being Yourself: How to Lose Your Mind and Create a New One*. Hay House, 2012.

Dobzhansky, T. 1973. "Nothing in Biology Makes Sense Except in the Light of Evolution." *American Biology Teacher*, 35(3), 125–129.

Doidge, Norman. *The Brain That Changes Itself: Stories of Personal Triumph from the Frontiers of Brain Science*. Viking, 2007.

Doidge, Norman. *The Brain's Way of Healing: Remarkable Discoveries and Recoveries from the Frontiers of Neuroplasticity*. Viking, 2015.

Duckworth, Angela. *Grit: The Power of Passion and Perseverance*. Scribner, 2016.

Duhigg, Charles. *The Power of Habit: Why We Do What We Do in Life and Business*. Random House 2012.

Dweck, Carol S. *Mindset: The New Psychology of Success*. Random House, 2006.

Eisenberger, N. I., and M. D. Lieberman. 2004. "Why It Hurts to Be Left Out: The Neurocognitive Overlap Between Physical Pain and Social Pain." *Trends in Cognitive Sciences* 8 (7), 294–300. https://doi.org/10.1016/j.tics.2004.05.012.

Ferrari, Joseph R. *Still Procrastinating: The No Regrets Guide to Getting It Done*. Wiley, 2010.

Ferrari, Joseph R., J. L. Johnson, & William G. McCown. *Procrastination and Task Avoidance: Theory, Research, and Treatment*. Springer, 1995.

Festinger, L. *A Theory of Cognitive Dissonance*. Stanford University Press, 1957.

Frankl, V. E. *Man's Search for Meaning*. Beacon Press, 2006.

Gilbert, Daniel. *Stumbling on Happiness*. Vintage, 2013.

Goleman, D. *Emotional Intelligence: Why It Can Matter More Than IQ*. Bantam Books, 1995.

Gottman, J., and N. Silver. *The Seven Principles for Making Marriage Work: A Practical Guide from the Country's Foremost Relationship Expert*. Harmony Books, 1999.

Grant, A. M. *Give and Take: A Revolutionary Approach to Success*. Viking, 2013.

Grant, A. M. *Think Again: The Power of Knowing What You Don't Know*. Viking, 2021.

Graybiel, Ann M. "Habits, Rituals, and the Evaluative Brain." *Annual Review of Neuroscience*, vol. 31, (2008): 359–387.

Hallowell, Edward M., and John J. Ratey. *ADHD 2.0: New Science and Essential Strategies for Thriving with Distraction.* Ballantine Books, 2021.

Hare, Brian, and Vanessa Woods. *Survival of the Friendliest: Understanding Our Origins and Rediscovering Our Common Humanity.* Random House, 2020.

Hatfield, Elaine, John T. Cacioppo, & Richard L. Rapson. *Emotional Contagion.* Cambridge University Press, 1994.

Heath, C., and D. Heath. *Switch: How to Change Things When Change Is Hard.* Crown Business, 2010.

Hebb, Donald O. *The Organization of Behavior: A Neuropsychological Theory.* Wiley, 1949.

Hofstede, Geert. *Culture's Consequences: Comparing Values, Behaviors, Institutions, and Organizations Across Nations.* Sage Publications, 2001.

"How to Work with the Inner Critic." NICABM. National Institute for the Clinical Application of Behavioral Medicine, n.d. https://www.nicabm.com/program/inner-critic/.

Huberman, Andrew, host. *Ask Huberman Lab*, podcast. "Embracing Curiosity." Huberman Lab Podcast AI Archive, n.d. https://ai.hubermanlab.com/clip?sids=chunk_3415398.

Huberman, Andrew. *Huberman Lab*, podcast. "Build or Break Habits Using Science-Based Tools." https://www.hubermanlab.com/newsletter/build-or-break-habits-using-science-based-tools.

Huberman, Andrew host. *Huberman Lab*, podcast. "Leverage Dopamine to Overcome Procrastination & Optimize Effort." 2023. https://www.hubermanlab.com/episode/leverage-dopamine-to-over-come-procrastination-and-optimize-effort.

Huberman, Andrew, host. *Huberman Lab*, podcast. "Using Failure to Learn & Dopamine to Drive Motivation." https://www.hubermanlab.com/episode/using-failure-to-learn-and-dopamine-to-drive-motivation.

Huberman, Andrew, host, and Charan Ranganath. *Huberman Lab*, podcast. "Dr. Charan Ranganath: How to Improve Memory & Focus Using Science-Based Tools." September 30, 2024. https://podcasts.apple.com/us/podcast/dr-charan-ranga-nath-how-to-improve-memory-focus-using/id1545953110?i=1000671263585.

Kahneman, Daniel. *Thinking, Fast and Slow*. Farrar, Straus and Giroux, 2011.

LeDoux, Joseph. *Anxious: Using the Brain to Understand and Treat Fear and Anxiety*. Viking, 2015.

LeDoux, Joseph E. *The Emotional Brain: The Mysterious Underpinnings of Emotional Life*. Simon & Schuster, 1996.

LeDoux, Joseph E. *The Synaptic Self: How Our Brains Become Who We Are*. Viking Adult, 2002.

Lembke, Anna. *Dopamine Nation: Finding Balance in the Age of Indulgence*. Dutton, 2021.

Lent, Ricardo. *The Human Brain: An Introduction to Its Functional Anatomy*. Cambridge University Press, 2010.

Levine, Peter A. *In an Unspoken Voice: How the Body Releases Trauma and Restores Goodness*. North Atlantic Books, 2010.

Lieberman, Matthew D. *Social: Why Our Brains Are Wired to Connect*. Crown, 2013.

McEwen, Bruce S. "Protective and Damaging Effects of Stress Mediators." *New England Journal of Medicine*, vol. 338, no. 3, (1998): 171–179.

McRaney, David. *You Are Not So Smart: Why You Have Too Many Friends on Facebook, Why Your Memory Is Mostly Fiction, and 46 Other Ways You're Deluding Yourself*. Gotham Books, 2011.

Merton, Robert K. *Social Theory and Social Structure*. New York: Free Press, 1948.

Merzenich, Michael M. *Soft-Wired: How the New Science of Brain Plasticity Can Change Your Life*. Parnassus Publishing, 2013.

Montague, P. R., and T. Lohrenz. "To Detect and Correct: Norm Violations and Their Enforcement." *Neuron, 56*1 (2007): 14–18.

Murray, S. L., and J. G. Holmes. *The Psychology of Close Relationships*. Guilford Press, 2011.

Porges, Stephen W. *The Polyvagal Theory: Neurophysiological Foundations of Emotions, Attachment, Communication, and Self-Regulation*. W.W. Norton & Company, 2011.

Pink, Daniel H. *Drive: The Surprising Truth About What Motivates Us*. Riverhead Books, 2009.

Raichle, Marcus E. *The Brain's Default Mode Network and Its Role in Self-Reflection and Mental Time Travel*. Academic Press, 2015.

Real, Terrance. *Us: Getting Past You & Me to Build a More Loving Relationship*. Random House, 2022.

Rosenthal, Robert, and Lenore Jacobson. *Pygmalion in the Classroom: Teacher Expectation and Pupils' Intellectual Development.* New York: Holt, Rinehart & Winston, 1968.

Rizzolatti, G., and C. Sinigaglia. *Mirrors in the Brain: How Our Minds Share Actions and Emotions.* Oxford University Press, 2008.

Rozin, P., J. Haidt, and C. R. McCauley. "Disgust." In *Handbook of Emotions*, 3rd ed. Guilford Press, 2008.

Sapolsky, Robert M. *Behave: The Biology of Humans at Our Best and Worst.* Penguin Press, 2017.

Sapolsky, Robert M. *Why Zebras Don't Get Ulcers: The Acclaimed Guide to Stress, Stress-Related Diseases, and Coping*, 3rd ed. Holt Paperbacks, 2004.

Seth, Anil. *Being You: A New Science of Consciousness.* Dutton, 2021.

Siegel, Daniel J. *The Developing Mind: How Relationships and the Brain Interact to Shape Who We Are.* Guilford Press, 2010.

Siegel, Daniel J. *Mindsight: The New Science of Personal Transformation.* Bantam Books, 2010.

Steel, Piers. *The Procrastination Equation: How to Stop Putting Things Off and Start Getting Stuff Done.* Harper, 2011.

Suler, John. *The Psychology of Cyberspace.* Rider, 2004.

Szczypka, M. S., M. A. Rainey, D. S. Kim, W. A. Alaynick, B. T. Marck, A. M. Matsumoto, & R. D. Palmiter. "Feeding Behavior in Dopamine-Deficient Mice." *Proceedings of the National Academy of Sciences*, 96(21) (1999): 12138–12143.

Tatkin, Stan. *In Each Other's Care: A Guide to the Most Common Relationship Conflicts and How to Work Through Them.* Sounds True, 2024.

Tatkin, Stan. *Wired for Love: How Understanding Your Partner's Brain and Attachment Style Can Help You Defuse Conflict and Build a Secure Relationship.* New Harbinger Publications, 2012.

Van der Kolk, Bessel. A. *The Body Keeps the Score: Brain, Mind, and Body in the Healing of Trauma.* Viking, 2014.

Young, S. N. "How to Increase Serotonin in the Human Brain Without Drugs." *Journal of Psychiatry & Neuroscience,* 326 (2007): 394–399.

Notes

Chapter 1: A Prehistoric Brain in a Modern World

1 Joseph LeDoux, *The Emotional Brain: The Mysterious Underpinnings of Emotional Life* (Simon & Schuster, 1996); Stephen W. Porges, *The Polyvagal Theory: Neurophysiological Foundations of Emotions, Attachment, Communication, and Self-Regulation* (W.W. Norton & Company, 2011).

2 Charles Duhigg, *The Power of Habit: Why We Do What We Do in Life and Business* (Random House, 2012).

3 Dan Ariely, *Predictably Irrational: The Hidden Forces That Shape Our Decisions* (HarperCollins, 2008).

4 Anil Seth, *Being You: A New Science of Consciousness* (Dutton, 2021).

5 Robert M. Sapolsky, *Why Zebras Don't Get Ulcers: The Acclaimed Guide to Stress, Stress-Related Diseases, and Coping*, 3rd ed. (Holt Paperbacks, 2004).

6 Sapolsky, *Why Zebras Don't Get Ulcers*.

7 LeDoux, *The Emotional Brain*; Lisa Feldman Barrett, *How Emotions Are Made: The Secret Life of the Brain* (Houghton Mifflin Harcourt, 2017).

8 Sapolsky, *Why Zebras Don't Get Ulcers*; Robert M. Sapolsky, *Behave: The Biology of Humans at Our Best and Worst* (Penguin Press, 2017).

9 Valerie Curtis, *Don't Look, Don't Touch, Don't Eat: The Science Behind Revulsion* (University of Chicago Press, 2013).

10 Sapolsky, *Behave*.

11 Ricardo Lent, *The Human Brain: An Introduction to Its Functional Anatomy* (Cambridge University Press, 2010).

12 Sapolsky, *Behave*.

13 Daniel Kahneman, *Thinking, Fast and Slow* (Farrar, Straus and Giroux, 2011).

14 Roy F. Baumeister and John Tierney, *Willpower: Rediscovering the Greatest Human Strength* (Penguin Press, 2011).

15 Stan Tatkin, *Wired for Love: How Understanding Your Partner's Brain and Attachment Style Can Help You Defuse Conflict and Build a Secure Relationship* (New Harbinger Publications, 2012).

16 Brian Hare and Vanessa Woods, *Survival of the Friendliest: Understanding Our Origins and Rediscovering Our Common Humanity* (Random House, 2020).

17 John Suler, *The Psychology of Cyberspace* (Rider, 2004).

18 Bessel Van der Kolk, *The Body Keeps the Score: Brain, Mind, and Body in the Healing of Trauma* (Viking, 2014).

Chapter 2: Whispers Across Time: How History and Memory Shape Us

1 Daniel J. Siegel, *The Developing Mind: How Relationships and the Brain Interact to Shape Who We Are* (Guilford Press, 2010).

2 Lisa Feldman Barrett, *How Emotions Are Made: The Secret Life of the Brain* (Houghton Mifflin Harcourt, 2017).

3 Barrett, *How Emotions Are Made*; Joseph LeDoux, *The Emotional Brain: The Mysterious Underpinnings of Emotional Life* (Simon & Schuster, 1996); Daniel J. Siegel, *The Developing Mind: How Relationships and the Brain Interact to Shape Who We Are* (Guilford Press, 2010).

4 John Bowlby, *Attachment and Loss: Vol. 1. Attachment* (Basic Books, 1969).

5 Peter A. Levine, *In an Unspoken Voice: How the Body Releases Trauma and Restores Goodness* (North Atlantic Books, 2010).

6 Bowlby, *Attachment and Loss*.

7 Geert Hofstede, *Culture's Consequences: Comparing Values, Behaviors, Institutions, and Organizations Across Nations* (Sage Publications, 2001).

8 Daniel Kahneman, *Thinking, Fast and Slow* (Farrar, Straus and Giroux, 2011).

9 Barrett, *How Emotions Are Made*.

10 Joseph LeDoux, *The Emotional Brain: The Mysterious Underpinnings of Emotional Life* (Simon & Schuster, 1996); Daniel Kahneman, *Thinking, Fast and Slow* (Farrar, Straus and Giroux, 2011).

11 Kahneman, *Thinking, Fast and Slow*

12 Leon Festinger, A Theory of Cognitive Dissonance (Stanford University Press, 1957); LeDoux, The Emotional Brain

13 Kahneman, *Thinking Fast and Slow*

14 Anil Seth, *Being You: A New Science of Consciousness* (New York: Dutton, 2021); Kahneman, *Thinking Fast and Slow*; LeDoux, *The Emotional Brain*

15 LeDoux, *The Emotional Brain*

16 Kahneman, *Thinking, Fast and Slow*; LeDoux, *The Emotional Brain*

17 Bessel Van der Kolk, *The Body Keeps the Score: Brain, Mind, and Body in the Healing of Trauma* (Viking, 2014).

18 Daniel J. Siegel, *The Developing Mind: How Relationships and the Brain Interact to Shape Who We Are* (Guilford Press, 2010).

19 Van der Kolk, *The Body Keeps the Score*.

20 Peter A. Levine, *In an Unspoken Voice: How the Body Releases Trauma and Restores Goodness* (North Atlantic Books, 2010).

21 Siegel, *The Developing Mind*.

Chapter 3: The Neuroscience of Motivation: Understanding Why You Feel Stuck

1 Daniel H. Pink, *Drive: The Surprising Truth About What Motivates Us* (Riverhead Books, 2009); Lisa Feldman Barrett, *How Emotions Are Made:*

279

The Secret Life of the Brain (Houghton Mifflin Harcourt, 2017); Joseph LeDoux, *The Emotional Brain: The Mysterious Underpinnings of Emotional Life* (Simon & Schuster, 1996).

2   Charles Duhigg, *The Power of Habit: Why We Do What We Do in Life and Business* (Random House, 2012).

3   Anna Lembke, *Dopamine Nation: Finding Balance in the Age of Indulgence* (Dutton, 2021).

4   M. S. Szczypka et al., "Feeding Behavior in Dopamine-Deficient Mice," *Proceedings of the National Academy of Sciences*, 96 (21), (1999): 12138–12143.

5   Robert M. Sapolsky, *Why Zebras Don't Get Ulcers: The Acclaimed Guide to Stress, Stress-Related Diseases, and Coping*, 3rd ed. (Holt Paperbacks, 2004).

6   Lembke, *Dopamine Nation*.

7   Sapolsky, *Why Zebras Don't Get Ulcers*.

8   Lembke, *Dopamine Nation*.

9   Sapolsky, *Why Zebras Don't Get Ulcers*; Bruce S. McEwen, "Protective and Damaging Effects of Stress Mediators," *New England Journal of Medicine*, vol. 338, no. 3, (1998): 171–179

10 Sapolsky, *Why Zebras Don't Get Ulcers*; McEwen, "Protective and Damaging Effects of Stress Mediators," 171–179; Lembke, *Dopamine Nation*.

Chapter 4: Your Brain's Power to Change

1   Norman Doidge, *The Brain's Way of Healing: Remarkable Discoveries and Recoveries from the Frontiers of Neuroplasticity* (Viking, 2015); Daniel J. Siegel, *The Developing Mind: How Relationships and the Brain Interact to Shape Who We Are* (Guilford Press, 2010).

2   Michael M. Merzenich, *Soft-Wired: How the New Science of Brain Plasticity Can Change Your Life* (Parnassus Publishing, 2013).

3   Charles Duhigg, *The Power of Habit: Why We Do What We Do in Life and Business* (Random House, 2012).

4   Andrew Huberman, host, and Charan Ranganath, *Huberman Lab*, podcast, "Dr. Charan Ranganath: How to Improve Memory & Focus Using Science-Based Tools," September 30, 2024, https://podcasts.apple.com/us/podcast/dr-charan-ranganath-how-to-improve-memory-focus-using/id1545953110?i=1000671263585; Andrew Huberman, *Ask Huberman Lab*, podcast, "Embracing Curiosity," Huberman Lab Podcast AI Archive, n.d., https://ai.hubermanlab.com/clip?sids=chunk_3415398.

5   Norman Doidge, *The Brain That Changes Itself: Stories of Personal Triumph from the Frontiers of Brain Science* (Viking, 2007).

6   Merzenich, *Soft-Wired*.

7   Doidge, *The Brain That Changes Itself*.

8 Ann M. Graybiel, "Habits, Rituals, and the Evaluative Brain," *Annual Review of Neuroscience*, vol. 31, (2008): 359–387.

9 Duhigg, *The Power of Habit*.

10 Duhigg, *The Power of Habit*; Anna Lembke, *Dopamine Nation: Finding Balance in the Age of Indulgence* (Dutton, 2021).

11 Joseph LeDoux, *The Emotional Brain: The Mysterious Underpinnings of Emotional Life* (Simon & Schuster, 1996).

12 LeDoux, *The Emotional Brain*.

13 Matthew D. Lieberman, *Social: Why Our Brains Are Wired to Connect* (Crown, 2013).

14 Louis Cozolino, *The Neuroscience of Human Relationships: Attachment and the Developing Social Brain* (W.W. Norton & Company, 2014).

15 Stephen W. Porges, *The Polyvagal Theory: Neurophysiological Foundations of Emotions, Attachment, Communication, and Self-Regulation* (W.W. Norton & Company, 2011); Daniel J. Siegel, *Mindsight: The New Science of Personal Transformation* (Bantam Books, 2010).

16 LeDoux, *The Emotional Brain*.

17 R. J. Davidson and S. Begley, *The Emotional Life of Your Brain* (Penguin Books, 2012).

18 G. Rizzolatti and C. Sinigaglia, *Mirrors in the Brain: How Our Minds Share Actions and Emotions* (Oxford University Press, 2008).

19 C. S. Carter, "Neuroendocrine Perspectives on Social Attachment and Love," *Psychoneuroendocrinology*, 23(8) (1998): 779–818.

20 P. R. Montague and T. Lohrenz, "To Detect and Correct: Norm Violations and Their Enforcement," *Neuron, 56*(1) (2007): 14–18.

21 S. N. Young, "How to Increase Serotonin in the Human Brain Without Drugs," *Journal of Psychiatry & Neuroscience*, 32(6) (2007): 394–399.

22 N. I. Eisenberger and M. D. Lieberman, "Why It Hurts to Be Left Out: The Neurocognitive Overlap Between Physical Pain and Social Pain," *Trends in Cognitive Sciences*, 8(7) (2004): 294–300.

Chapter 5: Why We Doubt Ourselves: Unpacking the Roots of Self-Doubt

1 Joseph LeDoux, *The Emotional Brain: The Mysterious Underpinnings of Emotional Life*, (Simon & Schuster, 1996).

2 Matthew D. Lieberman, *Social: Why Our Brains Are Wired to Connect* (Crown Publishers, 2013).

3 Robert M. Sapolsky, *Behave: The Biology of Humans at Our Best and Worst* (Penguin Press, 2007).

4 Albert Bandura, *Self-Efficacy: The Exercise of Control* (W.H. Freeman and Company, 1996).

5 "How to Work with the Inner Critic," NICABM, National Institute for the Clinical Application of Behavioral Medicine, n.d., https://www.nicabm.com/program/inner-critic/.

[6] S. B. Klein, *The Self: Science, Theory, and Practice* (Psychology Press, 2013).

[7] Donald O. Hebb, *The Organization of Behavior: A Neuropsychological Theory* (Wiley, 1949).

Chapter 6: When Relationships Hurt: Breaking the Patterns and Finding Connection

[1] Elaine Hatfield et al., *Emotional Contagion* (Cambridge University Press, 1994).

[2] S. L. Murray and J. G. Holmes, *The Psychology of Close Relationships* (Guilford Press, 2011).

[3] Stan Tatkin, *Wired for Love: How Understanding Your Partner's Brain and Attachment Style Can Help You Defuse Conflict and Build a Secure Relationship* (New Harbinger Publications, 2012).

[4] Norman Doidge, *The Brain That Changes Itself: Stories of Personal Triumph from the Frontiers of Brain Science* (Viking, 2007).

[5] Robert M. Sapolsky, *Why Zebras Don't Get Ulcers: The Acclaimed Guide to Stress, Stress-Related Diseases, and Coping*, 3rd ed. (Holt Paperbacks, 2004); Robert M. Sapolsky, *Behave: The Biology of Humans at Our Best and Worst* (Penguin Press, 2017).

Chapter 7: Why We Avoid: Overcoming Procrastination and Reclaiming Focus

[1] Anna Lembke, *Dopamine Nation: Finding Balance in the Age of Indulgence* (Dutton, 2021).

[2] Lembke, *Dopamine Nation*.

[3] Piers Steel, *The Procrastination Equation: How to Stop Putting Things Off and Start Getting Stuff Done* (Harper, 2011).

[4] Joseph R. Ferrari, *Still Procrastinating: The No Regrets Guide to Getting It Done* (Wiley, 2010).

[5] Joseph R. Ferrari et al., *Procrastination and Task Avoidance: Theory, Research, and Treatment* (Springer, 1995).

[6] J. N. Choi and A. Y. P. Chu, "The Motivational Dynamics of Unproductive Work Behavior: A Study of Procrastination," *Journal of Organizational Behavior*, 26(5) (2005): 485–507.

[7] Roy F. Baumeister and John Tierney, *Willpower: Rediscovering the Greatest Human Strength* (Penguin Press, 2011).

[8] Carol S. Dweck, *Mindset: The New Psychology of Success* (Ballantine Books, 2006).

[9] Anil Seth, *Being You: A New Science of Consciousness* (Faber & Faber, 2021).

[10] Joseph LeDoux, *Anxious: Using the Brain to Understand and Treat Fear and Anxiety* (Viking, 2015).

[11] Stephen R. Covey, *The 7 Habits of Highly Effective People: Powerful Lessons in Personal Change* (Free Press, 1989), 28

[12] Steel, *The Procrastination Equation.*

[13] George Ainslie, *Breakdown of Will* (Cambridge University Press, 2001).

[14] Marcus E. Raichle, *The Brain's Default Mode Network and Its Role in Self-Reflection and Mental Time Travel* (Academic Press, 2015).

[15] Robert Sapolsky, *Behave: The Biology of Humans at Our Best and Worst* (Penguin Press, 2017).

[16] Raichle, *The Brain's Default Mode Network and Its Role in Self-Reflection and Mental Time Travel.*

[17] Norman Doidge, *The Brain That Changes Itself: Stories of Personal Triumph from the Frontiers of Brain Science* (Penguin Books, 2007).

[18] Arnsten AF. Stress signalling pathways that impair prefrontal cortex structure and function. Nat Rev Neurosci. 2009 Jun;10(6):410-22. doi: 10.1038/nrn2648. PMID: 19455173; PMCID: PMC2907136.

[19] Robert M. Sapolsky, *Why Zebras Don't Get Ulcers: The Acclaimed Guide to Stress, Stress-Related Diseases, and Coping*, 3rd ed. (Holt Paperbacks, 2004).

[20] Andrew Huberman, host, *Huberman Lab*, podcast, "Leverage Dopamine to Overcome Procrastination & Optimize Effort," 2023, Retrieved from https://www.hubermanlab.com/episode/leverage-dopamine-to-overcome-procrastination-and-optimize-effort

[21] Huberman, "Leverage Dopamine to Overcome Procrastination & Optimize Effort," https://www.hubermanlab.com/episode/leverage-dopamine-to-overcome-procrastination-and-optimize-effort.

[22] Huberman, "Leverage Dopamine to Overcome Procrastination & Optimize Effort," https://www.hubermanlab.com/episode/leverage-dopamine-to-overcome-procrastination-and-optimize-effort.

[23] Huberman, "Leverage Dopamine to Overcome Procrastination & Optimize Effort," https://www.hubermanlab.com/episode/leverage-dopamine-to-overcome-procrastination-and-optimize-effort.

Chapter 8: Feeling Invisible: Breaking Free and Rebuilding Self-Worth

[1] Robert M. Sapolsky, *Behave: The Biology of Humans at Our Best and Worst* (Penguin, 2017).

[2] Brene Brown, *Braving the Wilderness: The Quest for True Belonging and the Courage to Stand Alone* (Random House, 2017).

[3] Andrew Huberman, *Huberman Lab*, podcast, "Build or Break Habits Using Science-Based Tools," https://www.hubermanlab.com/newsletter/build-or-break-habits-using-science-based-tools.

[4] Joseph LeDoux, *The Emotional Brain: The Mysterious Underpinnings of Emotional Life* (Phoenix, 2002).

5 Norman Doidge, *The Brain That Changes Itself: Stories of Personal Triumph from the Frontiers of Brain Science* (Viking, 2007).
6 Doidge, *The Brain That Changes Itself*.
7 Robert M. Sapolsky, *Why Zebras Don't Get Ulcers: The Acclaimed Guide to Stress, Stress-Related Diseases, and Coping*, 3rd ed. (Holt Paperbacks, 2004).
8 Edward M. Hallowell and John J. Ratey, *ADHD 2.0: New Science and Essential Strategies for Thriving with Distraction* (Ballantine Books, 2021).

Chapter 9: Struggling with Boundaries: Building Strength and Restoring Balance

1 Brené Brown, *Dare to Lead: Brave Work. Tough Conversations. Whole Hearts.* (Random House, 2018).
2 Terrance Real, *Us: Getting Past You & Me to Build a More Loving Relationship* (Random House, 2022).
3 David McRaney, *You Are Not So Smart: Why You Have Too Many Friends on Facebook, Why Your Memory Is Mostly Fiction, and 46 Other Ways You're Deluding Yourself* (Gotham Books, 2011).
4 E. M. Hallowell and J. J. Ratey, *ADHD 2.0: New Science and Essential Strategies for Thriving with Distraction* (Ballantine Books, 2021).

Chapter 10: The Inner Work of Professional Growth: Moving Beyond Self-Limiting Patterns

1 Brené Brown, *Dare to Lead: Brave Work. Tough Conversations. Whole Hearts.* (Random House, 2018).
2 Daniel Kahneman, *Thinking, Fast and Slow* (Farrar, Straus and Giroux, 2011).
3 Robert Sapolsky, *Behave: The Biology of Humans at Our Best and Worst* (Penguin Press, 2017).
4 Norman Doidge, *The Brain That Changes Itself: Stories of Personal Triumph from the Frontiers of Brain Science* (Viking Press, 2007).
5 Merton, Robert K. *Social Theory and Social Structure* (New York: Free Press, 1948); Robert Rosenthal and Lenore Jacobson, *Pygmalion in the Classroom: Teacher Expectation and Pupils' Intellectual Development* (Holt, Rinehart & Winston, 1968)
6 Andrew Huberman, host, *Huberman Lab*, podcast, "Using Failure to Learn & Dopamine to Drive Motivation," Retrieved from https://www.hubermanlab.com/episode/using-failure-to-learn-and-dopamine-to-drive-motivation.

Chapter 11: Resilience: The Foundation for Lasting Change

1 Lisa Feldman Barrett, *How Emotions Are Made: The Secret Life of the Brain* (Houghton Mifflin Harcourt, 2017).

2   Daniel J. Siegel, *The Developing Mind: How Relationships and the Brain Interact to Shape Who We Are* (Guilford Press, 2010).

3   Norman Doidge, *The Brain That Changes Itself: Stories of Personal Triumph from the Frontiers of Brain Science* (Viking, 2007).

4   Joseph LeDoux, *The Synaptic Self: How Our Brains Become Who We Are* (Viking Adult, 2002).

5   Daniel Kahneman, *Thinking, Fast and Slow* (Farrar, Straus and Giroux, 2011).

6   Michael Merzenich, *Soft-Wired: How the New Science of Brain Plasticity Can Change Your Life* (Parnassus Publishing, 2013).

7   Robert Sapolsky, *Behave: The Biology of Humans at Our Best and Worst* (Penguin Press, 2017).

8   Joseph LeDoux, Joseph (1996). *The Emotional Brain: The Mysterious Underpinnings of Emotional Life.* (Simon & Schuster, 1996).

9   Angela Duckworth, *Grit: The Power of Passion and Perseverance* (Scribner, 2016).

About the Author

Kira Kayler is a Licensed Marriage and Family Therapist with a private practice in Sonoma County, California, specializing in relationships, trauma, anxiety and personal transformation.

Kira Kayler is also a CAMFT Certified Clinical Supervisor, NeuroChange Practitioner and Functional Imagery Training facilitator. She is also an ADHD-Certified Clinical Services Provider (ADHD-CCSP) and Certified Mental Health and Nutrition Clinical Specialist (CMNCS). She is often accompanied by one of her dogs in the therapy office. She also employs and trains and assists associate therapists on their paths towards licensure.

As a mental health professional, Kira works with couples and individuals to overcome internal obstacles to having the life and relationship that they want. She helps people understand themselves, their histories, and how our minds, thoughts, emotions, and behaviors intersect to help them make informed and empowered choices about their decisions, behaviors and lives.

The principles Kira teaches are the very same tools and information that she applied to her own life, to overcome past failures, self-sabotage and limiting beliefs. Transformation resulted in the creation of a happy and fulfilling marriage to a wonderful man, three glorious dogs, a cat, and a wonderful son and a thriving private practice.

www.ingramcontent.com/pod-product-compliance
Lightning Source LLC
Chambersburg PA
CBHW021708120626
46545CB00004B/1454